MID-ATLANTIC
HOME LANDSCAPING

Fourth Edition

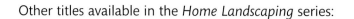

Other titles available in the *Home Landscaping* series:

CALIFORNIA
MIDWEST
including South-Central Canada
NORTHEAST
including Southeast Canada
NORTHWEST
SOUTHEAST
SOUTHERN COASTAL
TEXAS
WESTERN

CREATIVE HOMEOWNER®

MID-ATLANTIC
HOME LANDSCAPING

46 Landscape Designs
200+ Plants & Flowers for Your Region

Fourth Edition

Roger Holmes, Rita Buchanan

Technical Editor: Mark Wolfe

FOURTH EDITION

MANAGING EDITOR	Gretchen Bacon
EDITOR	Sherry Vitolo
TECHNICAL EDITOR	Mark Wolfe
DESIGNER	Freire Disseny*Comunicació

Mid-Atlantic Home Landscaping, 4th Edition
ISBN 978-1-58011-586-5

Library of Congress Control Number: 2023903977

We are always looking for talented authors. To submit an idea, please send a brief inquiry to acquisitions@foxchapelpublishing.com.

Printed in China

First Printing

Creative Homeowner®, *www.creativehomeowner.com*, is an imprint of New Design Originals Corporation and distributed exclusively in North America by Fox Chapel Publishing Company, Inc., 800-457-9112, 903 Square Street, Mount Joy, PA 17552, and in the United Kingdom by Grantham Book Service, Trent Road, Grantham, Lincolnshire, NG31 7XQ.

About the Authors

Roger Holmes is the founding editor of *Fine Gardening* magazine. He co-edited the monumental Taylor's *Master Guide to Gardening* and other highly regarded gardening books, and produced the landscaping series of which this book is part. He also co-wrote Creative Homeowner's *Creating Good Gardens.*

Rita Buchanan is a lifelong gardener with degrees in botany and an encyclopedic knowledge of plants. She worked with Roger Holmes to edit *Fine Gardening* magazine and co-edit several books, including Taylor's *Master Guide to Gardening.* She is the author of numerous award-winning books and is a contributor to many gardening magazines.

About the Technical Editor

Mark Wolfe is a garden and landscape content specialist based in Georgia, with an extensive background in the green industry. He works as an industry expert and commerce writer at BobVila.com, while contributing content and editing services for many other outlets. Mark graduated from Northland College in Ashland, Wisconsin with a degree in outdoor education. Early in his career, Mark fell in love with plants. Working on stream restoration and wetlands construction projects, he marveled at the willow's ability to quickly grow from a stem fragment and heal a sorely eroded streambank, and the ways that aquatic plants transform a suburban retention pond into a wildlife oasis. Over the next two decades, trees, shrubs, annuals, and perennials would dominate his working life as a landscaper and nursery manager. In the mid-twenty-teens, Mark co-founded a garden blog, ThePrudentGarden.com, and soon began contributing freelance work for dozens of lawn and garden websites and consumer brands. As a writer, his favorite topics are those that help people new to plants and gardening find success and seasoned plant people find new inspiration. As a gardener, he is passionate about establishing backyard habitats for wild birds and pollinators and growing his collection of native azaleas.

Safety First

Though all concepts and methods in this book have been reviewed for safety, it is not possible to overstate the importance of using the safest working methods possible. What follows are reminders—do's and don'ts for yard work and landscaping. They are not substitutes for your own common sense.

- *Always* use caution, care, and good judgment when following the procedures described in this book.

- *Always* determine locations of underground utility lines before you dig, and then avoid them by a safe distance. Buried lines may be for gas, electricity, communications, or water. Start research by contacting your local building officials. Also contact local utility companies; they will often send a representative free of charge to help you map their lines. In addition, there are private utility locator firms that may be listed in your Yellow Pages. Note: previous owners may have installed underground drainage, sprinkler, and lighting lines without mapping them.

- *Always* read and heed the manufacturer's instructions for using a tool, especially the warnings.

- *Always* ensure that the electrical setup is safe; be sure that no circuit is overloaded and that all power tools and electrical outlets are properly grounded and protected by a ground-fault circuit interrupter (GFCI). Do not use power tools in wet locations.

- *Always* wear eye protection when using chemicals, sawing wood, pruning trees and shrubs, using power tools, and striking metal onto metal or concrete.

- *Always* read labels on chemicals, solvents, and other products; provide ventilation; heed warnings.

- *Always* wear heavy rubber gloves rated for chemicals, not mere household rubber gloves, when handling toxins.

- *Always* wear appropriate gloves in situations in which your hands could be injured by rough surfaces, sharp edges, thorns, or poisonous plants.

- *Always* wear a disposable face mask or a special filtering respirator when creating sawdust or working with toxic gardening substances.

- *Always* keep your hands and other body parts away from the business ends of blades, cutters, and bits.

- *Always* obtain approval from local building officials before undertaking construction of permanent structures.

- *Never* work with power tools when you are tired or under the influence of alcohol or drugs.

- *Never* carry sharp or pointed tools, such as knives or saws, in your pockets. If you carry such tools, use special-purpose tool scabbards.

The Landscape Designers

Stephanie Cohen, of Collegeville, Penn., is a horticulturist and landscape designer specializing in herbaceous plants and plant ecology. A graduate of Temple University, she has worked at Barnes Arboretum in Pennsylvania. She is the education director for the Waterloo Gardens in Pennsylvania, as well as the Perennial Plant Association's director for the Mid-Atlantic region. Ms. Cohen's award-winning designs have appeared in Rodale's Illustrated Encyclopedia of Perennials, Fine Gardening magazine, and The American Herbarist. She is currently a contributing editor for Country Living Gardener. Her designs appear on pp. 33-37, 42-45, 62-65, and 82-85.

Bruce Crawford is president of Garden Architecture, a 12-year-old design-and-build firm in Upper Saddle River, N.J., that specializes in residential garden designs and installations. Mr. Crawford trained at Rutgers University and Cook College in landscape architecture and horticulture and has since taught courses in those subjects at Rutgers. A member of Hortus Club of New York, he has spoken to many organizations about herbaceous and woody plants. His designs appear on pp. 66-69, 78-81, 94-97, 102-105, and 106-109.

Brian Katen is a University of Virginia-trained landscape architect with extensive experience in education, large- and small-scale physical planning, landscape architectural design, and historic landscape preservation. He has worked on a wide range of projects, including design of private gardens, heritage landscapes, public parks, urban plazas and streetscapes, and commercial developments. An assistant professor of landscape architecture at Virginia Tech, he has served as advisor to the director at Dumbarton Oaks in Washington, D.C., and was director of the Landscape Design Program at the George Washington University Center for Career Education. His designs appear on pp. 30-33, 46-49, 54-57, 58-61, and 70-73..

Stratton Semmes operates her own landscape architecture firm in Annapolis, Md., doing residential, public, and commercial projects. She has taught landscaping at George Washington University and Morgan State University. Trained in urban design, she has designed projects for public parks, historic homes, housing developments, and public institutions and colleges. Recent projects include a street-tree master plan for the city of Annapolis and an over-structure plaza at the United States Naval Academy. Ms. Semmes is a recipient of numerous awards and public commendations, including Southern Living magazine's Southern Home Award and the IAA Merit Award. She serves on many advisory boards for the cities of Annapolis and Washington, D.C. Her designs appear on pp. 22-25, 86-89, 74-77, and 98-101.

Mark Willocks is the proprietor of Willocks Landscape Design, Washington, D.C. A graduate of the Landscape Design Program at George Washington University, Mr. Willocks worked as a designer for landscape design-and-build companies and a large retail nursery before setting up his own firm in 1991. His work to date has been almost exclusively residential. From 1991 to 1997, he served as president of the Landscape Designer's Group of Metro Washington. His designs appear on pp. 26-29, 38-41, 50-53, 90-93, and 110-113.

Contents

About This Book

Of all the home improvement projects homeowners tackle, few offer greater rewards than landscaping. Paths, patios, fences, arbors, and—most of all—plantings, can enhance home life in countless ways, large and small, functional and pleasurable, every day of the year. At the main entrance, an attractive brick walkway flanked by eye-catching shrubs and perennials provides a cheerful send-off in the morning and welcomes you home from work in the evening. A carefully placed grouping of small trees, shrubs, and fence panels creates privacy on the patio or screens a nearby eyesore from view. An island bed showcases your favorite plants, while dividing the backyard into several areas for a variety of activities.

Unlike some home improvements, the rewards of landscaping can lie as much in the activity as in the result. Planting and caring for lovely shrubs, perennials, and other plants can afford years of enjoyment. And for those who like to build things, outdoor construction projects can be a special treat.

While the installation and maintenance of plants and outdoor structures are within the means and abilities of most people, few of us are as comfortable determining exactly which plants or structures to use and how best to combine them. It's one thing to decide to dress up the front entrance or patio, another to come up with a design for doing so.

That's where this book comes in. Here, in the Portfolio of Designs, you'll find inspiration for nearly two dozen common home landscaping situations, created by landscape professionals who live and work in the Mid-Atlantic region. Drawing on years of experience, they balance functional requirements and aesthetic possibilities, choosing the right plant or structure for the task based on its proven performance in similar situations.

Complementing the Portfolio of Designs is the second section, Plant Profiles, which provides information on all the plants used in the book. The book's third section, the Guide to Installation, will help you to install and maintain the plants and structures described in the designs. The following discussions take a closer look at each section; we've also printed representative pages of the sections on pp. 9 and 10 and pointed out their features.

Portfolio of Designs

This is the heart of the book, providing examples of landscaping situations and solutions that are at once inspiring and accessible. Some are simple, others more complex, but each one can be installed in a few weekends by homeowners with no special training or experience.

For each situation, we present two designs, the second a variation of the first. As the sample pages on the facing page show, the first design is displayed on a two-page spread. A perspective illustration (called a "rendering") shows what the design will look like several years after installation, when the perennials and many of the shrubs have reached mature size. The rendering also shows the planting as it will appear at a particular time of year. (For more on how plantings change over the course of a year, see "Seasons in Your Landscape," pp. 14–17.) A site plan shows the positions of the plants and structures on a scaled grid. Text introduces the situation and the design and describes the plants and projects used.

The second design option, presented on the second two-page spread, addresses the same situation as the first but differs in one or more important aspects. It might show a planting suited for a shady rather than a sunny site; or it might incorporate different structures or kinds of plants (adding shrubs to a perennial border, for example). As for the first design, we present a rendering, site plan, and written information, but in briefer form. The second spread also includes photographs of landscapes in situations similar to those featured in the two designs. The photos showcase noteworthy variations or details that you may wish to use in the designs we show or in designs of your own.

Installed exactly as shown here, these designs will provide enjoyment for many years. But individual needs and properties will differ, so we encourage you to alter the designs to suit your site and desires. You can easily make changes. For example, you can add or remove plants and adjust the sizes of paths, patios, and fences to suit larger or smaller sites. You can rearrange groupings and substitute favorite plants to suit your taste. Or you can integrate the design with your existing landscaping. If you are uncertain about how to solve specific problems or about the effects of changes you are considering, consult with staff at a local nursery or with a landscape designer in your area.

PORTFOLIO OF DESIGNS

FIRST DESIGN OPTION

Summary
An overview of the
situation and the design.

Rendering
Shows how the design
will look when plants
are well established

Plants & Projects
Noteworthy qualities of
the plants and structures
and their contributions
to the design

Site Plan
Positions all plants
and structures on a
scaled grid

Concept Box
Summarizes an important aspect of the design;
tells whether the site is sunny or shady and
what season is depicted in the rendering

Rendering
Depicts the design when plants
are well established.

Variations on a Theme
Photos of inspiring designs in similar
situations.

SECOND DESIGN OPTION

Summary
Addressing the same
situation as the first design,
this variation may differ
in design concept, site
conditions, or plant selection.

Site Plan
Plants and structures
on a scaled grid.

Concept Box
Site, season, and design
summary.

PLANT PROFILES

Choices
Selections here help you choose from the many varieties of certain popular plants.

Plant Portraits
Photos of selected plants.

Detailed Plant Information
Descriptions of each plant's noteworthy qualities and requirements for planting and care.

GUIDE TO INSTALLATION

Sidebars
Detailed information on special topics, set within ruled boxes

Step-by-Step
Illustrations show process; steps are keyed by number to discussion in the main text.

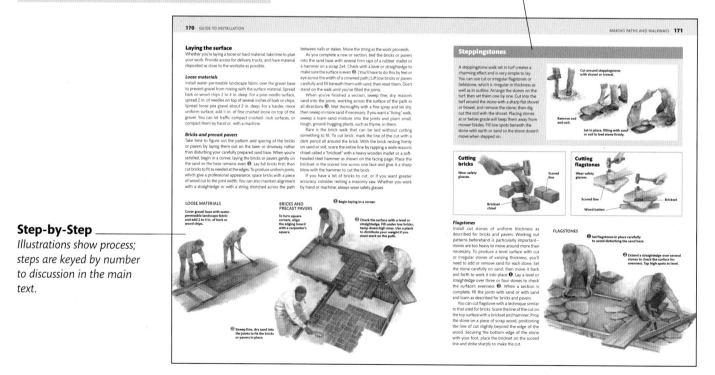

Plant Profiles

The second section of the book includes a description of each plant featured in the Portfolio. These outline each plant's basic preferences for environmental conditions, such as soil, moisture, and sun or shade, and give advice about planting as well as ongoing care.

Working with the book's landscape designers, we selected plants carefully, following a few simple guidelines: Every plant should be a proven performer in the region; once established, it should thrive without pampering. All plants should be available from a local nursery or garden center, or from online sellers; if they're not in stock, they can be ordered, or you can ask the nursery staff to recommend suitable substitutes.

In the Portfolio section, you'll note that plants are referred to by their common name but are cross-referenced to the Plant Profiles section by their botanical name. While common names are familiar to many people, they can be confusing. Distinctly different plants can share the same common name, or one plant can have several different common names. Botanical names, therefore, ensure greatest accuracy and are more appropriate for a reference section such as this. Although you can confidently purchase most of the plants in this book from local nurseries using the common name, knowing the botanical name allows you to make sure that the plant you're ordering is actually the one that is shown in our design.

Guide to Installation

In this section you'll find detailed instructions and illustrations covering all the techniques you'll need to install any design from start to finish. Here we explain how to think your way through a landscaping project and anticipate the various steps. Then you'll learn how to do each part of the job: preparing the site; laying out the design; choosing materials; building paths, trellises, or other structures; amending the soil for planting; buying the recommended plants and putting them in place; and caring for the plants to keep them healthy and attractive year after year.

We've taken care to make installation of built elements simple and straightforward. Hardscape elements such as paths, trellises, fences, and arbors all use basic materials available from local suppliers, and they can be assembled by people who have no special skills or tools beyond those commonly used for home maintenance. The designs can easily be adapted to meet specific needs or to fit in with the style of your house or other landscaping features.

Installing different designs requires different techniques. You can find what you need by following the cross-references in the Portfolio to pages in the Guide to Installation, or by skimming the Guide. If you continue to improve your landscape by adding more than one design, you'll find that many basic techniques are reused from one project to the next. You might want to start with one of the smaller, simpler designs. Gradually you'll develop the skills and confidence to do any project you choose.

Most of the designs in this book can be installed in a weekend or two; some will take a little longer. Digging planting beds, building retaining walls, and erecting fences and arbors can be strenuous work. If you lack the time or energy for the more arduous installation tasks, consider hiring a teenager to help out. Local landscaping services can provide any of the services you need help with.

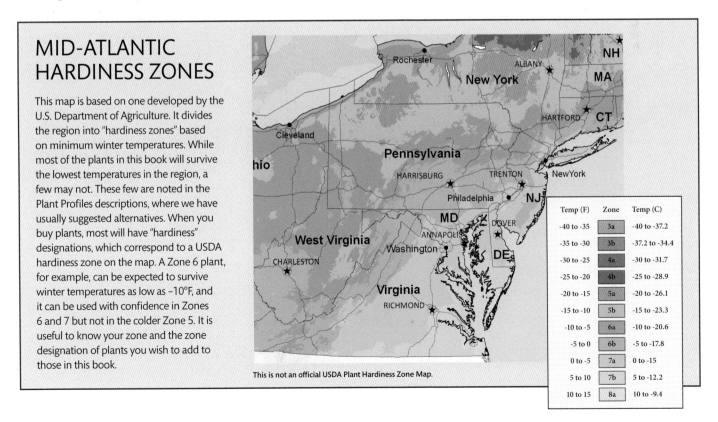

MID-ATLANTIC HARDINESS ZONES

This map is based on one developed by the U.S. Department of Agriculture. It divides the region into "hardiness zones" based on minimum winter temperatures. While most of the plants in this book will survive the lowest temperatures in the region, a few may not. These few are noted in the Plant Profiles descriptions, where we have usually suggested alternatives. When you buy plants, most will have "hardiness" designations, which correspond to a USDA hardiness zone on the map. A Zone 6 plant, for example, can be expected to survive winter temperatures as low as –10°F, and it can be used with confidence in Zones 6 and 7 but not in the colder Zone 5. It is useful to know your zone and the zone designation of plants you wish to add to those in this book.

This is not an official USDA Plant Hardiness Zone Map.

Temp (F)	Zone	Temp (C)
-40 to -35	3a	-40 to -37.2
-35 to -30	3b	-37.2 to -34.4
-30 to -25	4a	-30 to -31.7
-25 to -20	4b	-25 to -28.9
-20 to -15	5a	-20 to -26.1
-15 to -10	5b	-15 to -23.3
-10 to -5	6a	-10 to -20.6
-5 to 0	6b	-5 to -17.8
0 to -5	7a	0 to -15
5 to 10	7b	5 to -12.2
10 to 15	8a	10 to -9.4

Landscaping In an Unpredictable Climate

It's no secret that our dynamic climate is not the same today as it was 25, 50, or 100 years ago. The 30-year rolling temperature averages used to map USDA hardiness zones reveal cold winters moving steadily northward. Frost dates end earlier in spring and begin later in fall, extending the growing season. We've also experienced an increase in damaging storms and severe drought. On top of the infusion of beauty and the increase in property value that come with landscaping, these projects can also protect your property and neighborhood from the unpredictability of a changing climate.

The projects in this book can help you build a more resilient landscape. Well-chosen, well-placed shade trees cool the home, and reduce the energy used for air conditioning. Decreasing lawn area, and increasing the area planted with layers of low-maintenance trees, shrubs, and perennials cuts back energy used on mowing, edging, and blowing, improves the soil's ability to absorb rainfall, and conserves water. Choosing native plants that are adapted to the flooding and winds from tropical storms alleviates some of the risk of storm damage in coastal areas. Installing flagstone or pavers instead of a poured concrete slab patio or walkway means that more rainwater can soak into the ground rather than running off into the streets.

While the designs in this book were drawn up as easy-to-follow, broadly effective guides, you will gain even

Planting a low-maintenance shade tree within a reasonable distance of your house can reduce the energy used for air conditioning.

greater benefits by adapting the plant selections to your unique growing conditions. Consider the effects of intense rainfall, strong winds, severe drought, and inconsistent temperatures in your yard. If your property is exposed to wind, then choose deep-rooted, wind resistant trees and shrubs. For flood prone areas, plants must be able to withstand occasional root saturation, or even partial submersion. Hedge against wild temperature swings by selecting a diverse mix of plants with cold and heat tolerance. In any case, following the landscape maintenance best practices outlined later in the book will help you establish strong, healthy plants.

Few of us spend much time thinking about stormwater unless a flood threatens our home or contaminated runoff pollutes our drinking water. Unfortunately, urban and suburban development from the 1940s to the present day, throughout the Mid-Atlantic region, has increased the frequency and severity of these issues. Every new roof, driveway, street, and sidewalk covers soil that once absorbed rainfall with an impervious surface that increases the volume of runoff into storm drains, detention ponds, and ultimately natural waterways.

When a storm deposits 1 inch of rainfall on a 16 x 40-foot two-car driveway, more than 53 cubic feet (396.44 gallons) of water rush to the nearest storm drain as fast as possible. If the rain falls fast, flash flooding damages human property and infrastructure and scours streambanks. It may deposit excessive silt into streams as it recedes. Even in gentle rain events, runoff picks up pollutants like trash, chemicals, sediment, and animal waste, and carries them to waterways. State and municipal leaders have begun taking these environmental threats seriously, regulating development projects to reduce these negative effects and repairing severely degraded waterways, but private landscaping projects also have an important role to play.

Any hardscaping project comes with an array of material choices that affect stormwater issues. Conventional asphalt and concrete are impervious surfaces. Concrete patios, walkways, and driveways are cost-effective and extremely durable, but they directly contribute to environmental degradation. This goes for mortared stone and brick as well. Permeable pavements on the other hand offer the benefit of a solid surface with little or no runoff. These materials allow rainwater to flow down into open spaces in the surface instead of running off to a storm drain. The pavement surface lays atop a deep layer of compacted aggregate, such as sand and gravel, that allow water to filter down into the ground. Examples of permeable pavements include dry laid flagstone or pavers, crushed stone and gravel, and ground reinforcement grids. They can be used instead of impervious pavement in any residential landscaping project.

Strategically plant to limit the size of your lawn and cut back on the energy needed for mowing, edging, and blowing.

Permeable pavers create a solid surface, but allow rainwater to filter down to the ground through the compacted aggregate below.

Seasons in Your Landscape

One of the rewards of landscaping is watching how plants change through the seasons. During the dark winter months, you look forward to the bright, fresh flowers of spring. Then the lush green foliage of summer is transformed into the blazing colors of fall. Perennials that rest underground in winter can grow head-high by midsummer, and hence a flower bed that looks flat and bare in December becomes a jungle in July.

To illustrate typical seasonal changes, we've chosen one of the designs from this book (see p. 82) and shown here how it would look in spring, summer, fall, and winter. As you can see, this planting looks quite different from one season to the next, but it always remains interesting. Try to remember this example of transformation as you look at the other designs in this book. There we show how

the planting will appear in one season and indicate which plants will stand out at other times.

The task of tending a landscape also changes with the seasons. Below we've noted the most important seasonal jobs in the annual work cycle.

Spring

Crocus flowers and other signs of spring appear in late February in the Mid-Atlantic region. By early April it's time to start mowing the lawn, and by May all the trees have fresh new leaves. Many shrubs and perennials, such as the white azalea, white foamflower, and pink dianthus shown here, bloom in spring. Others that will bloom in summer are just low mounds of foliage now. Do a thorough garden cleanup in March or early April. Remove last year's perennial flower stalks and tattered foliage, cut ornamental grasses to the ground, prune shrubs and trees, renew the mulch, and neaten the edges between the lawn and the beds.

Dianthus

Evergreen azalea

Foamflower

SPRING

SUMMER

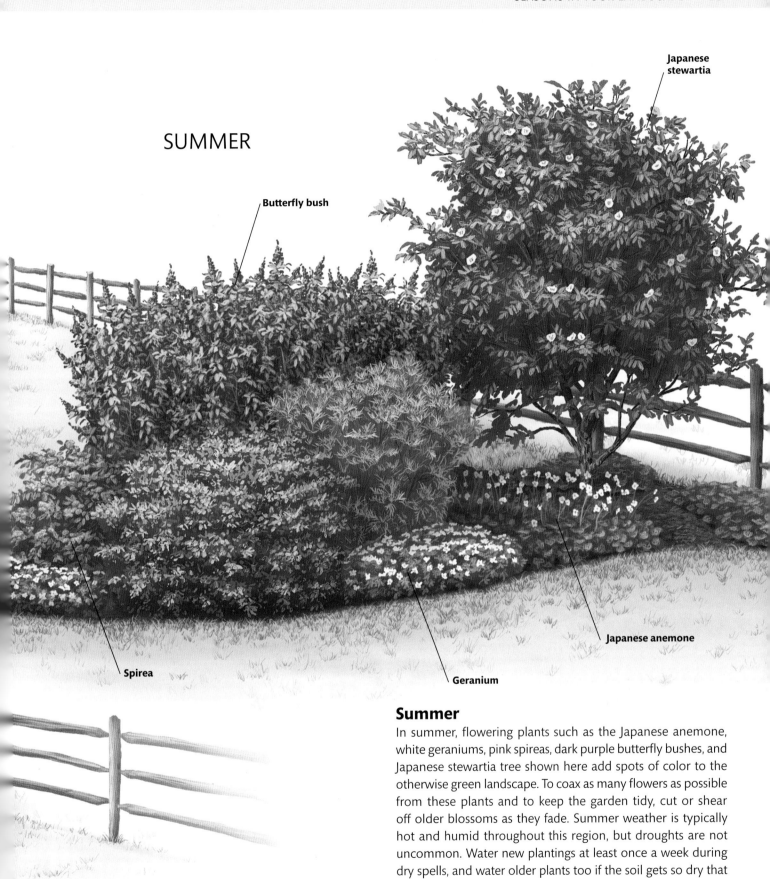

Japanese
stewartia

Butterfly bush

Spirea

Geranium

Japanese anemone

Summer

In summer, flowering plants such as the Japanese anemone, white geraniums, pink spireas, dark purple butterfly bushes, and Japanese stewartia tree shown here add spots of color to the otherwise green landscape. To coax as many flowers as possible from these plants and to keep the garden tidy, cut or shear off older blossoms as they fade. Summer weather is typically hot and humid throughout this region, but droughts are not uncommon. Water new plantings at least once a week during dry spells, and water older plants too if the soil gets so dry that they wilt. Pull any weeds that sprout up through the mulch. This is easiest when the soil is moist from rain or watering.

FALL

Japanese anemone

Dianthus

Fall

A few bright-colored leaves appear here and there in September, but fall foliage season doesn't peak until late October in the Mid-Atlantic region. While trees turn red, orange, and yellow overhead and roadside grasses dry to shades of russet and tan, perennials such as asters, chrysanthemums, or the Japanese anemones shown here provide fresh-looking flowers in the fall garden.

Sometime in October, the first hard frost will kill tender plants to the ground, signaling the time for fall cleanup. Toss frosted plants on the compost pile. Rake leaves into a pile or bin and save them to use as mulch in spring. Fall rains usually soak the ground, so you can stop watering.

Winter

In winter, when deciduous trees and shrubs are leafless and many perennials die down to the ground, you appreciate evergreen plants such as the shrubby dark green azaleas and gray-green southernwood, and the ground-covering dianthus and foamflowers shown here. Clumps of rustling grass or shrubs and trees with colorful twigs, unusual bark, or bright berries are welcome in winter, too.

Normally, garden plants don't need any care in winter. If heavy snow or an ice storm snaps or crushes some plants, you can trim away the broken parts as soon as it's convenient, but if plants get frozen during a severe cold spell, wait until spring to assess the damage before deciding how far to cut them back.

WINTER

Foamflower

Southernwood

Evergreen azalea

As Your Landscape Grows

Landscapes change over the years. As plants grow, the overall look evolves from sparse to lush. Trees cast cool shade where the sun used to shine. Shrubs and hedges grow tall and dense enough to provide privacy. Perennials and ground covers spread to form colorful patches of foliage and flowers. Meanwhile, paths, arbors, fences, and other structures gain the patina of age.

Constant change over the years—sometimes rapid and dramatic, sometimes slow and subtle—is one of the joys of landscaping. It is also one of the challenges. Anticipating how fast plants will grow and how big they will eventually get is difficult, even for professional designers, and was a major concern in formulating the designs for this book.

To illustrate the kinds of changes to expect in a planting, these pages show one of the designs (see p. 41) at three different "ages." Even though a new planting may look sparse at first, it will soon fill in. And because of careful spacing, the planting will look as good in ten to fifteen years as it does after three to five. It will, of course, look different, but that's part of the fun.

At Planting—Here's how the corner might appear in spring immediately after planting. The fence and mulch look conspicuously fresh, new, and unweathered. The fringe tree is only 4 to 5 ft. tall, with trunks no thicker than broomsticks. (With this or other trees, you can buy bigger specimens to start with, but they're a lot more expensive and sometimes don't perform as well in the long run.) The spireas and spreading English yews, transplanted from 2-gal. nursery containers, spread 12 to 18 in. wide. The perennials, transplanted from quart- or gallon-size containers, are just low tufts of foliage now, but they grow fast enough to produce a few flowers the first summer.

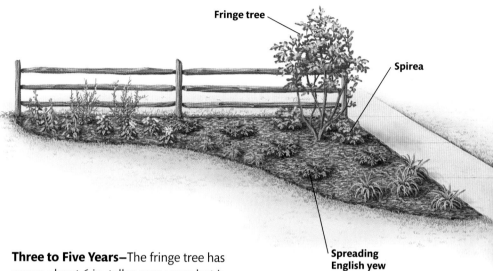

Fringe tree
Spirea
Spreading English yew

AT PLANTING

Three to Five Years—The fringe tree has grown about 6 in. taller every year but is still quite slender. Some trees would grow faster, as much as 1 to 2 ft. a year. The spireas, like many fast-growing shrubs, have reached almost full size. From now on, they'll get thicker but not much taller. The slower-growing English yews make a series of low mounds; you still see them as individuals, not a continuous patch. Most perennials, such as the coneflowers, Shasta daisies, daylilies, and dianthus shown here, grow so crowded after a few years that you will have to divide and replant them.

Ten to Fifteen Years—The fringe tree is becoming a fine specimen, 10 to 12 ft. wide and tall. Unless you prune away enough of its lower limbs to let some sunlight in, the spireas will gradually stop blooming, get weaker, and need to be replaced with shade-tolerant shrubs such as more English yews or with shade-loving perennials and ferns. The original English yews will have formed a continuous ground cover by now and may have spread enough to limit the space available for perennials. Since the perennials get divided every few years anyway, it's no trouble to rearrange or regroup them, as shown here.

THREE TO FIVE YEARS

Fringe tree

Spreading
English yew

Spirea

Coneflower

Shasta daisy

Dianthus

Daylily

Fringe tree

TEN TO FIFTEEN YEARS

Spreading
English yew

Portfolio
of Designs

This section presents ideas for nearly two dozen situations common in home landscapes. You'll find designs to enhance entrances, decks, and patios. There are gardens of colorful perennials and shrubs, as well as structures and plantings to create shady hideaways, dress up nondescript walls, and even make a centerpiece of a lowly mailbox. Large color illustrations show what the designs will look like, and site plans delineate the layout and planting scheme. The accompanying text explains the designs and describes the plants and projects appearing in them. Installed as shown or adapted to meet your site and personal preferences, these designs can make your property more attractive, more useful, and—most important—more enjoyable for you, your family, and your friends.

An Elegant Entry

SEASONAL COLOR BRIGHTENS SHEARED SYMMETRY

Formal gardens have a special appeal. Their simple geometry can be soothing in a hectic world, and the look is timeless, never going out of style. The front yard of a classical house, like the one shown here, with two identical rectangles of lawn either side of a central entry walk invites a formal makeover. (A house with a symmetrical facade in any style has similar potential.)

The layout of this elegant design keys off of and reinforces the symmetry of the house facade. Evergreens around the perimeter define the space, creating a sense of enclosure without shutting out the view of the street, or the view from it. The lawn has disappeared, replaced by rectangular flower beds. Framed with lilyturf, a low-growing evergreen perennial, the beds showcase seasonal plantings of colorful annuals. In the center of the design, a wide brick walkway forms a small courtyard, a pleasing setting for chatting with guests as they arrive or depart.

The design is easily altered to accommodate the character of your site and gardening preferences. The rectangular beds can be expanded or reduced to fit properties of differing sizes without losing the composition's balanced proportions. Dressed flagstones, neatly raked gravel, or precast pavers may be more in keeping with the materials used on your home's facade. If replanting annuals several times a year is more work than you care to tackle, you can substitute perennials such as 'Monch' aster, 'Dropmore' catmint, or 'May Night' salvia, which bloom through most of the summer. Finally, if you're a traditionalist, consider replacing the lilyturf edging with a low boxwood hedge.

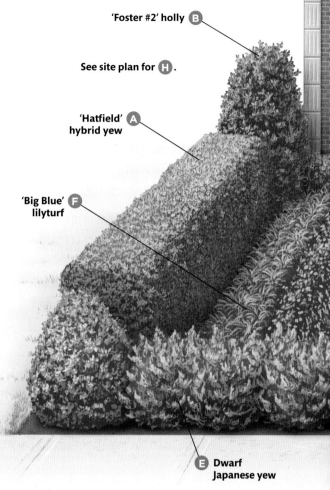

'Foster #2' holly **B**

See site plan for **H**.

'Hatfield' hybrid yew **A**

'Big Blue' lilyturf **F**

E Dwarf Japanese yew

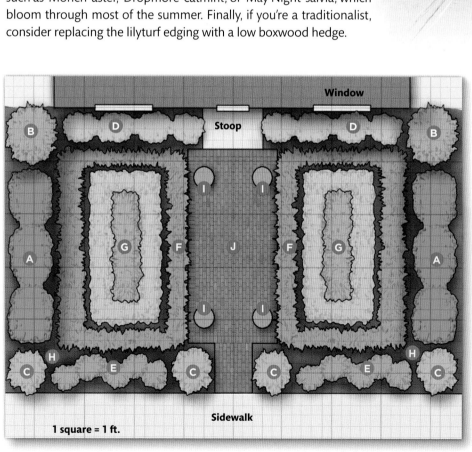

1 square = 1 ft.

Window

Stoop

Sidewalk

Plants & Projects

The evergreens in this design display a mixture of hues, from the dark blue-green 'Blue Princess' hollies to the bright green yews. Against this neatly clipped and subdued background the bright-colored annuals and red fall berries are a striking sight. While the evergreens are dependable problem-free performers, you'll need to attend to them regularly with clippers to keep them in shape.

A **'Hatfield' hybrid yew** (use 6 plants)
A slow-growing evergreen trained and sheared to form a dense hedge 4 ft. tall and 3 ft. wide. See *Taxus* x *media*, p. 157.

B **'Foster #2' holly** (use 2)
Pruned to form slender cones 12 ft. tall, these evergreen trees emphasize the corners of the house. Slim, spiny evergreen leaves look good year-round; masses of red berries enliven the winter scene. See *Ilex* x *attenuata*, p. 139.

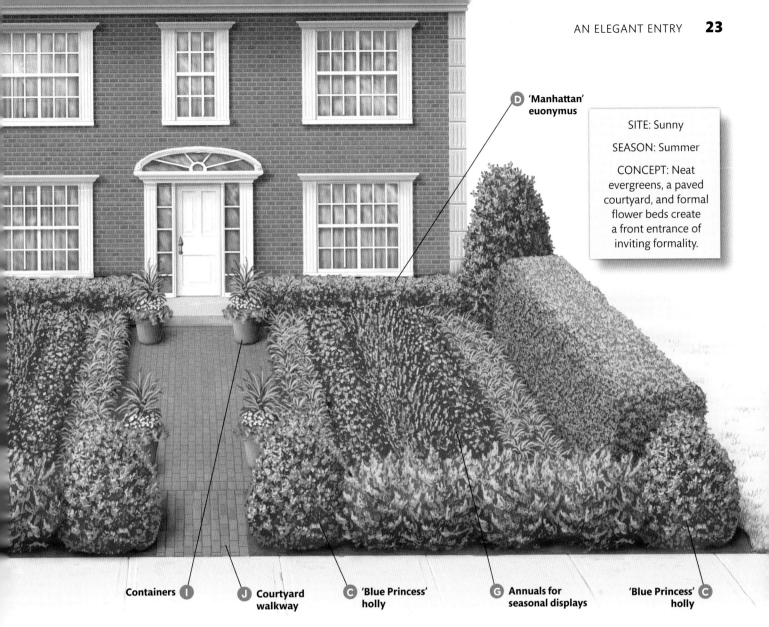

D 'Manhattan' euonymus

SITE: Sunny

SEASON: Summer

CONCEPT: Neat evergreens, a paved courtyard, and formal flower beds create a front entrance of inviting formality.

Containers **I**

J Courtyard walkway

C 'Blue Princess' holly

G Annuals for seasonal displays

'Blue Princess' holly **C**

C **'Blue Princess' holly** (use 4)
Waist-high sheared cones of lustrous dark blue-green leaves mark the front corners of the design and the entrance to the "courtyard." In fall and winter, these evergreen shrubs glow with abundant crops of bright red berries. (If there are no 'Blue Prince' hollies in your neighborhood, plant these pollinators at the corners to ensure berry production.) See *Ilex* x *meserveae*, p. 139.

D **'Manhattan' euonymus** (use 8)
These evergreen shrubs are sheared to form a block of greenery beneath the windows. Leaves hold their color through the region's mild winters; they're sprinkled in fall with eye-catching pinkish orange fruits. See *Euonymus kiautschovicus*, p. 131.

E **Dwarf Japanese yew** (use 10)
These compact evergreen shrubs contribute a modestly "natural" note in this geometric design. Their dense spreading form needs only a little pruning to keep the plants about

a foot lower than the nearby hollies. See *Taxus cuspidata* 'Nana', p. 157.

F **'Big Blue' lilyturf** (use 92)
❶ *This plant is locally invasive in the Mid-Atlantic.*
Planted about 1 ft. apart, these evergreen perennials outline the annual beds with a continuous ribbon of grassy foliage. Spikes of small blue flowers rise above the leaves in late summer. See *Liriope muscari*, p. 143.

G **Annuals for seasonal displays**
Possibilities are endless for creating a different carpet of color in these little "rooms" each season. To get started, try tulips in spring, a mixture of pink geraniums and blue salvias for summer (shown here), chrysanthemums for fall, and ornamental cabbage for winter.

H **'Bronze Beauty' bugleweed** (as needed)
❶ *This plant is locally invasive in the Mid-Atlantic.*
Planted as a ground cover under hedges and

shrubs, these vigorous perennials will form a handsome carpet of purple-bronze foliage. May be shaded out as shrubs mature. See *Ajuga reptans*, p. 119.

I **Containers**
Fill pots or urns with annuals to suit your taste. Here we show impatiens and trailing variegated vinca clustered around a dracaena spike. Change these seasonally, too, if you wish.

J **Courtyard walkway**
Select hard surface material to complement your house. Brick (shown here) or rectangular flagstones in random sizes reinforce the formal lines of the design. See p. 167.

 Plants with this symbol are considered invasive or are locally invasive, as noted. See the appropriate plant profile for suggested alternatives.

Not-so-plain geometry

Sheared greenery in a subtle variety of colors and textures gives this design a clean, uncluttered look. The sculpted forms gently play off one another. Matched pairs of conical yews and boxwoods mark the beginning and end of the walk, their shape echoed and enlarged by the hollies at the corners of the house. Contrasting with these rounded shapes are the rectilinear hedges that outline the lawn itself.

Offsetting all this solid geometry are the freer shapes of the sweet bay magnolias at the corners and the double row of azaleas. Their lovely white flowers make striking accents in spring and early summer.

The design is elegantly simple, but plants don't grow in such tidy shapes and will need frequent pruning to look their best. If maintaining the evergreens is enough work for you, consider replacing the lawn with a ground cover, such as ajuga, that won't need mowing.

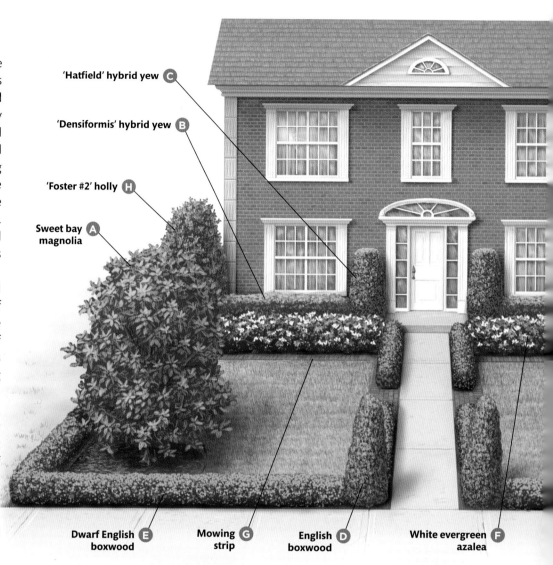

'Hatfield' hybrid yew **C**

'Densiformis' hybrid yew **B**

'Foster #2' holly **H**

Sweet bay magnolia **A**

Dwarf English boxwood **E**

Mowing strip **G**

English boxwood **D**

White evergreen azalea **F**

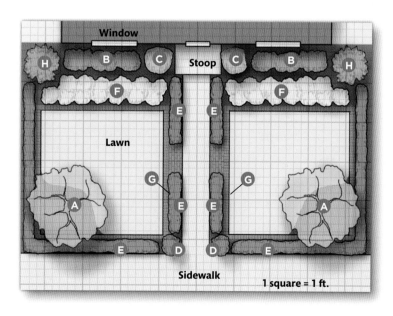

Window

H **B** **C** Stoop **C** **B** **H**

F **F**

E **E**

Lawn

G **G**

A **E** **E** **A**

E **D** **D** **E**

Sidewalk

1 square = 1 ft.

Plants & Projects

A **Sweet bay magnolia** (use 2 plants)
These graceful, slow-growing trees provide 2- to 3-in.-wide creamy white flowers in early summer. Glossy leaves may last through the winter. See *Magnolia virginiana*, p. 144.

B **'Densiformis' hybrid yew** (use 6)
Fast-growing and compact, this hardy evergreen makes a spreading mound low enough to stay beneath the windows without excessive pruning. Its foliage turns bronze when the weather turns cold. See *Taxus* x *media*, p. 157.

C **'Hatfield' hybrid yew** (use 2)
Neat cones of sheared evergreen foliage mirror the shape of the boxwoods at the other end of the walk. Slow-growing shrubs keep their bright green color all winter. See *Taxus* x *media*, p. 157.

D **English boxwood** (use 2)
The classic shrub for formal gardens. Small evergreen leaves give it a fine texture, and it can be sheared into any shape. Make these chubby

SITE: Sunny

SEASON: Spring

CONCEPT: Evergreen foliage sheared in geometric forms complements a formal facade.

H 'Foster #2' holly

A Sweet bay magnolia

E Dwarf English boxwood

VARIATIONS ON A THEME

Formal needn't mean square. A graceful air of formality can also be achieved with curves.

Masses of yellow and white daffodils brighten this front yard in spring. They can be underplanted with perennials, or the beds can be planted anew with annuals for another show in summer.

An urn provides a focal point and a splash of color in a classically formal design.

Neat edges outline a graceful curve that gives the mixed borders in this front yard a touch of formality.

cones about 5 to 6 ft. high. See *Buxus sempervirens*, p. 125.

E Dwarf English boxwood (use 68)
The best boxwood for low edging, compact and slow-growing. Plant these evergreen shrubs roughly 20 in. apart(15 in. to fill in faster), and prune to about 18 in. high with a rounded top. See *Buxus sempervirens* 'Suffruticosa', p. 125.

F White evergreen azalea (use 26)
In spring, these compact shrubs are covered with large white flowers that make a lovely show against the backdrop of dark yews. See *Rhododendron*, p. 150.

G Mowing strip
A brick or stone edging separates the lawn and surrounding hedge and makes mowing easier. See p. 198-199.

See pp. 22-23 for the following:
H 'Foster #2' holly (use 2)

Foundation with Flair

PLANT A FOUNDATION GARDEN

Homes on raised foundations usually have foundation plantings. These simple skirtings of greenery hide unattractive concrete-block underpinnings and help overcome the impression that the house is hovering a few feet above the ground. Useful as these plantings are, they are too often just monochromatic expanses of clipped junipers, dull as dishwater. But, as this design shows, a durable, low-maintenance foundation planting can be more varied, more colorful, and more fun.

Because a foundation planting should look good year-round, the design is anchored by a row of cherry laurels, broad-leaved evergreens covered each spring by heavily scented flowers. A small garden of shrubs, perennials, and a graceful arching grass will catch the eye of visitors approaching the front door. Colorful perennials bloom from spring to fall along the edge of the bed. At the far end is a tidy viburnum, whose spicy-scented flowers will encourage springtime strolls around that corner of the house.

'Autumn Joy' sedum   **E**

'Crimson Pygmy' Japanese barberry   **C**

Lamb's ears   **I**

Plants & Projects

From spring to fall, something is always blooming here, but foliage texture and color play an even greater role than flowers in this design. From the slender, shimmering leaves of Japanese silver grass rising behind mounded barberries, to furry lamb's ears, feathery coreopsis, and fleshy sedum, textures abound, colored in a variety of reds, greens, and silvers. Winter offers glossy green cherry laurels, the tawny leaves and striking seed heads of silver grass, and the rich russets of the sedum. Other than an annual cutback in spring and a little pruning to shape the viburnum, the planting requires little maintenance.

A **Korean spice viburnum** (use 1 plant)
At the corner of the house, this deciduous shrub produces spicy-scented flowers in spring (preceded by pretty pink buds) and dense green foliage in summer and fall. Shape by annual pruning. See *Viburnum carlesii*, p. 158.

B **'Otto Luyken' cherry laurel** (use 4)
The glossy dark leaves and spreading habit of these evergreen shrubs will clothe the foundation year-round. As a bonus, spring produces a profusion of fragrant white flowers in spikes. See *Prunus laurocerasus*, p. 150.

C **'Crimson Pygmy' Japanese barberry** (use 3)
❶ *This plant is considered invasive in the Mid-Atlantic.*
A compact deciduous shrub with small, teardrop-shaped maroon leaves that turn crimson in fall, when they are joined by bright red berries. See *Berberis thunbergii*, p. 122.

D **'Morning Light' Japanese silver grass** (use 1)
❶ *This plant is locally invasive in the Mid-Atlantic.*
A rustling sentinel by the door, this grass is silvery all summer, then turns tawny after frost. Its fluffy seed heads last through the winter. See *Miscanthus sinensis*, p. 145.

E **'Autumn Joy' sedum** (use 3)
Flat-topped flower clusters emerge in late summer above clumps of fleshy gray-green leaves, turning from white through shades of ever deeper pink to rust-colored seed heads that can stand through the winter. See *Sedum*, p. 155.

F **'East Friesland' salvia** (use 4)
Shown off against the green backdrop, reddish purple flower spikes cover these perennials off and on from May through fall. See *Salvia* x *superba*, p. 154.

G **'Longwood Blue' bluebeard** (use 1)
A small deciduous shrub with silvery gray foliage and fringed blue flowers from late summer to frost. See *Caryopteris* x *clandonensis*, p. 126.

H **'Moonbeam' coreopsis** (use 4)
A perennial with fine foliage and tiny pale yellow flowers from July into September. See *Coreopsis verticillata*, p. 128.

I **Lamb's ears** (use 3)
A perennial with fuzzy silver-white leaves. Use the large-leaved, wide-spreading cultivar 'Helene von Stein' (sometimes called 'Big Ears'). See *Stachys byzantina*, p. 156.

J **'Big Blue' lilyturf** (use 4)
❶ *This plant is locally invasive in the Mid-Atlantic.*
This grasslike evergreen perennial under the viburnum has dark blue flowers in summer. See *Liriope muscari*, p. 143.

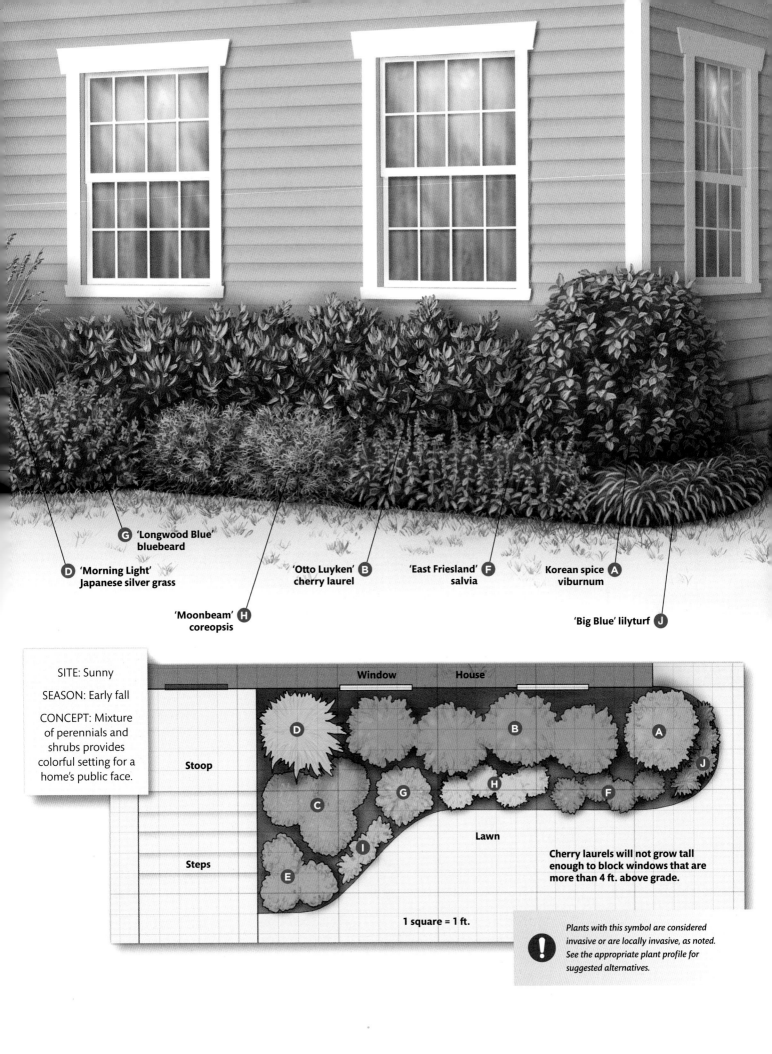

G 'Longwood Blue' bluebeard

D 'Morning Light' Japanese silver grass

'Otto Luyken' B cherry laurel

'East Friesland' F salvia

Korean spice A viburnum

'Moonbeam' H coreopsis

'Big Blue' lilyturf J

SITE: Sunny

SEASON: Early fall

CONCEPT: Mixture of perennials and shrubs provides colorful setting for a home's public face.

Window   House

Stoop

Steps

Lawn

Cherry laurels will not grow tall enough to block windows that are more than 4 ft. above grade.

1 square = 1 ft.

Plants with this symbol are considered invasive or are locally invasive, as noted. See the appropriate plant profile for suggested alternatives.

Brighten a shady porch

This foundation planting graces a front porch on a shady site, making it an even more welcome haven on a hot summer's day. Like the previous design, this one relies on evergreen plants, both shrubs and perennials, to look good in all four seasons. All the plants will thrive in a shady location.

The planting is in bloom from very early spring, in a range of reds, pinks, blues, whites, and lilacs. Baskets of petunias cascading from the porch columns provide people on porch swings and wicker chairs with a colorful sight throughout the summer.

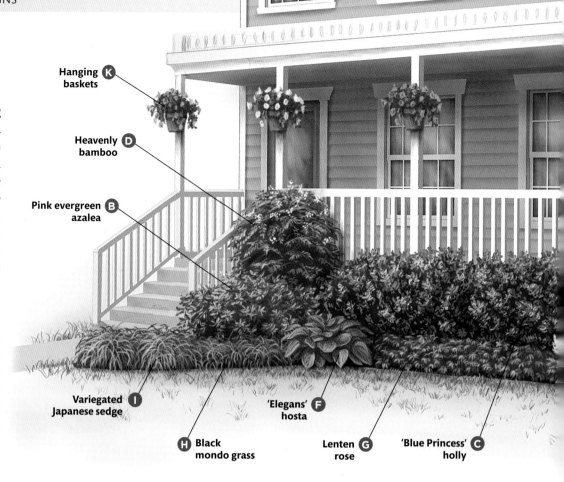

Hanging baskets **K**

Heavenly bamboo **D**

Pink evergreen azalea **B**

Variegated Japanese sedge **I**

'Elegans' hosta **F**

Black mondo grass **H**

Lenten rose **G**

'Blue Princess' holly **C**

Plants & Projects

A **'Nova Zembla' rhododendron** (use 1 plant)
Dark red flowers are strikingly displayed against large evergreen leaves in late spring. Growing 5 ft. tall and spreading as wide, this shrub anchors the corner of the design. See *Rhododendron*, p. 150.

B **Pink evergreen azalea** (use 3)
These compact shrubs bloom profusely in mid- to late spring, and they won't outgrow their space near the steps. An excellent pink-flowered cultivar is 'Nancy of Robin Hill'. See *Rhododendron*, p. 150.

C **'Blue Princess' holly** (use 5)
Handsome blue-green leaves make these evergreen shrubs standout winter plants. They produce bright red berries if there's a 'Blue Prince' holly nearby for pollination. Prune to control their height. See *Ilex* x *meserveae*, p. 139.

D **Heavenly bamboo** (use 1)
❶ *This plant is considered invasive in the Mid-Atlantic.*
This eye-catching evergreen shrub with straight, unbranched stems and layers

of lacy leaves isn't a bamboo at all. This is a truly colorful plant, with leaves changing with the seasons from copper to green to red, and white summer flowers followed by long-lasting red berries. See *Nandina domestica*, p. 146.

E **White astilbe** (use 5)
Decorative dark green foliage perfectly sets off the fluffy white flower spires on this rugged, elegant perennial. The 3-ft.-tall white spires of the hybrid cultivar 'Bridal Veil' bloom in midsummer and simply glow

in a shady spot. See *Astilbe* x *arendsii*, p. 122.

F **'Elegans' hosta** (use 1)
Huge blue puckered leaves give this perennial the stature of a shrub and look great from spring until frost. Small lilylike flowers peeking above the foliage are a bonus. See *Hosta sieboldiana*, p. 137.

G **Lenten rose** (use 5)
Some of the very first flowers of spring appear on these perennials. Large, nodding, cuplike blooms in pink, rosy, white, or greenish colors are

SITE: Partial shade

SEASON: Summer

CONCEPT: Hanging baskets and varied foliage make comfortable companions for a sociable porch.

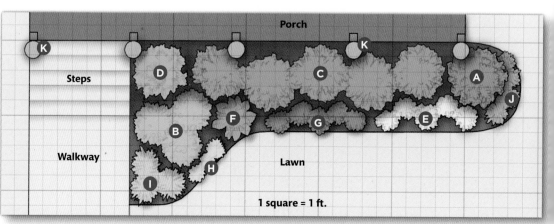

Porch

Steps

Walkway

Lawn

1 square = 1 ft.

White **E** astilbe
A 'Nova Zembla' rhododendron
J Variegated lilyturf

displayed for weeks against dark leathery leaves. See *Helleborus orientalis*, p. 135.

H **Black mondo grass** (use 3)
The unusual purple-black grassy foliage of this evergreen perennial is a striking accent next to the large hosta leaves. See *Ophiopogon planiscapus*, p. 147.

I **Variegated Japanese sedge** (use 3)
Vivid yellow and green, the swirling leaves of this evergreen perennial form neat grassy tufts that are perfect for edging the walk. See *Carex morrowii* 'Aureo-variegata', p. 126.

J **Variegated lilyturf** (use 4)
! *This plant is locally invasive in the Mid-Atlantic.*
The grassy evergreen leaves of this clump-forming perennial are edged with golden yellow stripes that age to a creamy white. Lilac-colored flowers bloom in late summer. See *Liriope muscari* 'Variegata', p. 143.

K **Hanging baskets**
Cascading petunias clothe the columns supporting the porch roof, providing a colorful frame for the view from the porch.

VARIATIONS ON A THEME

Anything but boring, the plantings shown here demonstrate the wide range of possibilities for foundations.

This house couldn't have a more natural setting than the rhododendrons and other woodland plants nestled by its walls.

Varied in color, texture, and shape, the shrubs in this foundation planting pack a big punch in a narrow space.

Attractive windows like these don't need to be hidden behind a bank of shrubs. Flowering annuals work well here. They'll disappear in winter, but all summer long they'll provide a glorious display that can be viewed from inside as well as outside.

A Welcoming Entry

MAKE A PLEASANT PASSAGE TO THE FRONT DOOR

First impressions are as important in the home landscape as they are on a blind date or a job interview. Why wait until a visitor reaches the front door to extend a warm greeting? Instead let your landscape offer a friendly welcome and a helpful "Please come this way." Well-chosen plants and a revamped walkway not only make a visitor's short journey a pleasant one, they can also enhance your home's most public face and help settle it comfortably in its immediate surroundings.

The ample bluestone walkway in this design invites visitors to stroll side by side through a small garden from the driveway to the entrance. The path is positioned to put the front door in full view of arriving guests. Its generous width allows for informal gatherings as guests arrive and leave, and well-chosen plants encourage lingering there to enjoy them.

Three small trees grace the entrance with spring and summer flowers, light shade, and superb fall color. Most of the perennials and shrubs are evergreen and look good year-round, providing a fine background to the flowers and an attractive foil to the fall color. In the winter, colorful tree bark and bright berries make gazing out the windows a pleasure.

'Natchez' **C**
crape myrtle

See site plan for **K** .

White evergreen azalea **B**

'Big Blue' lilyturf **D**

'Blue Prince' holly **H**

Blue oat grass **I**

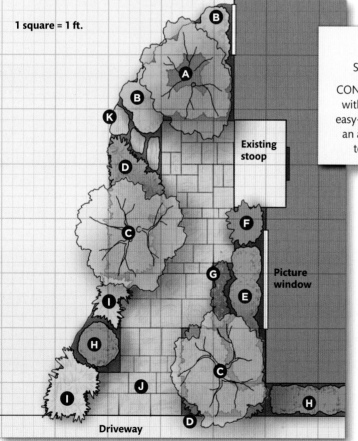

1 square = 1 ft.

Existing stoop

Picture window

Driveway

SITE: Sunny

SEASON: Summer

CONCEPT: New walkway with largely evergreen, easy-care plantings make an attractive approach to the main entry.

Plants & Projects

The predominantly evergreen foliage comes in a surprising range of blues and greens, accented by white and blue flowers in spring and summer. Once established, the planting requires regular pruning and shearing but little else.

A Serviceberry (use 1 plant)
This small deciduous, often multitrunked tree greets spring with clusters of white flowers. Edible blue-purple berries ripen in June or July; bright foliage enlivens the autumn. See *Amelanchier* x *grandiflora*, p. 119.

B White evergreen azalea
(use 11)
Low, mounding shrubs form a soft skirt beneath the serviceberry by the door. Try the cultivar 'Helen Curtis', with white flowers in mid- to late spring. See *Rhododendron*, p. 150.

C 'Natchez' crape myrtle (use 2)
Flanking the walk, these small multitrunked trees bear pure white crepe-papery flowers for weeks in summer. Colorful fall leaves drop to reveal attractive flaking bark in winter. See *Lagerstroemia indica*, p. 142.

A Serviceberry

Plants with this symbol are considered invasive or are locally invasive, as noted. See the appropriate plant profile for suggested alternatives.

G Christmas rose

F Heavenly bamboo

J Walkway

E 'Otto Luyken' cherry laurel

D 'Big Blue' lilyturf

C 'Natchez' crape myrtle

H 'Blue Prince' holly

D **'Big Blue' lilyturf** (use 40)
! *This plant is locally invasive in the Mid-Atlantic.*
These grassy evergreen perennials carpet the ground beneath the crape myrtles. Small spikes of blue flowers in summer produce shiny blue-black berries in fall. Brighten up spring by underplanting 75 white daffodil bulbs (*Narcissus*, p.120) in each lilyturf bed. See *Liriope muscari*, p. 143.

E **'Otto Luyken' cherry laurel** (use 4)
This evergreen shrub has thick glossy leaves and fragrant white spring flowers. Prune to form a neat block of greenery below the windows. See *Prunus laurocerasus*, p. 150.

F **Heavenly bamboo** (use 1)
! *This plant is considered invasive in the Mid-Atlantic.*
An evergreen shrub that packs four seasons of interest into the narrow space by the door. Tiers of lacy foliage turn from copper to green to rich crimson or purple. Summer's white flowers give way to heavy sprays of shiny red berries that may last until spring. See *Nandina domestica*, p. 146.

G **Christmas rose** (use 5)
Tucked in by the walk, this evergreen ground cover offers fine-toothed dark green leaves and white cup-size blossoms in winter and early spring. Underplant 20 white Grecian windflower bulbs (*Anemone blanda*, p. 120) to add to the spring display. See *Helleborus niger*, p. 135.

H **'Blue Prince' holly** (use 5)
An excellent evergreen foundation shrub between the drive and house; one is also used as a shaped specimen next to the walk. Features glossy blue-green foliage and purple twigs. Maintained by regular pruning. See *Ilex x meserveae*, p. 139.

I **Blue oat grass** (use 10)
The formality of the sheared holly is set off nicely by this small island of clump-forming grass. Blue-gray foliage looks good all year. See *Helictotrichon sempervirens*, p. 135.

J **Walkway**
Rectangular flagstones in random sizes; bluestone shown here. See p. 167.

K **Steppingstones**
Fieldstones provide easy access to the lawn. See p. 171.

A shady welcome

If your entry is shady, receiving less than six hours of sunlight a day, try this planting scheme, which replaces sun-loving plants from the previous design with others that prefer the shade. Overall, the emphasis is still on evergreen plants for year-round good looks.

New plants expand the color scheme and include fragrant summersweet by the drive, with rhododendron, foamflower, and Christmas fern, all handsome evergreens, alongside the walk. Flanking the door, a witch hazel unfolds sweet-scented flowers in early spring, and a Japanese andromeda becomes the four-season attraction by the door.

Plants & Projects

A **Vernal witch hazel**
(use 1 plant)
The fragrant reddish or gold flowers of this deciduous shrub perfume the entry in very early spring. Golden leaves in fall. See *Hamamelis vernalis*, p. 134.

B **Christmas fern** (use 65)
Easy-care evergreen ground cover with glossy fronds is at home beneath the serviceberries. See Ferns: *Polystichum acrostichoides*, p. 132.

C **'Spring Snow' Japanese andromeda** (use 1)
Glossy evergreen foliage heaves under masses of white flowers in early spring. New leaves bright gold or red. Annual pruning fits it into the corner. See *Pieris japonica*, p. 149.

D **Foamflower** (use 9)
Woodland ground cover spreads quickly, producing clumps of low evergreen foliage and plump spikes of white flowers in late spring. See *Tiarella cordifolia*, p. 157.

E **'PJM' rhododendron** (use 1)
This shrub greets visitors with handsome evergreen foliage year-round (leaves turn maroon in winter) and magenta flowers in very early spring. See *Rhododendron*, p. 150.

F **Summersweet** (use 4)
Pruned here as a foundation planting. Summersweet's small white or pink flowers will fill the entry garden with fragrance in August. Glossy dark deciduous foliage turns gold in fall. See *Clethra alnifolia*, p. 128.

G **Bulbs**
Scatter 150 Spanish bluebells (*Endymion hispanica*) among the ferns and lilyturf for a charming display of dangling bell-shaped blue flowers in April. See Bulbs, p. 124.

See pp. 30–31 for the following:

H **White evergreen azalea** (use 11)

I **Serviceberry** (use 2)

J **'Blue Prince' holly** (use 4)

K **'Big Blue' lilyturf** (use 20)
❗ *This plant is locally invasive in the Mid-Atlantic.*

L **Walkway**

M **Steppingstones**

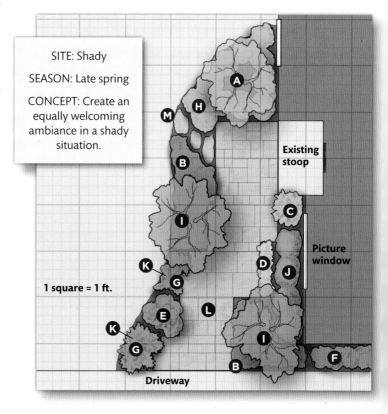

SITE: Shady

SEASON: Late spring

CONCEPT: Create an equally welcoming ambiance in a shady situation.

1 square = 1 ft.

Existing stoop

Picture window

Driveway

VARIATIONS ON A THEME

People visit a home year-round, so an entry garden should be welcoming in all seasons.

If you have little or no front yard, containers of showy annuals, such as this purple fountain grass, help extend a friendly greeting. Make new container arrangements for each season.

Evergreen foliage, bright flowers, attractive bark, and spring bulbs ensure that this entry is colorful all year.

A well-planned entry garden complements the architecture of this two-story house. Evergreen hedges help define the spacious entry area and serve as an attractive backdrop for a mixed-shrub border. The brick path and white bench echo the colors of the house, as do the white azaleas.

On the Street

GIVE YOUR CURBSIDE STRIP A NEW LOOK

Homeowners seldom think much about the area that runs between the sidewalk and street. At best it is a tidy patch of lawn; at worst, a weed-choked eyesore. But it is one of the most public parts of your property. Planting this strip with attractive perennials and shrubs can give pleasure to passersby and visitors who park next to the curb, as well as enhancing the streetscape you view from the house. (This strip is usually city-owned, so check local ordinances for restrictions before you start a remake.)

It might help to think of this curbside strip as an island bed between two defined boundaries: the street and the sidewalk. These beds are divided further by a wide pedestrian walkway, providing ample room for visitors to get in and out of front and rear car doors. The plantings on either side are balanced, but not rigidly symmetrical. You can expand the beds to fill a longer strip, or plant lawn next to the beds.

This can be a difficult site. Summer drought and heat, winter road salt, pedestrian and car traffic, and errant dogs are the usual conditions found along the street. Plants have to be tough to perform well here, but they need not look tough. These combine fine foliage and bright colors for a dramatic impact from spring until fall. Most of these plants die back in winter, so piles of snow won't hurt them.

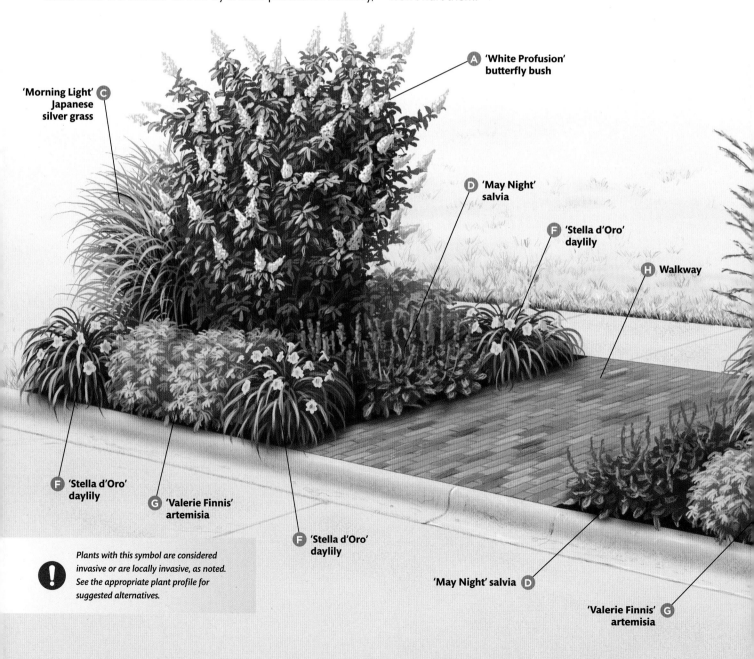

'Morning Light' **C**
Japanese
silver grass

A 'White Profusion'
butterfly bush

D 'May Night'
salvia

F 'Stella d'Oro'
daylily

H Walkway

F 'Stella d'Oro'
daylily

G 'Valerie Finnis'
artemisia

F 'Stella d'Oro'
daylily

! Plants with this symbol are considered invasive or are locally invasive, as noted. See the appropriate plant profile for suggested alternatives.

'May Night' salvia **D**

'Valerie Finnis' **G**
artemisia

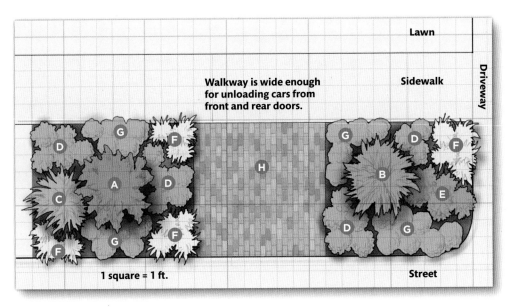

Lawn

Driveway

Sidewalk

Walkway is wide enough for unloading cars from front and rear doors.

1 square = 1 ft.

Street

Plants & Projects

Shrubs, grasses, and perennials in bright colors and a variety of forms and textures combine for a bold look. Foliage in a range of greens, silvers, and, late in the season, browns and golds join flowers in white, purple, pink, and yellow. While these hardy plants will need to be divided every few years, the only annual maintenance required is cutting everything to the ground in early spring. Spacing the plants close together, as shown on the plan, is one way to deter weeds.

A **'White Profusion' butterfly bush** (use 1)
! *This plant is considered invasive in the Mid-Atlantic.*
The arching shoots of this large deciduous shrub anchor the left side of the design. Clumps of fragrant small white flowers attract butterflies from mid-summer through autumn. See *Buddleia davidii*, p. 123.

B **'Karl Foerster' feather reed grass** (use 1)
This tall, upright perennial grass echoes the shape of the butterfly bush across the path. Midsummer flowers produce seed heads that look pretty for months as they ripen to a silvery beige. Leaves and seed heads can stand through the winter. See *Calamagrostis* x *acutiflora*, p. 125.

C **'Morning Light' Japanese silver grass** (use 1)
! *This plant is locally invasive in the Mid-Atlantic.*
The long slender blades of this perennial grass are edged with clear white, giving the lovely arching form a ghostly luminescence from a distance. Large red-bronze flower plumes wave above the foliage in late summer and dry to silvery gold for a show in winter. See *Miscanthus sinensis*, p. 145.

D **'May Night' salvia** (use 18)
This perennial's indigo-purple flower spikes dapple clumps of dark green foliage from May through fall. See *Salvia* x *superba*, p. 154.

E **Purple coneflower** (use 5)
A tough prairie perennial well suited to this site. Its large, pink, rough-hewn daisies add a splash of color from summer until fall. See *Echinacea purpurea*, p. 130.

F **'Stella d'Oro' daylily** (use 15)
Gold flowers flare like trumpets on sturdy stems rising above this small perennial's grassy leaves. Blooms from late spring through fall. See *Hemerocallis*, p. 136.

G **'Valerie Finnis' artemisia** (use 22)
An excellent perennial for color contrast. Forms a patch of silvery foliage that looks fresh and bright all season. See *Artemisia ludoviciana*, p. 121.

H **Walkway**
Brick pavers make a path through the planting for visitors getting out of cars parked by the curb. See p. 167.

B 'Karl Foerster' feather reed grass

SITE: Sunny

SEASON: Late summer

CONCEPT: Small but varied planting treats visitors and passersby to a colorful display.

D 'May Night' salvia

F 'Stella d'Oro' daylily

E Purple coneflower

Enliven a shady curb

This design features shade-loving plants for those who live on the cool shady streets that make many neighborhoods so pleasant. Emphasizing foliage more than flowers, the effect is more subdued than the previous design, but still cheerful.

Two deciduous shrubs, bayberry and summersweet, anchor the composition. Bayberry offers fragrant leaves; summersweet, scented flowers. Around them a mix of foliage in golds, purples, whites, and greens catches the eye, as does the contrast of slender and broad leaves. Unlike the drought-tolerant plants in the previous design, these shade lovers will need water during long dry spells. Other than that, maintenance is restricted to a little pruning and spring cleanup.

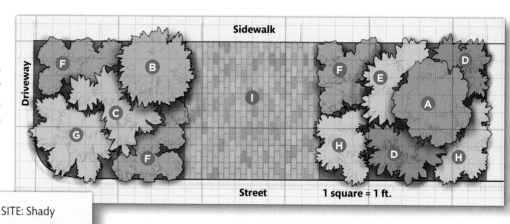

SITE: Shady

SEASON: Late summer

CONCEPT: Foliage colors and textures stand out on a shady site.

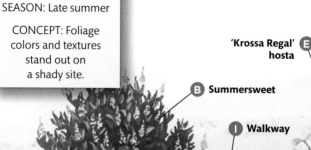

A **Bayberry**

E **'Krossa Regal' hosta**

B **Summersweet**

I **Walkway**

F **'Palace Purple' heuchera**

G **Gold-variegated hakonechloa**

C **'Aureo-marginata' hosta**

F **'Palace Purple' heuchera**

D **'Francee' hosta**

H **Variegated Japanese sedge**

Plants & Projects

A Bayberry (use 1 plant)
This low, mounded deciduous shrub is impervious to road salt. Fragrant glossy leaves turn purple in fall and hang on until winter. See *Myrica pensylvanica*, p. 145.

B Summersweet (use 1)
A deciduous native shrub that starts late in spring but bears numerous spikes of sweet-scented flowers in late summer. As a bonus, its leaves turn a lovely gold in autumn. See *Clethra alnifolia*, p. 128.

C 'Aureo-marginata' hosta (use 5)
These medium-size hostas form neat mounds of dark green foliage, each leaf edged with gold. See *Hosta*, p. 136.

D 'Francee' hosta (use 8)
Echoing the hostas across the path, these medium-size plants have forest green leaves edged with bright white. See *Hosta*, p. 136.

E 'Krossa Regal' hosta (use 3)
The largest hostas in the planting. Their large powdery

blue leaves arch, giving the plant a vase shape. Stalks bearing lavender flowers rise 5 ft. or more. See *Hosta*, p. 136.

F 'Palace Purple' heuchera (use 18)
This foot-tall clumping perennial carpets the edges of the beds with large dark purple leaves that look good all season. See *Heuchera*, p. 136.

G Gold-variegated hakonechloa (use 8)
The fine golden blades of this lovely shade-tolerant perennial

grass light up the shade and contrast nicely with the broad hosta leaves. See *Hakonechloa macra* 'Aureola', p. 134.

H Variegated Japanese sedge (use 10)
Neat evergreen tufts of brightly striped green-and-gold leaves make another nice contrast in texture with the neighboring hostas. See *Carex morrowii* 'Aureo-variegata', p. 126.

See p. 35 for the following:
I Walkway

VARIATIONS ON A THEME

Gardening right up to the edge of the street can be a challenge, but a thoughtful selection of plants can turn an awkward spot into a spectacular showpiece.

This simple design of brightly colored tulips is spectacular in spring. A mass planting of summer annuals maintains the show.

These eye-catching perennials and shrubs are as easy to appreciate when you're going 25 miles per hour as they are at a stroll.

Clump-forming ornamental grasses in a variety of colors and textures highlight this durable curbside planting.

A Neighborly Corner

BEAUTIFY A BOUNDARY WITH EASY-CARE PLANTS

Fringe tree **A**

'Anthony Waterer' spirea **B**

E Tamarix juniper

C 'Bronxensis' greenstem forsythia

Plants with this symbol are considered invasive or are locally invasive, as noted. See the appropriate plant profile for suggested alternatives.

The corner where your property meets your neighbor's and the sidewalk can be a kind of grassy no-man's-land. This design defines the boundary with a planting that can be enjoyed by the property owners as well as by people passing by. Good gardens make good neighbors, so we've used well-behaved plants that won't make extra work for the person next door—or for you. To keep you from having to haul water and supplies out to the corner too often, these are all tough, carefree plants.

Because of its exposed location, remote from the house and close to the street, this is a less personal planting than those in other more private and frequently used parts of your property. It is meant to be appreciated from a distance. Rising from low-growing shrubs to the lovely fringe tree near the sidewalk, the design draws the eye when viewed from the house. An existing split-rail fence on the property line serves as a backdrop for the plants without hiding them from the view of a neighbor or passerby. While not intended as a barrier, the planting also provides a modest psychological distraction, if not an actual physical screen from the activity on the street.

Plants & Projects

These plants offer pleasing foliage from spring through fall, when the barberries flame out in a blaze of crimson. While something is in flower from spring to midsummer, the high point is the fringe tree's distinctive display. Winter presents a tracery of bare stems and limbs above the junipers' evergreen carpet. All the plants can thrive on an open, sunny, dry site and require little care beyond some occasional pruning.

Ⓐ Fringe tree (use 1 plant)
An open, multistemmed form lets this small deciduous tree combine well with shrubs, but the profuse clusters of fringed, white, spring-blooming flowers with a spicy fragrance are its real attraction. See *Chionanthus virginicus*, p. 127.

Ⓑ 'Anthony Waterer' spirea (use 3)
❶ *This plant is considered invasive in the Mid-Atlantic.*
Spireas are among the toughest flowering shrubs. This cultivar forms a low mound of twiggy stems with small, fine, deciduous leaves and dark pink flowers in midsummer. See *Spiraea* x *bumalda*, p. 155.

Ⓒ 'Bronxensis' greenstem forsythia (use 3)
These diminutive shrubs grow only about a foot high, so they won't block your view of the sidewalk or other plants. Primrose yellow flowers bring spring color, and the deciduous leaves are a rich, glossy bright green. See *Forsythia viridissima*, p. 133.

Ⓓ 'Crimson Pygmy' Japanese barberry (use 4)
❶ *This plant is considered invasive in the Mid-Atlantic.*
Forming a low cushionlike mass at one end of the planting, these hardy deciduous shrubs are a clear contrast to the neighboring junipers in both texture and color. Leaves are maroon through the summer, turning crimson in fall. See *Berberis thunbergii*, p. 122.

Ⓔ Tamarix juniper (use 6)
Like all junipers, this is a rugged plant that thrives on dry, open sites. A low evergreen spreader, it will form a blue-green mat about 18 in. tall beneath the fringe tree. See *Juniperus sabina* 'Tamariscifolia', p. 141.

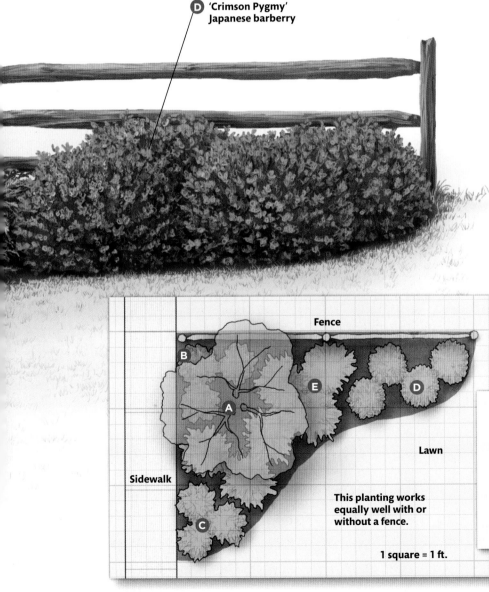

Ⓓ **'Crimson Pygmy' Japanese barberry**

Fence

B

E

A

D

Lawn

Sidewalk

C

This planting works equally well with or without a fence.

1 square = 1 ft.

SITE: Sunny

SEASON: Late spring

CONCEPT: Define the property line with a low-maintenance, neighbor-friendly planting of trees and shrubs.

VARIATIONS ON A THEME

Like the designs featured in the previous pages, these are bold enough
to catch the eye from a distance and interesting at close range.

This colorful corner incorporates a small pond and water plants. The rail fence provides the visual scaffolding that holds the design together.

Demonstrating how less can be more, a limited palette of plants creates considerable drama beneath a young blue spruce.

Situated near the street, the bold foliage of a Japanese maple offers attractions to passing drivers, while the daintier ground covers give strollers something to enjoy.

Add a touch of color

If you prefer more color in your corner, try this design. Here we've replaced some shrubs with tough, durable perennial flowers that light up the bed from spring through fall.

Low-growing yews join the fringe tree and spireas from the preceding design in defining the space and giving year-round structure. Two daisies—one yellow, one white—brighten one end of the bed. Behind these large flowers, with their coarse low-mounding foliage, a wispy silver-gray Russian sage is sprinkled for months with tiny blue blossoms. At the other end of the bed, daylilies bloom from early summer through fall, their cascading foliage contrasting nicely with the yews.

All these plants catch the eye at a distance. Dianthus, the last addition, handsomely repays closer inspection. These tough but dainty-looking plants have small, deliciously fragrant pink flowers. Stroll down and cut a few to perfume an entire room.

H Fringe tree

B Russian sage

G 'Anthony Waterer' spirea

C 'Goldsturm' coneflower

D 'Silver Princess' Shasta daisy

F 'Bath's Pink' dianthus

A Spreading English yew

E 'Stella d'Oro' daylily

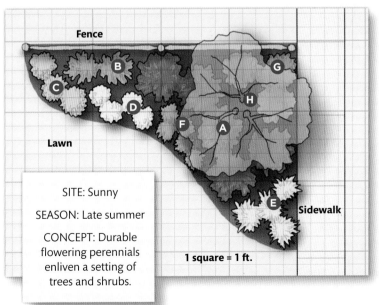

Fence

Lawn

Sidewalk

1 square = 1 ft.

SITE: Sunny

SEASON: Late summer

CONCEPT: Durable flowering perennials enliven a setting of trees and shrubs.

Plants & Projects

A Spreading English yew (use 5 plants)
Replacing the junipers at the foot of the fringe tree are low-growing, wide-spreading yews. The large evergreen needles are an excellent backdrop for the perennial flowers, and they retain their green color year-round. See *Taxus baccata 'Repandens'*, p. 157.

B Russian sage (use 2)
This shrubby perennial's many small blue flowers create an airy haze of blue when seen from a distance. Silvery gray, aromatic foliage complements the flowers and nearby plants. Russian sage is in bloom for weeks during the summer and fall. See *Perovskia atriplicifolia*, p. 148.

C 'Goldsturm' coneflower (use 3)
Making an eye-catching display at the corner of the bed, this perennial is an improved version of the reliable old black-eyed Susan. 'Goldsturm' produces large gold-yellow daisylike flowers with black centers. Masses of flowers hover over clumps of large dark green leaves from late July until October. See *Rudbeckia fulgida*, p. 153.

D 'Silver Princess' Shasta daisy (use 4)
Large showy white flowers (excellent for cutting) appear in June and July above a mat of glossy leaves. This dwarf perennial is only about 1 ft. tall, providing a nice contrast in stature as well as flower color

to the larger coneflower next door to it. See *Chrysanthemum x superbum*, p. 127.

E 'Stella d'Oro' daylily (use 4)
This exceptional daylily bears gold-orange trumpetlike flowers from early summer through fall—a remarkable feat, considering the flowers last only one day each. Flowers and the compact clumps of straplike arching leaves hold up admirably through heat and drought, succumbing only to hard frost. See *Hemerocallis*, p. 136.

F 'Bath's Pink' dianthus (use 5)
The clear pink, late-spring flowers of these small perennials have a wonderful fragrance. (Clip the spent flower stalks and they may rebloom.) The fine-textured foliage forms an evergreen ground cover at the feet of the yews. See *Dianthus*, p. 130.

See p. 39 for the following:

G 'Anthony Waterer' spirea (use 3)
❶ *This plant is considered invasive in the Mid-Atlantic.*

H Fringe tree (use 1)

A Pleasing Postal Planting

PROVIDE A LEAFY SETTING FOR THE DAILY MAIL

For some, the lowly mailbox may seem a surprising candidate for landscaping. But posted like a sentry by the driveway entrance, it is highly visible to visitors and passersby. And it is one of the few places on your property that you visit every day. A pretty planting like the one shown here pleases the passing public and rewards your daily journey (and that of your friendly letter carrier).

Foliage provides months of interest in this planting. Large clumps of feather reed grass are eye-catching from early summer through winter, with graceful leaves and plumes of flowers that rustle in the wind. At their feet, the grayish foliage of yarrow, catmint, and beach wormwood contrasts with reddish sedum and the grassy blue leaves of the cottage pinks. When the pinks are in bloom, take one or two of these sweet-scented flowers back to the house with you each day; they'll perfume a whole room. For a quick olfactory fix, rub your fingers on the aromatic catmint leaves.

Plants & Projects

Despite the frequent visits, this is not a spot for a high-maintenance garden. The plants selected here are carefree, able to withstand summer drought and piles of winter snow. A heavy mulch will control weeds not crowded out by the vigorous plants.

Ⓐ 'Karl Foerster' feather reed grass (use 3 plants)
This perennial grass is the focal point of the planting. Slender leaves arch but don't flop. Narrow flower plumes rise above the foliage from midsummer on. Seed heads and leaves turn a lovely tan in fall, fare well in winter conditions. See *Calamagrostis* x *acutiflora*, p. 125.

Ⓑ 'Coronation Gold' yarrow (use 5)
A perennial, it forms a clump of lacy but tough green-gray foliage. In midsummer thick flower stalks support clusters of very bright golden yellow flowers. See *Achillea*, p. 118.

Ⓒ 'Dropmore' catmint (use 7)
A perennial that forms a casual, sometimes floppy mound of arching stems and small gray leaves. Airy clouds of small violet-blue flowers seem to hover over the plant from early summer on. See *Nepeta* x *faassenii*, p. 146.

Ⓓ 'Silver Brocade' beach wormwood (use 3)
A low, spreading perennial grown here for its striking silver-gray foliage, which offers a nice contrast in color and texture to the nearby sedum and feather reed grass. See *Artemisia stelleriana*, p. 121.

Ⓔ 'Vera Jameson' sedum (use 5)
A perennial forming a low mound of distinctive, dusty gray-purple succulent leaves on stout stalks. Domed clusters of small pink flowers hover over the foliage in late summer. See *Sedum*, p. 155.

Ⓕ 'Aqua' cottage pink (use 5)
A perennial with grassy bluish evergreen foliage and deliciously scented frilly white flowers in late spring. See *Dianthus*, p. 130.

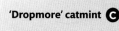

'Aqua' cottage pink Ⓕ

'Dropmore' catmint Ⓒ

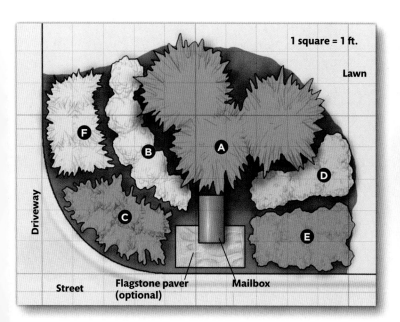

1 square = 1 ft.

Lawn

Driveway

Street

Flagstone paver (optional)

Mailbox

SITE: Sunny

SEASON: Summer

CONCEPT: Striking foliage accented by pretty flowers makes the mailbox a favorite destination.

'Karl Foerster' **A**
feather reed grass

'Coronation **B**
Gold'
yarrow

**Fill area between post and
curb with flagstone paver
or extend the plantings
from either side.**

'Vera Jameson' **E**
sedum

'Silver Brocade' **D**
beach wormwood

Plants with this symbol are considered
invasive or are locally invasive, as noted.
See the appropriate plant profile for
suggested alternatives.

Flowers by mail

In this planting, long-blooming shrubs and perennials back up the mailbox with a months-long display of color. Lower-growing spireas replace the grasses as the centerpiece. Their pink midsummer flowers are joined by rosy pink yarrow and violet-blue catmint. Mixing it up with these rather dainty flowers are large rustic purple coneflowers. Like their counterparts in the previous design, these are all tough plants, requiring only a bit of tidying up in fall and spring.

SITE: Sunny

SEASON: Summer

CONCEPT: Easy-care flowering shrubs and perennials provide a long season of bloom.

A 'Little Princess' Japanese spirea

C Purple coneflower

B See site plan for

E 'Dropmore' catmint

D Evergreen candytuft

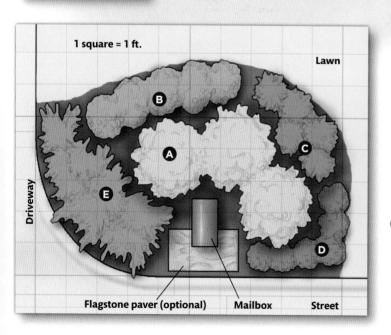

1 square = 1 ft.

Lawn

Driveway

Flagstone paver (optional)   Mailbox   Street

Plants & Projects

A **'Little Princess' Japanese spirea** (use 3 plants)
! *This plant is considered invasive in the Mid-Atlantic.* Well-behaved deciduous shrub that forms a tidy mound of fine-textured dark green leaves draped in summer with small rounded clusters of light pink flowers. Prune hard in early spring to remove winter-damaged stems and to keep the growth habit compact. See *Spiraea japonica*, p. 155.

B **'Appleblossom' yarrow** (use 5)
A vigorous perennial with sprawling gray-green ferny leaves that form an aromatic ground cover. Flat clusters of pink flowers rise above the foliage on stiff stalks and make good cut flowers; the more flowers you pick, the longer it blooms. See *Achillea*

millefolium, p. 118.

C **Purple coneflower** (use 5)
A perennial prairie wildflower, good for sunny open sites. In midsummer, sturdy stalks rise above the clump of dark green leaves, carrying cheerful outsize daisylike flowers. Leave the stalks standing in winter so goldfinches and other songbirds can eat the seeds. See *Echinacea purpurea*, p. 130.

D **Evergreen candytuft** (use 6)
A spreading perennial, it forms a tough mat of glossy evergreen leaves along (and over) the curb. Bright white flowers cover the dark foliage for several weeks in spring and may reappear in fall. See *Iberis sempervirens*, p. 139.

See p. 42 for the following:

E **'Dropmore' catmint** (use 7)

VARIATIONS ON A THEME

We've featured designs that will enhance any postbox.
But here are a few in which the box itself is an attraction.

This streaky blue box is an excellent foil for the red-orange flowers of the honeysuckle twined around the post.

The colors of this box and post, rather than their form, work nicely with the surrounding floral display.

White-flowering clematis highlights the old-fashioned charm of this antique postbox.

Gateway Garden

SIMPLE STRUCTURE AND PLANTINGS MAKE A PLEASING PASSAGE

Entrances are an important part of any landscape. They can welcome visitors onto your property; highlight a special feature, such as a rose garden; or mark passage between two areas with different character or function. The design shown here can serve in any of these situations. A picket fence and perennial plantings create a friendly attractive barrier, just enough to signal the confines of the front yard or contain the family dog. The simple vine-covered arbor provides welcoming access.

The design combines uncomplicated elements imaginatively, creating interesting details to catch the eye and a slightly formal but comfortable overall effect. Picketed enclosures and compact evergreen shrubs broaden the arbor, giving it greater presence. The wide flagstone apron, flanked by

neat deciduous shrubs, reinforces this effect and frames the entrance. Massed perennial plantings lend substance to the fence, which serves as a backdrop to their handsome foliage and colorful flowers.

J Arbor

A White clematis

B 'Green Beauty' littleleaf boxwood

C Pale yellow daylily

A White clematis

C Pale yellow daylily

B 'Green Beauty' littleleaf boxwood

G Evergreen candytuft

I White bugleweed

L Walkway

G Evergreen candytuft

F 'Autumn Joy' sedum

D 'Longwood Blue' bluebeard

See site plan for H .

! *Plants with this symbol are considered invasive or are locally invasive, as noted. See the appropriate plant profile for suggested alternatives.*

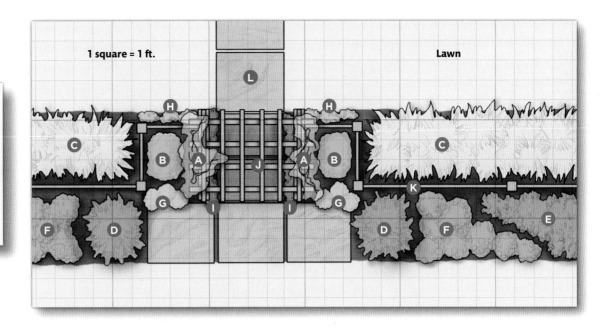

SITE: Sunny

SEASON: Late summer

CONCEPT: Perennials and flowering vines accent traditional fence and entry arbor.

1 square = 1 ft.

Lawn

Plants & Projects

K Picket fence

E 'Wargrave Pink' geranium

F 'Autumn Joy' sedum

D 'Longwood Blue' bluebeard

For many people, a picket fence and vine-covered arbor represent old-fashioned neighborly virtues. The plantings here further encourage this feeling. Pretty white flowers cover the arbor for much of the summer, while the canopy of foliage creates a cool spot for exchanging neighborhood news.

Massed plantings of daylilies, geraniums, and sedums along the fence produce wide swaths of flowers and attractive foliage from early summer to fall. Plant drifts of snowdrops in these beds; their late-winter flowers are a welcome sign that spring will soon come.

The structures and plantings are easy to build, install, and care for. You can extend the fence and plantings as needed. To use an existing concrete walk, just pour pads either side to create the wide apron in front of the arbor.

A White clematis (use 4 plants)
Four of these deciduous climbing vines, one at each post, will cover the arbor in a few years. For lovely large white flowers, try the cultivar 'Henryi', which blooms in early and late summer. See *Clematis*, p. 128.

B 'Green Beauty' littleleaf boxwood (use 2)
This evergreen shrub forms a neat ball of small bright green leaves without shearing. It is colorful in winter when the rest of the plants are dormant. See *Buxus microphylla*, p. 125.

C Pale yellow daylily (use 24)
A durable perennial whose cheerful trumpet-shaped flowers nod above clumps of arching foliage. Choose from the many yellow-flowered cultivars (some fragrant); mix several to extend the season of bloom. See *Hemerocallis*, p. 136.

D 'Longwood Blue' bluebeard (use 2)
A pair of these small deciduous shrubs with soft gray foliage frame the entry. Sky blue late-summer flowers cover the plants for weeks. See *Caryopteris x clandonensis*, p. 126.

E 'Wargrave Pink' geranium (use 9)
This perennial produces a mass of bright green leaves and a profusion of pink flowers in early summer. Cut it back in July and it will bloom intermittently until frost. See *Geranium endressii*, p. 134.

F 'Autumn Joy' sedum (use 13)
This perennial forms a clump of upright stems with distinctive fleshy foliage. Pale flower buds in summer are followed by rosy pink flowers in fall and rusty seed heads that stand up in winter. See *Sedum*, p. 155.

G Evergreen candytuft (use 12)
A perennial ground cover that spreads to form a small welcome mat at the foot of the boxwoods. White flowers stand out against glossy evergreen leaves in spring. See *Iberis sempervirens*, p. 139.

H Lamb's ears (use 6)
Favorites of children, the long woolly gray leaves of this perennial form a soft carpet. In early summer, thick stalks carry scattered purple flowers. See *Stachys byzantina*, p. 156.

I White bugleweed (use 20)
❶ *This plant is locally invasive in the Mid-Atlantic.*
Edging the walk under the arbor, this perennial ground cover has pretty green leaves and, in late spring, short spikes of white flowers. See *Ajuga reptans* 'Alba', p. 119.

J Arbor
Thick posts give this simple structure a sturdy visual presence. Paint or stain it, or make it of cedar and let it weather as shown here. See p. 194–195.

K Picket fence
Low picket fence adds character to the planting; materials and finish should match the arbor. See p. 194–195.

L Walkway
Flagstone walk can be large pavers, as shown here, or made up of smaller rectangular flags. See p. 167.

VARIATIONS ON A THEME

Gateways mark boundaries, but entice passage, too. These gates, with their attendant hedges and plantings, provide transition between different areas on a property.

An eye-catching gate marks a boundary between the wild and the cultivated.

An impressive piece of architecture on its own, this arch is the right size and style for the wide, formal planting beds that flank it.

Elaborate and substantial borders funnel strollers toward a small gate in a large hedge.

A perennial "hedge"

Not every situation calls for a fence or a year-round enclosure. In this simpler design, massed plantings of perennials replace the fence. In summer and fall, the plants form a wide, hedgelike thicket of upright leafy stems topped from midsummer on by flowers of white or dark red. The arbor punctuates the line of the "hedge" and is covered all summer with large fragrant yellow roses.

In winter, the arbor is now the focal point, flanked by evergreen shrubs and ground covers. Cut to the ground, the perennials lie dormant, their beds coming to life in late winter with a flush of crocuses.

This seasonal design is useful for areas where summer boundaries are important but winter ones are not. Install it as a border and entrance to a vegetable garden, for example, or where a fence or permanent boundary would interfere with sledding or other winter activities.

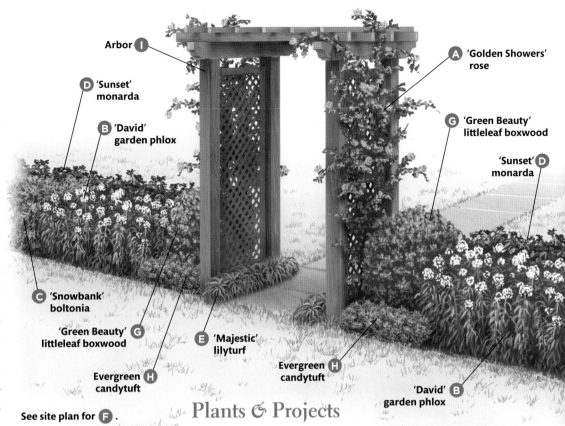

Arbor **I**

D 'Sunset' monarda

B 'David' garden phlox

A 'Golden Showers' rose

G 'Green Beauty' littleleaf boxwood

D 'Sunset' monarda

C 'Snowbank' boltonia

'Green Beauty' **G** littleleaf boxwood

Evergreen **H** candytuft

E 'Majestic' lilyturf

Evergreen **H** candytuft

'David' **B** garden phlox

See site plan for **F** .

SITE: Sunny

SEASON: Late summer

CONCEPT: Dense planting of perennials makes an attractive seasonal "hedge" either side of rose-covered entry.

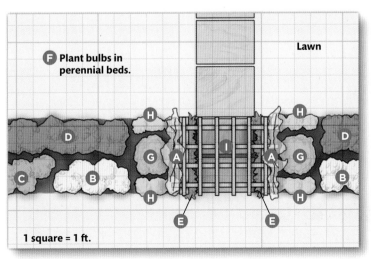

F Plant bulbs in perennial beds.

Lawn

1 square = 1 ft.

Plants & Projects

A **'Golden Showers' rose** (use 2 plants)
A deciduous climber featuring large, fragrant, double yellow flowers that bloom abundantly through the growing season. Tie canes to the arbor as they grow, positioning them to cover the structure. Enjoy the flowers and fragrance beside or beneath the arbor, or clip flowers and float them in a bowl indoors. See *Rosa*, pp. 152–153.

B **'David' garden phlox** (use 9)
A popular perennial forming a dense patch of upright leafy stems topped in late summer by clusters of scented white flowers. Foliage looks good throughout the season. See *Phlox paniculata*, p. 148–149.

C **'Snowbank' boltonia** (use 5)
This clump-forming perennial spreads to produce a tall hedgelike thicket of upright stems and pleasant blue-green leaves. For weeks in fall the plants are blanketed by small white flowers with yellow centers. See *Boltonia asteroides*, p. 123.

D **'Sunset' monarda** (use 10)
A perennial with cheerful, very showy flowers that attract hummingbirds. Large, shaggy, deep red flowers perch on long leafy stems for about a month in midsummer. The foliage has a rich aroma. See *Monarda didyma*, p. 145.

E **'Majestic' lilyturf** (use 12)
! *This plant is locally invasive in the Mid-Atlantic.*
Perennial evergreen ground cover that makes tall clumps of arching grassy leaves, rather like a small daylily. In late summer, cigar-shaped spikes of small purple flowers mingle with the foliage. See *Liriope muscari*, p. 143.

F **Spring bulbs**
Drifts of crocuses (and other spring bulbs if you like) fill the beds in spring before the perennial foliage pushes above ground. In late winter there are few more reassuring sights than the lovely cup-shaped flowers of crocuses peeking through a light snow cover. See Bulbs, pp. 124–125.

See p. 47 for the following:

G **'Green Beauty' littleleaf boxwood** (use 2)

H **Evergreen candytuft** (use 12)

I **Arbor**

A Garden Path

RECLAIM A NARROW SIDE YARD FOR A SHADE GARDEN

Many residential lots include a slim strip of land between the house and a property line. Usually overlooked by everyone except children and dogs racing between the front yard and the back, this often shady corridor can become a valued addition to the landscape. In the design shown here, a steppingstone path curves gently through a selection of shade-loving shrubs and perennials to make a garden that invites adults (as well as children) to linger as they stroll from one part of the property to another.

The wall of the house and a tall, opaque fence on the property line shade the space most of the day and give it a closed-in feeling, like a long empty hallway or narrow room. The design uses plants to enlarge these confines in the same way that comfortable furniture, floor coverings, and pictures on the walls seem to enlarge a small room in a house.

Large shrubs with striking foliage and spring flowers mark each entrance to this narrow "outdoor room." Handsome vines hang from the fence like three-dimensional floral prints. The foliage and flowers of good-size shrubs are nicely displayed against the wall opposite. (In spring the daphne's pale flowers fill the entire area with a delicious aroma.) On the "floor," the steppingstones are flanked by broad-leaved and grassy ground-cover "throw rugs" along the path. Ferns and perennials with pretty flowers and interesting foliage complete the furnishings.

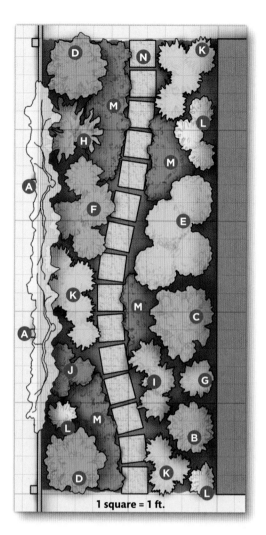

1 square = 1 ft.

Plants & Projects

Foliage distinguishes this planting in all seasons, from brilliant emerging leaves in spring to glossy summer greens and winter-defying evergreens. Flowers bloom from spring through fall in white, lilac, and shades of pink. Maintenance includes seasonal cleanup and shrub pruning to direct growth and to control size.

A Climbing hydrangea
(use 2 plants)
This deciduous vine brightens June with mildly fragrant white flowers. Glossy leaves and dark brown papery bark look good the rest of the year. See *Hydrangea petiolaris*, p. 138.

B 'Carol Mackie' daphne (use 1)
An evergreen shrub prized for its intensely fragrant bursts of starry light pink spring flowers and beautiful variegated green-and-cream leaves. See *Daphne x burkwoodii*, p. 130.

C Garden hydrangea (use 1)
A deciduous shrub with shiny green leaves and large clusters of pink or blue flowers throughout the summer. See *Hydrangea macrophylla*, p. 138.

D 'Mountain Fire' Japanese andromeda (use 2)
The leaves of this evergreen shrub emerge fiery red, then mature to glossy green. In spring, clusters of buds that have dangled from branch tips since autumn open in a blizzard of white flowers. See *Pieris japonica*, p. 149.

E White evergreen azalea (use 4)
This shrub's semievergreen, fine-textured leaves contrast nicely with nearby foliage. Large, frilly white flowers lighten the shade in early summer. See *Rhododendron:* Evergreen azaleas, p. 151.

F 'Halcyon' hosta (use 4)
Grown for its low mounding foliage, this perennial's large, lush blue leaves become greener as the season progresses. See *Hosta*, pp. 136–137.

G 'Royal Standard' hosta (use 1)
Another hosta with lovely foliage, this time bright green. In addition, this cultivar's trumpetlike white flowers will perfume the path in August and September. See *Hosta*, pp. 136–139.

H Japanese autumn fern (use 3)
Tall clumps of glossy fronds start out copper-colored and turn dark green as they mature. Semievergreen. See Ferns: *Dryopteris erythrosora*, p. 132.

I Japanese painted fern (use 3)
Eye-catching deciduous fern. The delicately painted fronds blend gray-green, silver, and maroon. See Ferns: *Athyrium goeringianum* 'Pictum', p. 132.

J 'Palace Purple' heuchera (use 3)
A tough perennial with unusually dark purple-bronze foliage. Forms low mounds of large, lobed leaves and wiry stalks of tiny flowers in summer. See *Heuchera*, p. 136.

K Variegated lilyturf (use 12)
❶ This plant is locally invasive in the Mid-Atlantic.
The grassy evergreen foliage of this low mounding perennial is striped green and yellow. Small spikes of lilac flowers appear in late summer. See *Liriope muscari* 'Variegata', p. 143 .

L White astilbe (use 5)
The white spires of this perennial brighten the shade in early summer. Dark green, lacy foliage is pleasing all season. The 18-in.-tall 'Deutschland' is a good size for this planting. See *Astilbe x arendsii*, p. 122.

M Pachysandra (as needed)
This durable perennial ground cover forms a dense mat of glossy evergreen leaves. See *Pachysandra terminalis*, p. 147.

N Path
Use pavers or flagstones 18 in. square. Bluestone is attractive with the blue-tinted foliage of the planting. See p. 167.

SITE: Shady

SEASON: Early summer

CONCEPT: Plants with colorful foliage of varying textures make an enticing stroll garden in a frequently neglected area.

See site plan for **G** **J** .

Plants with this symbol are considered invasive or are locally invasive, as noted. See the appropriate plant profile for suggested alternatives.

H Japanese autumn fern

F 'Halcyon' hosta

D 'Mountain Fire' Japanese andromeda

C Garden hydrangea

A Climbing hydrangea

E White evergreen azalea

K Variegated lilyturf

N Path

'Mountain Fire' **D** Japanese andromeda

Pachysandra **M**

Japanese **I** painted fern

Variegated **K** lilyturf

'Carol Mackie' **B** daphne

L White astilbe

VARIATIONS ON A THEME

From formal to fanciful, these pathways that meander through side gardens show some of the range of possibilities.

A sunny side yard provides an opportunity for a colorful perennial border. Irregular flagstones, lattice fence, and carved weathered door contribute to the air of friendly informality.

A brick walk edged in fine-textured ferns adds interest to a shady passage walk.

A gate like this attractive structure smothered in roses is an enticement to make the journey through it.

Sunny side of the path

In this design, a low picket fence opens up the space and lets in more sunlight. The area next to the house is still shady, and the plants there remain mostly the same. Two new shrubs—mock orange and weigela—replace the daphne and garden hydrangea to offer a different look.

Flanked by taller shrubs at each end, low-growing perennials line the fence. Purple irises, pink peonies, and blue ajuga combine for a colorful spring display. Astilbes, sedums, and asters provide bloom from early summer until frost.

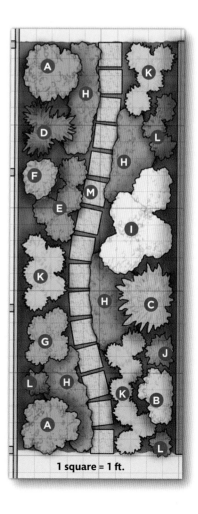

1 square = 1 ft.

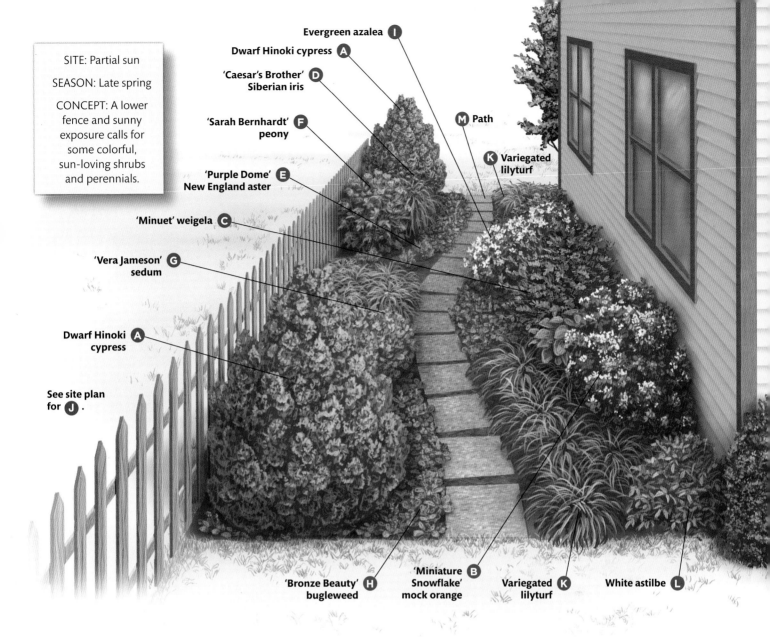

SITE: Partial sun

SEASON: Late spring

CONCEPT: A lower fence and sunny exposure calls for some colorful, sun-loving shrubs and perennials.

Evergreen azalea **I**

Dwarf Hinoki cypress **A**

'Caesar's Brother' Siberian iris **D**

'Sarah Bernhardt' peony **F**

'Purple Dome' New England aster **E**

'Minuet' weigela **C**

'Vera Jameson' sedum **G**

Dwarf Hinoki cypress **A**

See site plan for **J** .

M Path

K Variegated lilyturf

'Bronze Beauty' bugleweed **H**

'Miniature Snowflake' mock orange **B**

Variegated lilyturf **K**

White astilbe **L**

Plants & Projects

A Dwarf Hinoki cypress (use 2 plants)
Unusual foliage draws attention to these evergreen shrubs at the entrances to the path. Tiny dark green leaves are arranged in whorled clusters, densely packed on the pyramidal shrub. See *Chamaecyparis obtusa* 'Nana Gracilis', p. 127.

B 'Miniature Snowflake' mock orange (use 1)
The delightful fragrance of this deciduous shrub's double snow-white flowers rewards a late-spring stroll down the path. The remainder of the season it is a pleasing small mound of green foliage. See *Philadelphus x virginalis*, p. 148.

C 'Minuet' weigela (use 1)
Like the mock orange, this is a compact form of an old-fashioned favorite. It has handsome purple-green deciduous leaves and deep red flowers in early summer. See *Weigela florida*, p. 159.

D 'Caesar's Brother' Siberian iris (use 3)
These perennials form generous clumps of arching straplike leaves that look good all summer. Dark indigo-purple flowers make a fine display for a few weeks in May or June. See *Iris sibirica*, p. 140.

E 'Purple Dome' New England aster (use 4)
During the summer, this perennial edges the path with neat low mounds of dark green leaves. Masses of bright purple flowers totally cover the foliage in September. See *Aster novae-angliae*, p. 121.

F 'Sarah Bernhardt' peony (use 1)
Another old favorite, this bushy perennial produces fragrant double pink flowers in May and attractive foliage through the summer. Watch for the foliage as it emerges in spring—it's fascinating and colorful. See *Paeonia*, p. 148.

G 'Vera Jameson' sedum (use 4)
Low, mounding perennial with succulent purplish foliage contrasts nicely with the grassy lilyturf nearby. Rose-pink flowers appear in late summer. See *Sedum*, p. 155.

H 'Bronze Beauty' bugleweed (as needed)
! *This plant is locally invasive in the Mid-Atlantic.*
The dark purplish foliage of this perennial ground cover is evergreen in mild winters. Spikes of sky blue flowers rise above the leaves in late spring. See *Ajuga reptans*, p. 119.

See p. 50 for the following:

I White evergreen azalea (use 4)

J 'Royal Standard' hosta (use 1)

K Variegated lilyturf (use 12)
! *This plant is locally invasive in the Mid-Atlantic.*

L White astilbe (use 5)

M Path

"Around Back"

DRESS UP THE FAMILY'S DAY-TO-DAY ENTRANCE

When people think of landscaping the entrance to their home, the public entry at the front of the house comes immediately to mind. It's easy to forget that the back door often gets more use. If you make the journey between back door and driveway or garage many times each day, why not make it as pleasant a trip as possible? For many properties, a simple planting can transform the space bounded by the house, garage, and driveway, making it at once more inviting and more functional.

In a high-traffic area frequented by ball-bouncing, bicycle-riding children as well as busy adults, delicate, fussy plants have no place. The design shown here employs a few types of tough low-care plants, all of which look good year-round. The low yew hedge links the house and the garage and separates the more private backyard from the busy driveway. The star magnolia is just the right size for its spot. Its early-spring flowers will be a delight whether viewed coming up the driveway or from a window overlooking the backyard. The wide walk makes passage to and from the car easy—even with your arms full of groceries.

A Star magnolia

See site plan for **F** .

SITE: Sunny

SEASON: Summer

CONCEPT: This planting raises spirits weighed down by shopping bags and separates activities in the backyard from the driveway.

'Steeds' **C**
Japanese holly

B 'Hicksii'
hybrid yew

'Hidcote' **D**
hypericum

'Big Blue' **E**
lilyturf

Walkway **G**

'Big Blue' **E**
lilyturf

Plants & Projects

The watchword in this planting is evergreen. Except for the magolia, all the plants here are fully evergreen or are nearly so. Spring and summer see lovely flowers from the magnolia and hypericum, and the carpet of lilyturf turns a handsome blue in August. For a bigger splash in spring, underplant the lilyturf with daffodils. Choose a single variety for uniform color, or select several varieties for a mix of colors and bloom times. Other than shearing the hedge, the only maintenance required is cutting back the lilyturf and hypericum in late winter.

A Star magnolia (use 1 plant)
Lovely white flowers cover this small deciduous tree before the leaves appear. Starlike blooms, slightly fragrant and sometimes tinged with pink, appear in early spring and last up to two weeks. In summer, the dense leafy crown of dark green leaves helps provide privacy in the backyard. A multitrunked specimen will fill the space better and display more of the interesting winter bark. See *Magnolia stellata*, p. 144.

B 'Hicksii' hybrid yew (use 9)
A fast-growing evergreen shrub that is ideal for this 3-ft.-tall, neatly sheared hedge. Needles are glossy dark green and soft, not prickly. Eight plants form the L-shaped portion, while a single sheared plant extends the hedge on the other side of the walk connecting it to the house. (If the hedge needs to play a part in confining a family pet, you could easily set posts either side of the walk and add a gate.) See *Taxus* x *media*, p. 157.

C 'Steeds' Japanese holly (use 3 or more)
Several of these dense, upright evergreen shrubs can be grouped at the corner as specimen plants or to tie into an existing foundation planting. You could also extend them along the house to create a foundation planting, as shown here. The small dark green leaves are thick and leathery and have tiny spines. Plants attain a pleasing form when left to their own devices. Resist the urge to shear them; just prune to control size if necessary. See *Ilex crenata*, p. 139.

D 'Hidcote' hypericum (use 1)
All summer long, clusters of large golden flowers cover the arching stems of this tidy semievergreen shrub, brightening the entrance to the backyard. See *Hypericum*, p. 138.

E 'Big Blue' lilyturf (use 40 or more)
❗ This plant is locally invasive in the Mid-Atlantic.
Grasslike evergreen clumps of this perennial ground cover grow together to carpet the ground flanking the driveway and walk. (Extend the planting as far down the drive as you like.) Slim spires of tiny blue flowers rise above the dark green leaves in June. Lilyturf doesn't stand up to repeated tromping. If the drive is also a basketball court, substitute periwinkle (*Vinca minor*, p. 154), a tough ground cover with late-spring lilac flowers. See *Liriope muscari*, p. 143.

F Stinking hellebore (use 5 or more)
This clump-forming perennial is ideal for filling the space between the walk and house on the backyard side of the hedge. (You might also consider extending the planting along the L-shaped side of the hedge.) Its pale green flowers are among the first to bloom in the spring and continue for many weeks; dark green leaves are attractive year-round. See *Helleborus foetidus*, p. 135.

G Walkway
Precast concrete pavers, 2 ft. by 2 ft., replace an existing walk or form a new one. See p. 167.

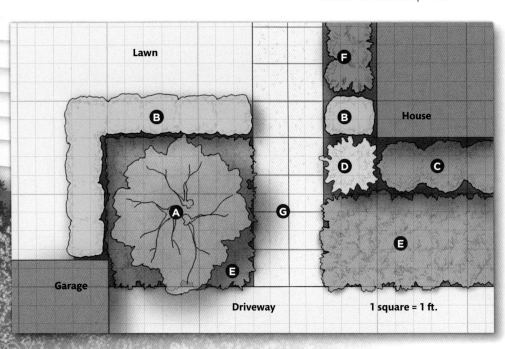

Lawn

House

Garage

Driveway

1 square = 1 ft.

Plants with this symbol are considered invasive or are locally invasive, as noted. See the appropriate plant profile for suggested alternatives.

VARIATIONS ON A THEME

Designs like these can make any journey to the back door a pleasure.

A border of colorful annuals and perennials brightens an otherwise businesslike back-door walkway.

A lattice fence and evergreen arborvitae screen this backyard from the driveway. A simple bench provides an opportunity to stop and appreciate the view.

Patio pots enhance an entry in no time. And they offer the opportunity to bring plants right up to the back door.

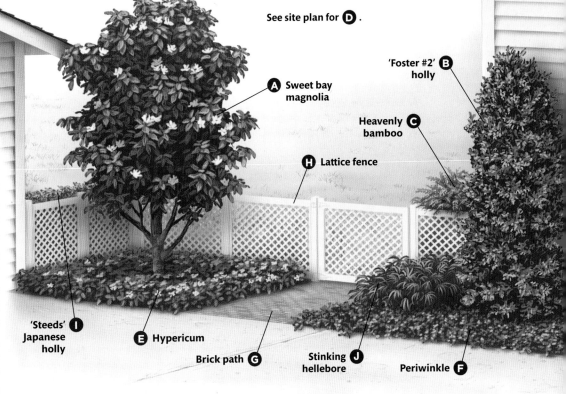

See site plan for **D**.

A Sweet bay magnolia

B 'Foster #2' holly

C Heavenly bamboo

H Lattice fence

I 'Steeds' Japanese holly

E Hypericum

G Brick path

J Stinking hellebore

F Periwinkle

Fence and flora

If you can't wait for a hedge to mature, try the lattice fence shown here. It looks good and provides enclosure right away; decorative 'Steeds' holly and lavender hedges on the backyard side will eventually enhance the effect. Ambitious home landscapers may want to replace a concrete walkway with bricks (as shown here), stone, or pavers to further dress up the "family entrance."

Evergreen ground covers and foundation shrubs give this planting, like the previous one, a year-round presence. Flowers and berries brighten the seasons, from lilac-colored periwinkle blossoms in spring to the bright red berries of the Foster holly and heavenly bamboo in fall and winter. In early summer the sweet bay magnolia and lavender will fill the entrance with fragrance. Golden yellow hypericum blossoms appear throughout the summer.

Plants & Projects

A **Sweet bay magnolia**
(use 1 plant)
This small multitrunked tree produces fragrant cream-colored flowers in early summer. Glossy leathery leaves last partway through the winter. See *Magnolia virginiana*, p. 144.

B **'Foster #2' holly** (use 1)
A small evergreen tree with a slender upright habit and red berries in winter. Easily kept pruned to fit its spot. See *Ilex x attenuata*, p. 139.

C **Heavenly bamboo**
(use 2 or more)
! *This plant is considered invasive in the Mid-Atlantic.*
This upright evergreen shrub fits nicely between the walk and the house. Fine-textured leaves on upright stems change color from gold to green to red with the seasons. Red berries are a treat in winter. See *Nandina domestica*, p. 146.

D **'Munstead' English lavender**
(use 7)
A small shrub with silver-gray foliage makes a low hedge that blooms in early summer. Leaves and flowers are scented; stop for a refreshing sniff on your way by. Foliage is evergreen in mild areas. See *Lavandula angustifolia*, p. 142–143.

E **Hypericum** (use 38)
A cousin of the 'Hidcote' hypericum in the previous design, this small semievergreen shrub fills in quickly beneath the magnolia. Large golden flowers will carpet the ground through the summer. See *Hypericum calycinum*, p. 138.

F **Periwinkle** (use 65 or more)
A short, tough evergreen ground cover, ideal for this high-traffic area. In spring, lilac flowers are sprinkled over the leathery green leaves. See *Vinca minor*, p. 158.

G **Brick path**
If it suits your house (and energies), smarten up the entry with a 4-ft.-wide brick walk like this one. See p. 170.

H **Lattice fence**
Adds good looks while corralling family pets and balls from driveway games. See p. 188.

See p. 55 for the following:

I 'Steeds' Japanese holly (use 3)

J Stinking hellebore (use 5)

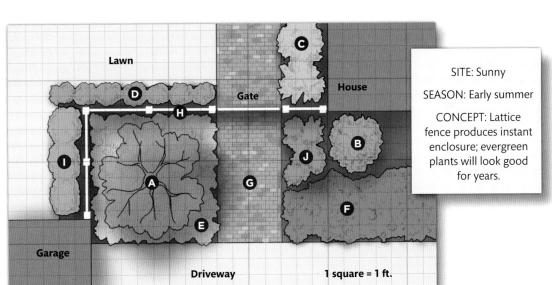

Lawn

C

D

Gate

House

H

B

I

J

A

G

E

F

Garage

Driveway

1 square = 1 ft.

SITE: Sunny

SEASON: Early summer

CONCEPT: Lattice fence produces instant enclosure; evergreen plants will look good for years.

Angle of Repose

MAKE A BACK-DOOR GARDEN IN A SHELTERED NICHE

Many homes offer the opportunity to tuck a garden into a protected corner. In the front yard, such spots are ideal for an entry garden or a landscaping display that showcases your house when viewed from the sidewalk or the street. If it is in the backyard, like the site shown here, the planting can be more intimate, part of a comfortable outdoor room you can stroll through at leisure or enjoy from a nearby terrace or window.

This planting has been specially designed with spring in mind, so we're showing that season here. (For a look at the planting later on, when perennials and shrubs take over the show, see p. 58.) Hundreds of spring bulbs light up the corner from February through May, assisted by several early-blooming perennials and a handsome backdrop of evergreen shrubs. Early flowers aren't the only pleasures of spring, though. Watch buds fatten and burst into leaf on the Japanese maple, and mark the progress of the season as new, succulent shoots of summer perennials emerge. Step along the fieldstone path to appreciate the magic of spring at closer range.

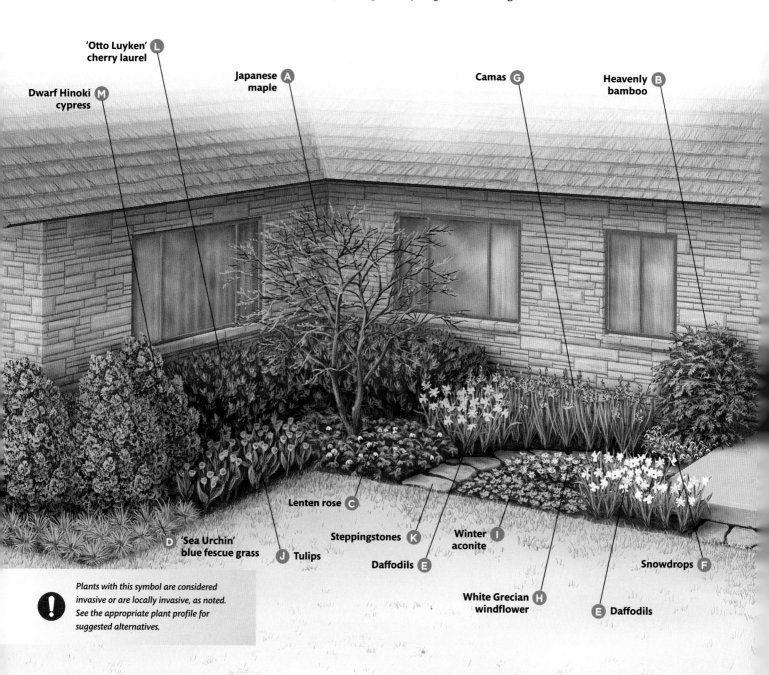

'Otto Luyken' cherry laurel **L**

Dwarf Hinoki **M** cypress

Japanese maple **A**

Camas **G**

Heavenly bamboo **B**

Lenten rose **C**

'Sea Urchin' **D** blue fescue grass

Tulips **J**

Steppingstones **K**

Daffodils **E**

Winter aconite **I**

Snowdrops **F**

White Grecian **H** windflower

Daffodils **E**

Plants with this symbol are considered invasive or are locally invasive, as noted. See the appropriate plant profile for suggested alternatives.

Plants & Projects

Snowdrops and winter aconites provide the first inklings of spring, often breaking through a February snow to do so. Lenten rose joins in March, followed by daffodils, tulips, and camas in April. Later the flowers of bigroot geranium (see p. 58) and cherry laurel mark the transition to summer.

Ⓐ Japanese maple (use 1 plant)
The bare branches of this small graceful tree form a tracery above the spring garden, and the fat leaf buds delight children (and adults). Delicate leaves and pleasing form provide a focal point through summer and fall. A variety with green summer leaves (red-leaved varieties are available) will look best in this design. See *Acer palmatum*, p. 118.

Ⓑ Heavenly bamboo (use 1)
❶ This plant is considered invasive in the Mid-Atlantic. This shrub's lacy evergreen leaflets have a golden hue in spring, turn a lovely green in summer and red in fall and winter. White flowers in summer precede heavy sprays of red berries that last through the winter. See *Nandina domestica*, p. 146.

Ⓒ Lenten rose (use 8)
A clump-forming perennial with clusters of cup-shaped flowers in early spring; its glossy leaves make a lovely ground cover under the maple for most of the year. See *Helleborus orientalis*, p. 135.

Ⓓ 'Sea Urchin' blue fescue grass (use 15)
Appearing in early spring, the fine blue blades of this perennial add attractive color and texture throughout the growing season. See *Festuca ovina* var. *glauca* 'Sea Urchin', p. 133.

Ⓔ Daffodils (use 75)
This spring garden gets an equal measure of fragrant yellow and white daffodils. For yellow, try the low-growing 'February Gold' and the larger 'Carlton'. 'Mount Hood', 'Ice Follies', and 'Thalia' are all good whites. Plant patches of individual colors or mix colors; underplant low-growing summer plants with low-growing daffodils to ensure that the fading bulb foliage is hidden. See Bulbs: *Narcissus*, p. 124.

Ⓕ Snowdrops (use 150)
Small white flowers dangle above dense clumps of grassy foliage in February. Use 75 under the heavenly bamboo and 75 under the maple. See Bulbs: *Galanthus nivalis*, p. 124.

Ⓖ Camas (use 20)
Uncommon but lovely, with long spikes of starry blue flowers in late spring. You should substitute early tulips if the soil under the eaves of the house is dry. See Bulbs: *Camassia esculenta*, p. 124.

Ⓗ White Grecian windflower (use 150)
Daisylike white flowers with yellow centers carpet the ground near the steppingstones in April. See Bulbs: *Anemone blanda*, p. 124.

Ⓘ Winter aconite (use 120)
Among the first bulbs to bloom, they form a low patch of golden flowers on the edge of the bed. See Bulbs: *Eranthis hyemalis*, p. 124.

Ⓙ Tulips (use 30)
Choose pastel colors rather than bold reds and yellows. If you substitute early tulips for the camas, use late ones here. See Bulbs: *Tulipa*, p. 124.

Ⓚ Steppingstones
A path of fieldstone slabs helps keep your feet dry on dewy mornings as you stroll through the garden. See p. 171.

See p. 56 for the following:
Ⓛ 'Otto Luyken' cherry laurel (use 3)
Ⓜ Dwarf Hinoki cypress (use 3)

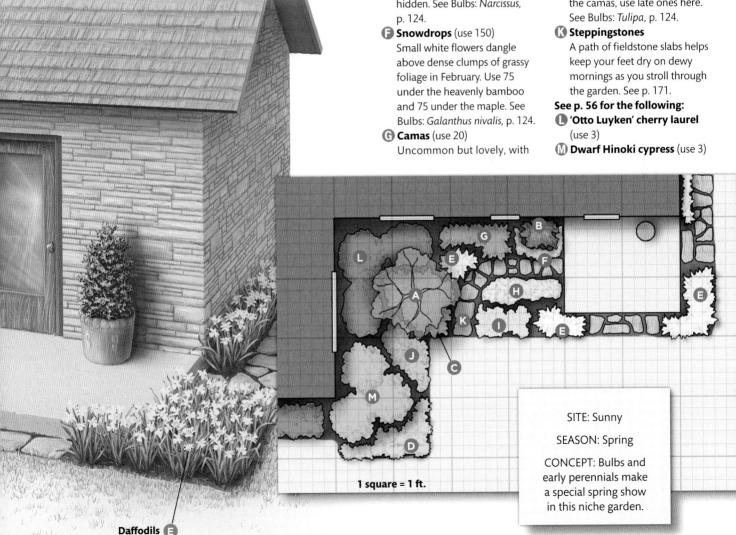

1 square = 1 ft.

Daffodils Ⓔ

SITE: Sunny

SEASON: Spring

CONCEPT: Bulbs and early perennials make a special spring show in this niche garden.

The scene in summer

There's no drop-off in interest or enjoyment as this planting moves from spring (shown on previous pages) to summer and fall. Now perennials join shrubs in a tapestry of varied foliage accented by a succession of flowers in shades of white, blue, and yellow.

Foliage textures include a selection of delicate lacy leaves and grassy foliage contrasting with more robust foliage. Autumn brings shades of red to the Japanese maple and dwarf plumbago and red berries on the heavenly bamboo. Note that the plants chosen here prefer some afternoon shade in summer, cast perhaps by the house or a nearby tree.

Plants & Projects

A Bigroot geranium (use 9 plants)
This perennial ground cover hides the spent foliage of the winter aconite and Grecian windflower. Its semievergreen leaves are fragrant; it flowers in early summer. See *Geranium macrorrhizum*, p. 134.

B 'Otto Luyken' cherry laurel (use 3)
Leathery dark evergreen leaves give this shrub year-round presence. Spikes of fragrant white flowers open in May. See *Prunus laurocerasus*, p. 150.

C Dwarf Hinoki cypress (use 3)
Slow-growing conifers feature rich-textured foliage and a naturally conical shape. See *Chamaecyparis obtusa* 'Nana Gracilis', p. 127.

D Dwarf plumbago (use 5)
These spreading perennials provide clear blue flowers from summer through fall, when the deep green leaves turn crimson. See *Ceratostigma plumbaginoides*, p. 126.

E Interrupted fern (use 7)
This deciduous native fern tolerates the dry soil likely under the eaves. See Ferns: *Osmunda claytoniana*, p. 132.

F Pale yellow daylily (use 6)
Grasslike foliage and cheerful flowers of this perennial brighten the planting. Try 'Hyperion', with fragrant light yellow flowers in midsummer. See *Hemerocallis*, p. 136.

G 'Royal Standard' hosta (use 8)
Growing up through the tulips, this perennial offers fragrant white flowers that rise above mounds of handsome foliage. See *Hosta*, pp. 136–137.

H 'Majestic' lilyturf (use 65)
❶ *This plant is locally invasive in the Mid-Atlantic.*
A perennial with evergreen clumps of grassy foliage, purple flowers in summer, and navy berries in fall. See *Liriope muscari*, p. 143.

See p. 55 for the following:

I Japanese maple

J Heavenly bamboo
❶ *This plant is considered invasive in the Mid-Atlantic.*

K Lenten rose

L 'Sea Urchin' blue fescue grass

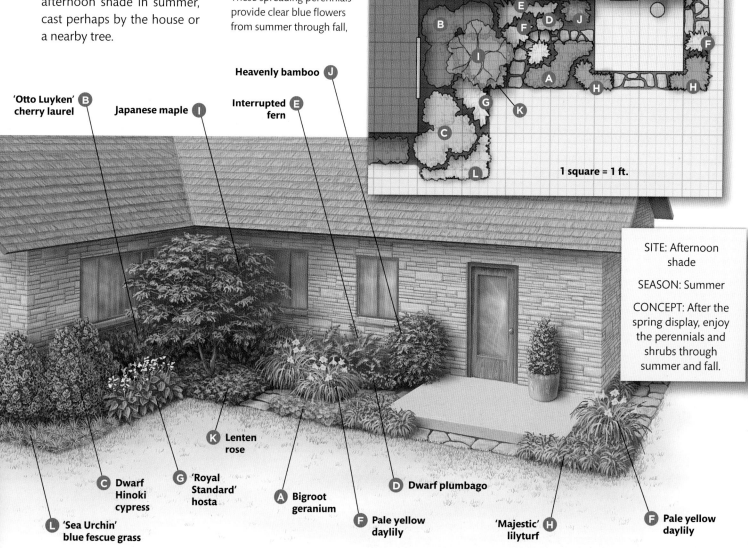

1 square = 1 ft.

'Otto Luyken' cherry laurel **B**

Japanese maple **I**

Heavenly bamboo **J**

Interrupted fern **E**

K Lenten rose

C Dwarf Hinoki cypress

G 'Royal Standard' hosta

A Bigroot geranium

F Pale yellow daylily

D Dwarf plumbago

L 'Sea Urchin' blue fescue grass

'Majestic' lilyturf **H**

F Pale yellow daylily

SITE: Afternoon shade

SEASON: Summer

CONCEPT: After the spring display, enjoy the perennials and shrubs through summer and fall.

VARIATIONS ON A THEME

The corners and little niches around a house are wonderful places for plantings and small garden retreats.

Combining simple shapes and a limited range of colors in a relatively small area, this corner courtyard has a comfortable, spacious feel.

Tucked into a corner formed by a high wall and the house, this little water garden makes the most of limited space.

This sheltered corner, viewed from a picture window and accessed by a glassed-in porch, is a perfect spot for a patio garden.

Landscaping a Low Wall

TWO-TIER GARDEN REPLACES A SHORT SLOPE

Some things may not love a wall, but plants and gardeners do. For plants, walls offer warmth for an early start in spring and good drainage for roots. Gardeners appreciate the rich visual potential of composing a garden on two levels, as well as the practical advantage of working on two relatively flat surfaces instead of a single sloping one. If you have a wall, or have a place to put one, grasp the opportunity for some handsome landscaping.

This design places two complementary perennial borders above and below a wall bounded at one end by a set of stairs. While each bed is relatively narrow (and therefore easy to maintain), when viewed from the lower level they combine to form a border that is almost 8 ft. deep, with plants rising to eye level or more. The planting can be extended with more of the same or similar plants.

Building the wall that makes this impressive sight possible doesn't require the time or skill it once did. Nor is it necessary to scour the countryside for tons of fieldstone or to hire an expensive contractor. Thanks to precast retaining-wall systems, a knee-high do-it-yourself wall can be installed in as little as a weekend. More experienced or ambitious wall builders may want to tackle a natural stone wall, but anyone with a healthy back (or access to energetic teenagers) can succeed with a prefabricated system.

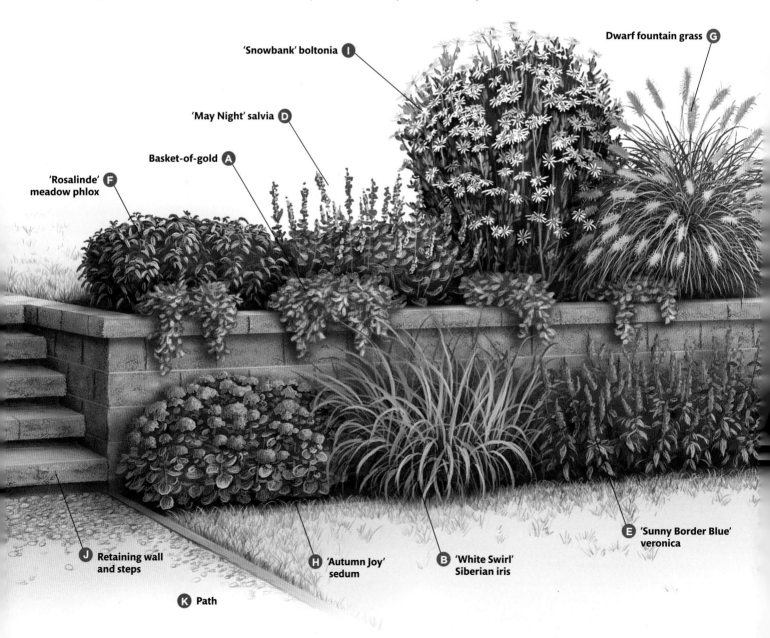

'Snowbank' boltonia **I**

Dwarf fountain grass **G**

'May Night' salvia **D**

Basket-of-gold **A**

'Rosalinde' meadow phlox **F**

J Retaining wall and steps

H 'Autumn Joy' sedum

B 'White Swirl' Siberian iris

E 'Sunny Border Blue' veronica

K Path

Plants & Projects

Chosen for their refined foliage and flowers, the plants in this design will put on an elegant display from spring through fall. Basket-of-gold is the first to bloom, followed through spring and into the summer by Siberian iris, bellflower, salvia, veronica, and phlox, in a swirl of gold, white, blue, and pink flowers.

The shapes and textures of the plants complement and contrast within beds and between levels. Grassy iris foliage echoes the arching fountain grass. Slender leaves on numerous stalks characterize boltonia and phlox. The attractive gray foliage of basket-of-gold spills down the face of the wall long after its flowers have disappeared.

All the plants in this design are perennials or grasses that need little maintenance. Remove old flower stalks regularly to keep things tidy and to promote more flowers on the veronica and salvia. Cut everything to the ground in late fall or winter. A spade-cut edge and fresh mulch each spring will keep the beds neat.

Ⓐ Basket-of-gold (use 6 plants)
This low-growing plant bears dense masses of fragrant gold flowers in early spring. Its attractive gray foliage will cascade down the wall through summer and fall. See *Aurinia saxatilis*, p. 122.

Ⓑ 'White Swirl' Siberian iris (use 5)
The exceptional pure white flowers of this perennial grace the planting in early summer. Its slender dark green leaves form an eye-pleasing arching clump. See *Iris sibirica*, p. 140.

Ⓒ 'Blue Clips' Carpathian bellflower (use 3)
A short compact plant ideal for the end of the lower bed, it produces sky blue flowers all summer. See *Campanula carpatica*, p. 126.

Ⓓ 'May Night' salvia (use 3)
Numerous spikes of indigo-purple flowers shoot up above a mass of dark green foliage off and on from May to frost. Flowers are set off nicely by the gray leaves of the basket-of-gold at their feet. See *Salvia x superba*, p. 154.

Ⓔ 'Sunny Border Blue' veronica (use 5)
Echoing the salvia on the level above, this plant produces deep purplish blue flower spikes all summer. Flowers combine with the basal clump of glossy green leaves to reach 2 ft. tall, a good height for this low wall. See *Veronica*, p. 157.

Ⓕ 'Rosalinde' meadow phlox (use 3)
Impressive stands of lilac-pink flowers bloom abundantly in midsummer, offering a pleasant scent to passersby on the neighboring steps. Foliage stays healthy and green all summer. See *Phlox* 'Rosalinde', p. 149.

Ⓖ Dwarf fountain grass (use 1)
A compact clump of this handsome perennial grass punctuates the end of the upper bed. Brushy spikes of flowers wave above the fine arching blades from midsummer into autumn, when the leaves turn gold or tan. See *Pennisetum alopecuriodes* 'Hameln', p. 148.

Ⓗ 'Autumn Joy' sedum (use 5)
Plump gray-green leaves on thick stems look good all summer and make a striking contrast to the phlox on the level above. Broad flat clusters of buds turn from pink to rust from late summer through fall. See *Sedum*, p. 155.

Ⓘ 'Snowbank' boltonia (use 1)
This large erect clump covered for weeks with white asterlike blooms is the planting's late-summer focal point. Slender pale green leaves on a profusion of stems look healthy all summer. See *Boltonia asteroides*, p. 123.

Ⓙ Retaining wall and steps
The precast wall shown here is typical of the ones you'll find at garden centers, nurseries, and local landscaping suppliers. See pp. 178–181.

Ⓚ Path
Whether you choose crushed stone (as shown here), precast pavers, or flagstones, select a color that complements that of the wall. See p. 167.

> SITE: Sunny
>
> SEASON: Fall
>
> CONCEPT: Low retaining wall creates easy-to-maintain beds for a distinctive two-level planting of perennials.

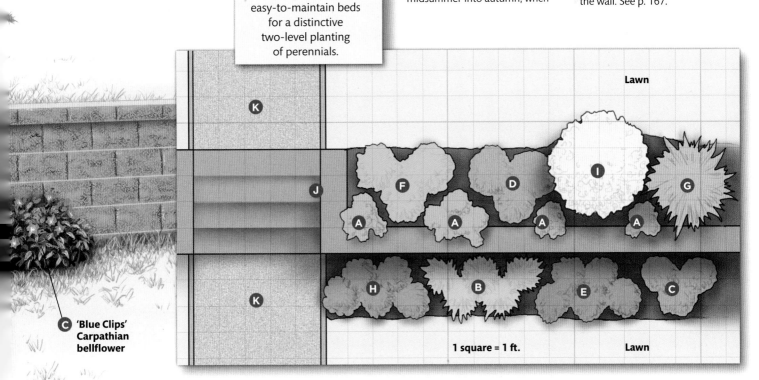

Ⓒ 'Blue Clips' Carpathian bellflower

1 square = 1 ft.

Lawn

VARIATIONS ON A THEME

A low wall provides all sorts of gardening opportunities as well as eliminating the need to push a mower up and down a slope.

Nestled in a stone-walled niche, a sitter here has a wealth of plants to contemplate.

This very low wall (not even knee-high) serves to retain a slope, provide a neat edge for the lawn, and showcase a handsome collection of shrubs and perennials.

This fieldstone wall has provided the opportunity for a beautiful two-tier combination of foliage textures and colors.

Shrubs change the scene

Carefree roses, lavender, and daisies look lovely along a wall, perhaps because they're reminiscent of plants seen along walls bordering old fields and meadows. The combination of shrubs and perennials gives this planting a look distinctly different from that of the perennial border of the previous design.

Something is in bloom from spring through fall. ('The Fairy' rose and 'Becky' Shasta daisy bloom the entire time.) Flowers in pink, white, and a range of blues are displayed against handsome green and silver-gray foliage as well as against the retaining wall. Maintenance is limited to snipping spent flowers and cutting plants back in either fall or spring.

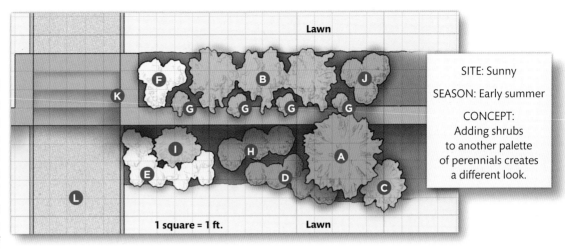

SITE: Sunny

SEASON: Early summer

CONCEPT: Adding shrubs to another palette of perennials creates a different look.

1 square = 1 ft.

Plants & Projects

(A) 'Miss Kim' lilac (use 1 plant)
A bushy but compact deciduous shrub graced with fragrant pale blue flowers in late spring. Leaves turn purple in fall. See *Syringa patula*, p. 156.

(B) 'The Fairy' rose (use 3)
The centerpiece of the upper level, these low, spreading shrub roses are laden with masses of dainty pink flowers from early summer until hard frost. See *Rosa*, p. 153.

(C) 'Festiva Maxima' peony (use 1)
An especially fragrant old-fashioned perennial bearing large double white blooms in late spring. Dark foliage looks good through the remainder of the season. See *Paeonia*, p. 148.

(D) 'Munstead' English lavender (use 5)
A dwarf shrub whose dense, fragrant, pale lavender flower spikes top slender stalks in early summer. Silver-gray leaves look good into the winter. See *Lavandula angustifolia*, p. 142–143.

(E) 'Silver Princess' Shasta daisy (use 11)
The dwarf form of this popular perennial forms a low mat of glossy leaves at the foot of the steps. Bears large white daisies in June and July. See *Chrysanthemum* x *superbum*, p. 127.

(F) 'Becky' Shasta daisy (use 3)
This taller daisy will bloom all through summer, providing long-stemmed white flowers for cutting. See *Chrysanthemum* x *superbum*, p. 127.

(G) 'Dropmore' catmint (use 4)
Bushy mounds of gray foliage spaced along the edge of the wall produce a heavy crop of blue flowers in June and again in late summer if sheared. See *Nepeta* x *faassenii*, p. 146.

(H) 'David' garden phlox (use 3)
A new perennial phlox with mildew-resistant foliage on vigorous, sturdy, and erect stems that withstand wind and rain. Fragrant white flowers appear in August and last well into September. See *Phlox*, p. 148–149.

(I) 'Longwood Blue' bluebeard (use 1)
Clusters of sky blue flowers on this small deciduous shrub attract butterflies in late summer. Soft gray foliage looks good with the colors of the surrounding plants. See *Caryopteris* x *clandonensis*, p. 126.

(J) Nippon daisy (use 3)
A shrubby perennial with thick stems and large glossy leaves. White daisies top the stems in late fall. See *Chrysanthemum nipponicum*, p. 127.

See p. 63 for the following:

(K) Retaining wall and steps

(L) Path

(F) 'Becky' Shasta daisy

(G) 'Dropmore' catmint

(B) 'The Fairy' rose

(J) Nippon daisy

(A) 'Miss Kim' lilac

(K) Retaining wall and steps

(L) Path

(E) 'Silver Princess' Shasta daisy

(I) 'Longwood Blue' bluebeard

(H) 'David' garden phlox

(D) 'Munstead' English lavender

(C) 'Festiva Maxima' peony

Beautify a Blank Wall

PAINT A PICTURE WITH PLANTS

Just as you enhance your living room by hanging paintings on the walls, you can decorate blank walls in your outdoor "living rooms." The design shown here transforms a nondescript garage wall into a living fresco, showcasing lovely plants in a framework of roses and flowering vines. Instead of a view of peeling paint, imagine gazing at this scene from a nearby patio, deck, or kitchen window.

This symmetrical composition frames two crape myrtles between arched latticework trellises. Handsome multitrunked shrubs, the crape myrtles perform year-round, providing sumptuous pink flowers in summer, orange-red foliage in fall, and attractive bark in winter. On either side of the crape myrtles, roses and clematis scramble over the trellis in a profusion of yellow and purple flowers.

A tidy low boxwood hedge sets off a shallow border of shrubs and perennials at the bottom of the "frame." Cheerful long-blooming daylilies and asters, airy Russian sage, and elegant daphne make sure that the ground-level attractions hold their own with the aerial performers covering the wall above. The flowers hew to a color scheme of yellows, pinks, blues, and purples.

Wider or narrower walls can be accommodated by expanding the design to include additional "panels," or by reducing it to one central panel. To set off the plants, consider painting or staining the wall and trellises in an off-white, an earth tone, or a light gray color.

Jackman clematis **D**

'Golden Showers' rose **B**

'Carol Mackie' daphne **F**

'Happy Returns' daylily **H**

'Green Beauty' littleleaf boxwood **E**

Plants & Projects

These plants will all do well in the hot, dry conditions often found near a wall with a sunny exposure. Other than training and pruning the vines, roses, and hedge, maintenance involves little more than fall and spring cleanup. The trellises, supported by 4x4 posts and attached to the garage, are well within the reach of average do-it-yourselfers.

A 'Hopi' crape myrtle (use 2 plants) Large multitrunked deciduous shrubs produce papery pink flowers for weeks in summer. They also contribute colorful fall foliage and attractive flaky bark for winter interest. See *Lagerstroemia indica*, p. 142.

B 'Golden Showers' rose (use 3) Tied to each trellis, the long canes of these climbers display large, fragrant, double yellow flowers in abundance all summer long. See *Rosa*, p. 153.

C Golden clematis (use 1) Twining up through the rose canes, this deciduous vine adds masses of small yellow flowers to the larger, more elaborate roses all summer. Feathery silver seed heads in fall. See *Clematis tangutica*, p. 128.

D Jackman clematis (use 2) These deciduous vines clamber among the rose canes at the corners of the wall. The combination of their large but simple purple flowers and the double yellow roses is spectacular. See *Clematis* x *jackmanii*, p. 128.

E 'Green Beauty' littleleaf boxwood (use 15) Small evergreen leaves make this an ideal shrub for this neat hedge. The leaves stay bright green all winter. Trim it about 12 to 18 in. high so it won't obscure the plants behind. See *Buxus microphylla*, p. 125.

F 'Carol Mackie' daphne (use 2) This small rounded shrub marks the far end of the bed with year-round green-and-cream variegated foliage. In spring, pale pink flowers fill the yard with their perfume. See *Daphne* x *burkwoodii*, p. 130.

G Russian sage (use 7) Silver-green foliage and tiers of tiny blue flowers create a light airy effect in the center of the design from midsummer until fall. Cut stems back partway in early summer to control the size and spread of this tall perennial. See *Perovskia atriplicifolia*, p. 148.

H 'Happy Returns' daylily (use 6) These compact grassy-leaved perennials provide yellow trumpet-shaped flowers from early June to frost. A striking combination of color and texture with the Russian sage behind. See *Hemerocallis*, p. 136.

I 'Monch' aster (use 4) Pale purple daisylike flowers bloom gaily from June until frost on these knee-high perennials. Cut stems partway back in midsummer if they start to flop over the hedge. See *Aster* x *frikartii*, p. 121.

J Trellis Simple panels of wooden lattice frame the crape myrtles while supporting the roses and clematis. See p. 189.

K Steppingstones Rectangular flagstone slabs provide a place to stand while pruning and tying nearby shrubs and vines. See p. 171.

J Trellis

D Jackman clematis

B 'Golden Showers' rose

A 'Hopi' crape myrtle

C Golden clematis

B 'Golden Showers' rose

G Russian sage

G Russian sage

H 'Happy Returns' daylily

F 'Carol Mackie' daphne

'Monch' aster **I**

See site plan for **K** .

SITE: Sunny

SEASON: Late summer

CONCEPT: Perennials, vines, and shrubs in a narrow bed make a focal point of an uninteresting wall.

Garage

J **B** **D** **G** **A** **J** **B** **C** **G** **A** **G** **D** **B** **J**

F **H** **G** **F**

K **I** **K** **I** **K**

E

Lawn

1 square = 1 ft.

Grow a living sculpture

A large empty wall is a perfect opportunity to try the art of espalier, where a woody plant is trained to grow flat against a wall in a formal pattern. The striking geometric array of branches looks much more difficult to achieve than it really is. (See p. 206 for instructions.)

The centerpiece of this design is an espaliered Sargent crab apple tree. Its branching arms are covered in late spring with fragrant white flowers, clothed in summer with attractive foliage, and dappled in fall with small bright red fruits. In winter its bare branches against the wall have a special beauty.

It takes four to five years for an espalier to fill out, but the rest of the planting will hold your interest in the meantime with pink flowers and foliage in shades of blue and green that will be in their prime in just a few years.

SITE: Sunny

SEASON: Late summer

CONCEPT: An espaliered crab apple is the centerpiece of this vertical garden.

Trellis **I**
Goldflame honeysuckle **B**
D 'Blue Star' juniper
H 'Carol Mackie' daphne
C 'Betty Prior' rose
Pink grapeleaf anemone **E**
'Sea Urchin' blue fescue grass **F**
A Sargent crab apple
Blue oat grass **G**
'Carol Mackie' daphne **H**

Plants & Projects

The espalier might appear difficult to make, but it requires only two to three hours of work each month from May through August. The vines will need some tying and pruning, but the shrubs and perennials are easy to grow and care for.

A Sargent crab apple
(use 1 plant)
This small deciduous tree offers simple white spring flowers, attractive foliage, and small bright red fruits all winter. See *Malus sargentii*, p. 144.

B Goldflame honeysuckle
(use 2)
These fast-growing but well-behaved woody vines will quickly cover the trellises at each end of the planting. They bear heavy crops of sweet-smelling pink-and-yellow

flowers in spring and fall, with lighter displays in between. See *Lonicera x heckrottii*, p. 144.

C 'Betty Prior' rose (use 2)
Old-fashioned shrub roses flank the espalier, blooming from early summer to late fall with fragrant pink single roses that resemble dogwood blossoms. See *Rosa*, p. 153.

D 'Blue Star' juniper (use 6)
The rich blue color and irregular, low mounded form of this evergreen shrub are a nice foil for the pink-flowered honeysuckle and roses behind. See *Juniperus squamata*, p. 141.

E Pink grapeleaf anemone
(use 6)
Pink daisylike flowers float above this perennial's dark green foliage in late summer.

See *Anemone vitifolia* 'Robustissima', p. 120.

F 'Sea Urchin' blue fescue grass
(use 9)
The fine blue leaves of this perennial grass complement the color while contrasting with the texture of the neighboring juniper. Makes a pleasing low edging for the center of the bed. See *Festuca ovina* var. *glauca*, p. 133.

G Blue oat grass (use 6)
Another grass with slender blue evergreen leaves, it echoes the blue fescue but in bigger, tufted mounds. See *Helictotrichon sempervirens*, p. 135.

See p. 66 for the following:

H 'Carol Mackie' daphne (use 2)
I Trellis
J Steppingstones

See site plan for **J** .

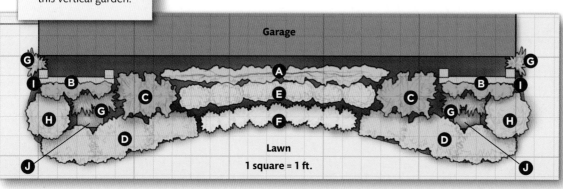

Garage

G
I B C A E B I
H G F C G H
D D
J Lawn J
1 square = 1 ft.

VARIATIONS ON A THEME

Running out of garden space? Here are some ideas to help you garden up as well as out.

Roses and delphiniums cover this wall beautifully. In front is 'Constance Spry', a shrub rose with a pink blush. The climbing rose, 'Johann Strauss', offers the same color but more delicate flowers for contrasting texture.

Although they don't actually grow on the wall, the billowy forms and colorful confetti-like blossoms of hydrangea dress it very nicely.

The wall in this design forms the backdrop for a larger garden that extends out into the lawn. Eventually, the clematis and other vines will cover the entire roof with flowers via the trellises.

Swags of ivy decorate this shady fence, conjuring fairytale landscapes a child would love.

Make a No-Mow Slope

A TERRACED GROVE TRANSFORMS A STEEP SLOPE

SITE: Sunny

SEASON: Early summer

CONCEPT: Retaining walls and a low-maintenance planting of trees and shrubs tame this slope.

A Kousa dogwood

See site plan for **G** .

F Lady's mantle

B 'Boule de Neige' rhododendron

E Dwarf plumbago

D 'Bronxensis' greenstem forsythia

H Retaining wall

! Plants with this symbol are considered invasive or are locally invasive, as noted. See the appropriate plant profile for suggested alternatives.

Loved by children with sleds, steep slopes can be a landscape headache for adults. They're a chore to mow, and they can present problems of erosion and maintenance if you try to establish other ground covers or plantings. One solution to this dilemma is shown here—tame the slope with low retaining walls, and plant the resulting flat (or flatter) beds with interesting low-care shrubs and perennials.

Steep slopes near the house are common on houses with walk-out basements or lower-level garages. Here, two low retaining walls create three terraces that mirror the curve of the driveway. A perennial ground cover and low-growing shrub carpet the lower and middle levels. On the top level, two small multistemmed trees and an informal underplanting of shrubs and perennials give the appearance of a small grove. Farther from the house, where the pitch of the slope lessens, the upper-level shrubs spill down the hill, marking the transition to the front lawn.

The planting is attractive whether viewed from above or below, providing good-looking flowers and foliage from spring through fall and a tracery of woody branches through the winter. When viewed from the sidewalk, it frames the house and directs attention to the front entrance. It also screens the semiprivate area of drive and garage from the more public entrance. The planting can be easily extended along the facade of the house with the addition of more rhododendrons and hostas.

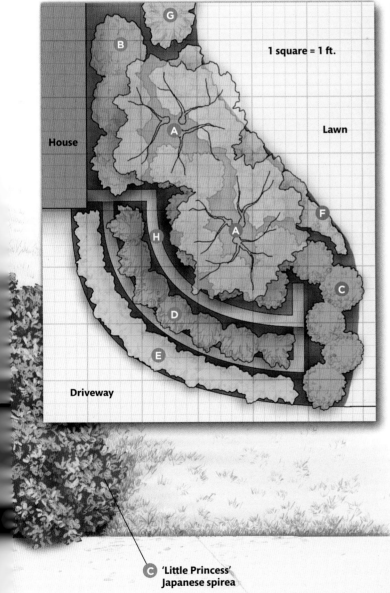

1 square = 1 ft.

House

Lawn

Driveway

C 'Little Princess' Japanese spirea

Plants & Projects

Building the retaining walls, reshaping the slope, and preparing the planting beds is a big job, so you might want to line up some energetic helpers or hire someone with a small earthmover such as a Bobcat. Once that job is done and the plants are established, this design will provide years of enjoyment and needs almost no maintenance—just snap the fading flowers off the rhododendrons in June, and trim the lady's mantle and spireas in early spring. Underplanting with spring bulbs is optional, but it's an easy way to add lots more color.

A **Kousa dogwood** (use 2 plants)
This small deciduous tree offers large creamy flowers for many weeks in early summer, showy edible fruits in late summer, bright fall foliage, and colorful flaky bark in winter. Two multitrunked trees will give the appearance of a small grove. See *Cornus kousa*, p. 129.

B **'Boule de Neige' rhododendron** (use 3)
Clusters of striking white flowers stand out against this shrub's glossy dark evergreen foliage in May or June. Its tidy rounded habit looks good against the house. See *Rhododendron*, p. 150.

C **'Little Princess' Japanese spirea** (use 12)
! *This plant is considered invasive in the Mid-Atlantic.*
A staggered row of these neat, low deciduous shrubs makes a casual edging along the upper wall. Pretty foliage topped with lots of pink flowers in June. See *Spiraea japonica*, p. 155.

D **'Bronxensis' greenstem forsythia** (use 7)
Low-growing deciduous shrub forms a tangle of attractive glossy foliage that will cascade over the lower wall with a little training. Pale yellow flowers in midspring. See *Forsythia viridissima*, p. 133.

E **Dwarf plumbago** (use 66)
Small blue flowers cover the dark green leaves of this perennial ground cover all summer. Foliage turns crimson in fall. Dies down in winter, so snow from the driveway won't hurt it. You can plant drifts of daffodils or other bulbs in the same bed; they will have plenty of time to bloom before the plumbago leafs out in May. See *Ceratostigma plumbaginoides*, p. 126.

F **Lady's mantle** (use 30)
Broad mounds of this perennial's attractive pleated leaves make an informal edging by the lawn. Billows of chartreuse flowers in summer. Underplant with drifts of white daffodils. See *Alchemilla mollis*, p. 119.

G **'Royal Standard' hosta** (use 3)
The arching clusters of this perennial's green leaves stay fresh even in the sun. Its fragrant trumpetlike white flowers bloom on tall stems in August and September. Underplant with pink tulips, which will bloom above emerging hosta foliage. See *Hosta*, p. 136.

H **Retaining wall**
Curving walls built of prefabricated blocks are 18 in. tall, 4 ft. apart. See p. 180.

VARIATIONS ON A THEME

These photos show very effective, though very different, ways of taming a slope. Each responds to its site and the functional requirements (if any) of the situation.

Terraced beds filled with roses, shrubs, and perennials turn an awkward slope next to the side of a house into a showpiece.

A simple, but lovely, combination of paving and plants transforms the gently sloping entrance to this modest house.

This splendid border makes superb use of its sloping site. Walking along its edge, a visitor is rewarded with something of interest on every sight line, from foot-height to treetop.

Planting for a shady slope

If your slope is shaded by the house or a large tree nearby, here's the same design with a selection of shade-tolerant trees, shrubs, and perennials.

Replacing the dogwoods are two redbuds, small Mid-Atlantic natives whose graceful branches lend an Asian flavor to the planting. Beneath them, an informal line of evergreen shrubs edges the house and the upper wall, tying the two together visually. Two ground covers—one woody, one grassy—fill the beds below with foliage and flowers of green and gold. Spring (shown here) is the most colorful season, but the planting looks good year-round.

A Redbud
F White astilbe
C 'Carol Mackie' daphne
'Brouwer's Beauty' Japanese andromeda B
Retaining wall G
E Variegated Japanese sedge
D Winter jasmine

SITE: Shady

SEASON: Early spring

CONCEPT: Shade-tolerant trees, shrubs, and perennials adapt the design to a site with little sun.

House

1 square = 1 ft.

Lawn

Driveway

Plants & Projects

A Redbud (use 2 plants)
This small deciduous tree greets spring with a striking display of tiny purple-pink flowers that cling to its bare branches. Heart-shaped leaves turn gold in autumn. Prune thoughtfully, removing lower and inner branches, to improve the winter silhouette. See *Cercis canadensis*, p. 126.

B 'Brouwer's Beauty' Japanese andromeda (use 4)
Evergreen shrubs with whorls of glossy oblong leaves make an informal foundation planting next to the house. Attractive maroon flower buds are visible all winter, producing clusters of white flowers in spring. See *Pieris japonica*, p. 149.

C 'Carol Mackie' daphne (use 7)
A neat evergreen shrub with outstanding foliage and flowers. Small oval leaves are green with gold edges. Very fragrant pale pink flowers bloom for several weeks in spring. See *Daphne x burkwoodii*, p. 130.

D Winter jasmine (use 7)
The trailing, bright green stems of this deciduous shrub root easily, quickly filling the second level and tumbling over the wall. Pale yellow flowers appear in late winter. See *Jasminum nudiflorum*, p. 141.

E Variegated Japanese sedge (use 60)
Grassy tufts of striped yellow-and-green leaves fill the lower level. This perennial is evergreen, although heavy snow may flatten it. See *Carex morrowii* 'Aureo-variegata', p. 126.

F White astilbe (use 60)
A dwarf variety of this popular shade-loving perennial makes an attractive ground cover beneath the redbuds. In summer, dark glossy foliage is topped with plumes of white flowers. Underplant with drifts of white daffodils for a springtime show. See *Astilbe simplicifolia*, p. 122.

See p. 71 for the following:

G Retaining wall

A Beginning Border

FLOWERS AND A FENCE MAKE A TRADITIONAL DESIGN

A perennial border can be one of the most delightful of all gardens. Indeed, that's usually its sole purpose. Unlike many other types of landscape plantings, a traditional border is seldom yoked to any function beyond that of providing as much pleasure as possible. From the first neat mounds of foliage in the spring to the fullness of summer bloom and autumn color, the mix of flowers, foliage, textures, tones, and hues brings enjoyment.

This border is designed for a beginning perennial gardener, using durable plants that are easy to establish and care for. Screening out distraction xbehind the planting is a simple fence. The planting is meant to be viewed from the front, so tall plants go at the back. A pair of graceful grasses mark the rear corners of the symmetrical design, with a slightly shorter grass as a leafy backdrop between them. Front corners are defined by the leaves of yucca.

Within this frame, a handsome collection of flowering perennials offers a long season of bloom and attractive foliage in a range of greens and grays. Low-growing plants edge the front of the border with blue and yellow flowers all summer. In the middle of the bed, loose spikes of catmint, upright spires of veronica, and the airy lavender flowers of Russian sage continue the blue theme. Autumn flowers add a burst of color, with deep purple asters, pink mums, and rosy sedums set against a tan and gold backdrop of grasses.

Ⓜ **Fence**

Ⓐ **'Autumn Light'**
Japanese silver grass

Plants & Projects

No perennial garden is carefree, but this one comes very close. Veronica blooms longer and pincushion flowers look better when spent flowers are clipped off. If you cut back catmint by about one-third after flowering, it will make a return performance, but don't cut back the grasses or sedum until spring, or you'll miss their buff and brown winter hues.

Ⓐ **'Autumn Light' Japanese silver grass** (use 2 plants)
❶ *This plant is locally invasive in the Mid-Atlantic.*
Tall clumps of narrow leaves produce silvery flower plumes in late summer that mature to fluffy seed heads. See *Miscanthus sinensis*, p. 145.

Ⓑ **'Karl Foerster' feather reed grass** (use 5)
In midsummer, thin stalks rise high above upright clumps of slender green leaves, carrying narrow flower spikes that ripen, along with the leaves, to a warm tan color. See

Calamagrostis x *acutiflora*, p. 125.

Ⓒ **Yucca** (use 4)
A dramatic shrub with spiky evergreen leaves and clusters of creamy white flowers that tower over the foliage in June on thick, branched stalks. See *Yucca filamentosa*, p. 159.

Ⓓ **Russian sage** (use 4)
This shrubby perennial's sparse, fragrant gray-green leaves and tiers of small blue late-summer flowers hover like an airy cloud in the border. See *Perovskia atriciplifolia*, p. 148.

Ⓔ **'Purple Dome' New England aster** (use 2)
A perennial whose mound of handsome deep green foliage is blanketed with rich purple flowers in early fall. See *Aster novae-angliae*, p. 121.

Ⓕ **'Sheffield' chrysanthemum** (use 2)
The large, single, light pink flowers produced by this perennial last from late September to early November.

See *Dendranthema* x *grandiflorum*, p. 130.

Ⓖ **'Sunny Border Blue' veronica** (use 3)
At the center of the planting, this perennial blooms all summer, with intense blue-purple flower spikes rising above a low bushy clump of glossy green foliage. See *Veronica*, p. 157.

Ⓗ **'Goodness Grows' veronica** (use 6)
A shorter veronica, its low mat of lustrous foliage defining the front edge of the bed. Slender spikes of lavender-blue flowers bloom all summer. See *Veronica*, p. 157.

Ⓘ **'Butterfly Blue' pincushion flower** (use 6)
Another season-long bloomer, this perennial produces masses of light blue flowers on neat, compact clumps of bright green leaves. See *Scabiosa columbaria*, p. 154.

Ⓙ **'Dropmore' catmint** (use 5)
This perennial's soft gray leaves

are nicely set off by the foliage and flowers of its neighbors. Clusters of small blue flowers repeat (if sheared) from early summer on. See *Nepeta* x *faassenii*, p. 146.

Ⓚ **'Vera Jameson' sedum** (use 4)
Short sturdy stalks with succulent purplish leaves support flat-topped clusters of rosy pink flowers in late summer. A perennial, it forms neat, compact clumps near the front of the bed. See *Sedum*, p. 155.

Ⓛ **'Moonbeam' coreopsis** (use 3)
This perennial's tiny pale yellow flowers float over a mound of delicate dark green foliage from midsummer into fall. See *Coreopsis verticillata*, p. 128.

Ⓜ **Fence**
A 6-ft.-tall fence provides a backdrop for the border and privacy for you. See p. 192.

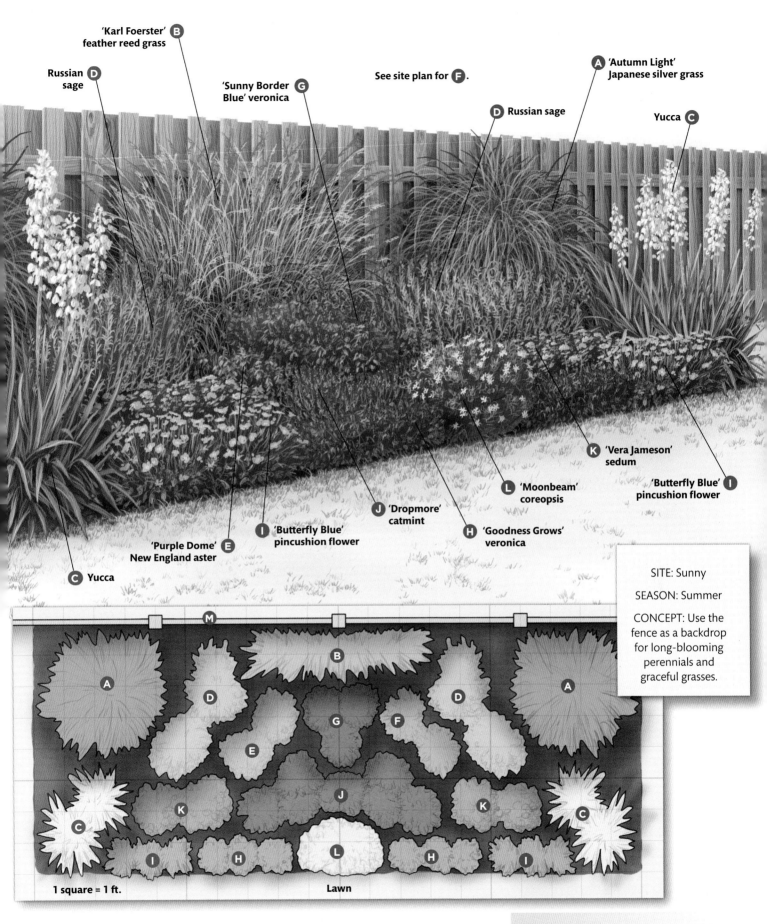

'Karl Foerster' **B**
feather reed grass

Russian **D**
sage

'Sunny Border **G**
Blue' veronica

See site plan for **F**.

A 'Autumn Light'
Japanese silver grass

D Russian sage

Yucca **C**

K 'Vera Jameson'
sedum

L 'Moonbeam'
coreopsis

'Butterfly Blue' **I**
pincushion flower

J 'Dropmore'
catmint

H 'Goodness Grows'
veronica

I 'Butterfly Blue'
pincushion flower

'Purple Dome' **E**
New England aster

C Yucca

SITE: Sunny

SEASON: Summer

CONCEPT: Use the
fence as a backdrop
for long-blooming
perennials and
graceful grasses.

1 square = 1 ft.

Lawn

 *Plants with this symbol are considered
invasive or are locally invasive, as noted.
See the appropriate plant profile for
suggested alternatives.*

Mixing it up

In a mixed border, shrubs and small trees join perennials, seasonal bulbs, and even annuals. Because of the all-season physical presence of woody plants, mixed borders are sometimes called upon to perform functional tasks, such as for screens or barriers.

This design, however, like the previous one, is intended primarily to be beautiful. Now butterfly bushes and shrub roses stand tall across the back of the planting, while fountainlike ornamental grasses mark the bed's front corners.

The long-blooming shrubs provide a colorful backdrop for the perennials at their feet, which fill the border with flowers in shades of blue and pink during the summer months. The show continues through fall into winter, with rustling tan leaves of the grasses, showy orange rose hips, and rusty brown seed heads of the coneflowers and sedum. When bulbs herald the arrival of spring, the cycle resumes.

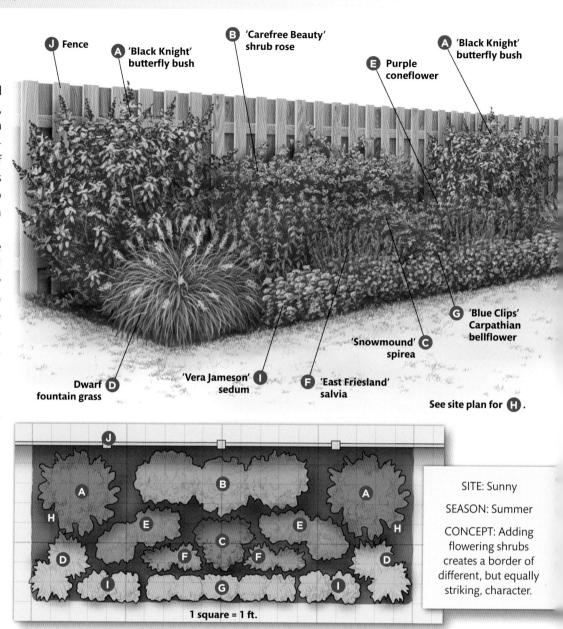

J Fence
A 'Black Knight' butterfly bush
B 'Carefree Beauty' shrub rose
E Purple coneflower
A 'Black Knight' butterfly bush
G 'Blue Clips' Carpathian bellflower
C 'Snowmound' spirea
I 'Vera Jameson' sedum
F 'East Friesland' salvia
D Dwarf fountain grass
See site plan for **H**.

1 square = 1 ft.

SITE: Sunny

SEASON: Summer

CONCEPT: Adding flowering shrubs creates a border of different, but equally striking, character.

Plants & Projects

A **'Black Knight' butterfly bush** (use 2 plants)
❶ *This plant is considered invasive in the Mid-Atlantic.* This eye-catching deciduous shrub forms a fountain of arching shoots tipped with spikes of small purple flowers from midsummer through fall. See *Buddleia davidii*, p. 123.

B **'Carefree Beauty' shrub rose** (use 3)
Clusters of fragrant semidouble flowers in a pretty shade of pink cover this disease-resistant deciduous shrub all summer. See *Rosa*, p. 153.

C **'Snowmound' spirea** (use 1)
❶ *This plant is considered*

invasive in the Mid-Atlantic. Arching branches give this deciduous shrub a mounded profile. In May the branches are lined with round clusters of white flowers. See *Spiraea nipponica*, p. 155.

D **Dwarf fountain grass** (use 4)
This perennial's tidy cascade of green leaves turns a warm buff-orange in fall. Fluffy flower spikes rise above the foliage in midsummer, turn tan in autumn, and persist into winter. See *Pennisetum alopecuroides* 'Hameln', p. 148.

E **Purple coneflower** (use 4)
A perennial with rosy pink flowers that rise on stiff stalks

above coarse green foliage from midsummer on. Flowers have prominent orange centers that turn brown as they mature. See *Echinacea purpurea*, p. 130.

F **'East Friesland' salvia** (use 4)
This perennial's spiky reddish purple flowers begin in early summer and continue until frost if you keep removing faded blossoms. Their dark foliage and numerous flowers make a mass of color near the front of the border. See *Salvia x superba*, p. 154.

G **'Blue Clips' Carpathian bellflower** (use 5)
Cup-shaped blue flowers float above a mat of attractive dark

green leaves for most of the summer. An excellent perennial for the border's edge. See *Campanula carpatica*, p. 126.

H **Bulbs**
The butterfly bushes are cut back to 1 ft. tall in early spring, so plant bulbs there to brighten the spot. Plant crocuses by the handful and white or yellow daffodils in groups of three or more. The new growth of the butterfly bushes will cover the fading bulb foliage. See Bulbs: *Crocus* and *Narcissus*, p. 124.

See p. 74 for the following:

I **'Vera Jameson' sedum** (use 4)

J **Fence**

Daffodils put on a springtime show in this border while the summer attractions are pushing up out of the ground.

VARIATIONS ON A THEME

Whether your taste runs to native grasses or formal English perennial gardens, there are countless ways to create an attractive border.

Borders also offer small-scale pleasures among their bounty, rewarding closer looks as well as overall appreciation.

Masses of flowers are a showcase against a tall evergreen hedge—a traditional perennial border in its glory.

Ornamental grasses add year-round structure and texture to any garden. But they take on a leading role in the sandy soil of this beach-front property, creating a beautiful, low-maintenance border.

Down to Earth

HARMONIZE YOUR DECK WITH ITS SURROUNDINGS

A second-story deck is a perfect spot for viewing your garden and yard. Too often, however, the view of the deck from the yard is less pleasing. Perched atop skinny posts, towering over a patch of lawn, an elevated deck looks out of place, an ungainly visitor that is uncomfortable in its surroundings.

In the design shown here, attractive landscaping brings the deck, house, and yard into balance. Plants, combined with lattice panels attached to the posts, form a broad pedestal of visual support for the deck. Decreasing in height from the deck to the yard, the planting makes it easier for our eyes to move between the levels.

The planting is as pretty as it is functional. At one corner, a fringe tree provides delightful scented spring flowers that can be enjoyed from the deck above or lawn below. Clematis climbs lattice panels on the sides of the deck, while an espaliered flowering dogwood fans out across its support in front.

Wrapping around the deck at ground level, a selection of shrubs, grasses, and perennials offers colorful flowers and foliage throughout the growing season. Grass paths lead to the enclosed area beneath the deck. Cover the ground there with wood chips and use the space to store garden tools or bicycles.

See site plan for **E**.

Fringe tree **A**   Dwarf Hinoki **D** cypress

Gold-variegated **G** hakonechloa

Hollyhock **H** mallow   'Karl Foerster' **I** feather reed grass

Plants & Projects

In this design, flowers in shades of blue, pink, and white bloom in sequence from spring to fall, complemented by green, gold, and purple foliage. The lattice provides instant screening, and the clematis vine, perennials, and grasses will flower and fill their space in just a year or two; the trees will take several years to grow as large as we've shown here. Annual maintenance includes cutting back the perennials and grasses in fall or spring and training the espaliered dogwood, a process that takes patience but is fun to do.

A Fringe tree (use 1 plant)
A small multitrunked deciduous tree, it is festooned with spectacular fleecy clusters of fragrant flowers in late spring. Leaves turn gold in the autumn. See *Chionanthus virginicus*, p. 127.

B Kousa dogwood (use 1)
Espaliered below the deck, this deciduous tree displays large white flowers in early summer, followed by red fruits and red-purple fall color. (See p. 206 for how to espalier.) Flaking multicolored bark looks interesting all year. See *Cornus kousa*, p. 129.

C Sweet autumn clematis (use 2)
A vigorous deciduous vine covered with

fragrant white flowers in late summer and puffy silvery seed heads in fall. See *Clematis terniflora*, p. 128.

D Dwarf Hinoki cypress (use 2)
A small pyramidal conifer with curly sprays of dark green foliage. See *Chamaecyparis obtusa* 'Nana Gracilis', p. 127.

E False indigo (use 5)
Candlelike spikes of sky blue flowers stand out in early summer above dense clumps of blue-green foliage. Big gray seedpods follow on this native perennial. See *Baptisia australis*, p. 122.

F Gaura (use 4)
Delicate white and pink flowers on arching stems sparkle from early summer to frost on this tough perennial wildflower. See *Gaura lindheimeri*, p. 133.

G Gold-variegated hakonechloa (use 12)
Arching gracefully from thin stems, the long tapering leaves of this perennial grass have a creamy background overlaid with green and traces of bronze. See *Hakonechloa macra* 'Aureola', p. 134.

H Hollyhock mallow (use 7)
For weeks in midsummer, a thicket of tall stems carry fresh pink flowers. The bright green foliage looks good in spring and fall. See *Malva alcea* 'Fastigiata', p. 144.

I 'Karl Foerster' feather reed grass (use 10)
This clumping perennial grass pushes stalks of slender silvery seed heads well above its leaves in midsummer. Handsome in winter. See *Calamagrostis* x *acutiflora*, p. 125.

J 'Longwood Blue' bluebeard (use 4)
Fluffy blue flowers on this deciduous shrub attract lots of butterflies in late summer. Gray-green foliage is attractive, too. See *Caryopteris* x *clandonensis*, p. 126.

K 'Palace Purple' heuchera (use 8)
A broad patch of this perennial ground cover fills the front of the bed. Dark purple-bronze foliage contrasts with the other plants and the lawn. See *Heuchera*, p. 136.

L Peony (use 3)
A bushy perennial with lovely foliage all season and beautiful flowers in late May. Try a single pink form here; it won't flop like the heavier double-flowered kinds. See *Paeonia*, p. 148.

M Lattice panels
Wooden lattice panels enclose the base of the deck and support the espalier and vines. See p. 192.

M Lattice panels

C Sweet autumn clematis

K 'Palace Purple' heuchera

B Kousa "dogwood

J 'Longwood Blue' bluebeard

I 'Karl Foerster' feather reed grass

F Gaura

D Dwarf Hinoki cypress

Peony **L**

Deck

Lawn

1 square = 1 ft.

SITE: Sunny

SEASON: Spring

CONCEPT: A pleasing mix of woody plants, perennials, and grasses leads the eye from ground to deck.

A shady understory

This planting also integrates the deck with its surroundings, but it does so in a shady environment, produced perhaps by large trees nearby. The design has a similar layout, but the plants—shade lovers from the woodland understory—reflect the altered conditions.

In February and March, the witch hazel tree's small yellow flowers perfume the whole area with a delicious sweet scent, and the vivid red twigs of the variegated Siberian dogwood gleam on sunny spring days. Later in the spring and then throughout the summer and fall, variegated green-and-white leaves and a succession of white flowers brighten this shady site, joined by a patch of cheerful pink astilbe blossoms in August.

The climbing hydrangea will slowly spread up and across the latticework, covering it with glossy leaves all season and lacy white flowers in June. It needs no ongoing care; the other plants need attention only once or twice a year, in spring or fall.

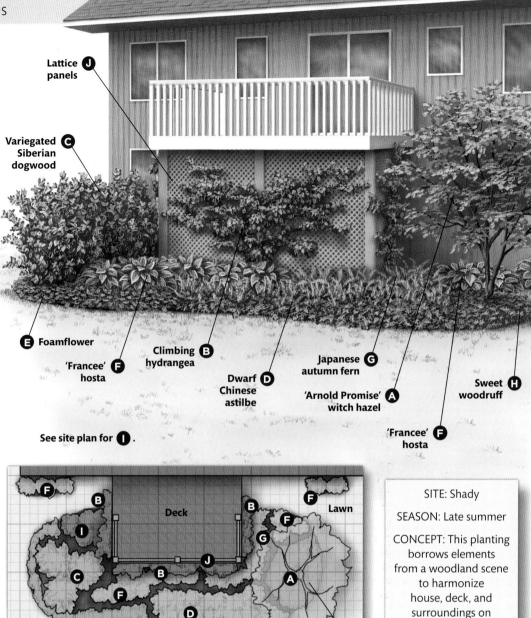

Lattice panels **J**
Variegated Siberian dogwood **C**
Foamflower **E**
'Francee' hosta **F**
Climbing hydrangea **B**
Dwarf Chinese astilbe **D**
Japanese autumn fern **G**
'Arnold Promise' witch hazel **A**
Sweet woodruff **H**
'Francee' hosta **F**
See site plan for **I**.

F **B** Deck **B** Lawn **F**
I **F** **G**
C **J** **A**
F **B**
E **D** **H**
1 square = 1 ft.

SITE: Shady

SEASON: Late summer

CONCEPT: This planting borrows elements from a woodland scene to harmonize house, deck, and surroundings on a shady site.

Plants & Projects

A **'Arnold Promise' witch hazel** (use 1 plant) A multitrunked tree with very fragrant flowers that reward early-spring visits to the deck. Deciduous leaves turn gold in fall. See *Hamamelis x intermedia*, p. 134.

B **Climbing hydrangea** (use 3) A deciduous vine with clusters of white flowers, handsome leaves, and peeling bark on the thick trunk and branches. See *Hydrangea petiolaris*, p. 138.

C **Variegated Siberian dogwood** (use 3) This large deciduous shrub is always attractive, providing white spring flowers, green-and-white leaves and blue berries in summer, brilliant fall foliage, and bright red stems in winter. See *Cornus alba* 'Elegantissima', p. 129.

D **Dwarf Chinese astilbe** (use 12) A low-growing perennial, it spreads to form a mat of ferny dark green leaves. Fuzzy spikes of tiny pink flowers cover the foliage in summer. See *Astilbe chinensis* var. *pumila*, p. 122.

E **Foamflower** (use 17) Spreading by underground runners, this native woodland perennial makes a good ground cover. Fluffy spikes of small white flowers float above broad, dark evergreen leaves in late spring. See *Tiarella cordifolia*, p. 157.

F **'Francee' hosta** (use 17) A perennial grown for its handsome foliage. Forms a low, spreading mound of large dark green leaves edged with white. See *Hosta*, p. 136.

G **Japanese autumn fern** (use 8) Forming a characteristic woodland ground cover next to the deck, this fern's upright fronds emerge in spring a copper color, then darken with maturity to a glossy green. See Ferns: *Dryopteris erythrosora*, p. 132.

H **Sweet woodruff** (use 13) Starry white flowers cover this low perennial ground cover in May. The dainty leaves look fresh from spring until frost. See *Galium odoratum*, p. 133.

I **'White Pearl' bugbane** (use 5) Slender wands of white flowers arch above the jagged dark green leaves in late fall. See *Cimicifuga simplex*, p. 127.

See p. 78 for the following:
J **Lattice panels**

VARIATIONS ON A THEME

These designs success-fully blend decks of dif-ferent heights into their surrounding landscapes.

Perennials and dwarf evergreen shrubs edge this low deck with flowers and year-round greenery.

This well-thought-out design highlights, rather than hides, the handsome architectural features of the second-story deck and helps tie it visually to the ground-level patio.

A terraced garden makes the transition up a slope from a low-lying lawn to this substantial deck.

Garden in the Round

CREATE A PLANTING WITH SEVERAL ATTRACTIVE FACES

(!) *Plants with this symbol are considered invasive or are locally invasive, as noted. See the appropriate plant profile for suggested alternatives.*

Plantings in domestic landscapes are usually "attached" to something. Beds and borders hew to property lines, walls, or patios; foundation plantings skirt the house, garage, or deck. Most are meant to be viewed from the front, rather like a wall-mounted sculpture in raised relief.

On the other hand, the planting shown here is only loosely moored to a low fence, forming a peninsula jutting into the lawn. It is an excellent option for those who want to squeeze more gardening space from a small lot, add interest to a rectangular one, or divide a large area into smaller "outdoor rooms." Because you can walk around most of the bed, plants can be displayed "in the round," and they can be combined to present different scenes from several vantage points.

Without a strong connection to a structure or other landscape feature, a bed like this (or its close cousin, the island bed) requires a sensitivity to scale. To be successful, the bed must neither dominate its surroundings nor be lost in them. This planting was designed with a modest or larger suburban property in mind. A combination of large and small, subtle and bold plants makes this attractive up close or viewed from a distance, and there's always something to admire as you stroll by.

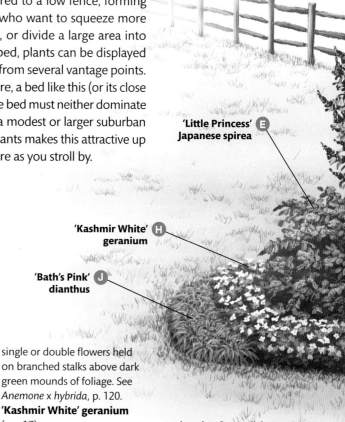

'Little Princess' Japanese spirea **E**

'Kashmir White' geranium **H**

'Bath's Pink' dianthus **J**

Plants & Projects

A handsome collection of woody plants garnished by complementary perennials gives this bed its character. There are flowers from spring to fall (and sometimes in winter), in whites, pinks, and purples. All of the plants have attractive foliage, including a number with evergreen leaves, and all grow well with a minimum of fuss.

A Japanese stewartia
(use 1 plant)
This small tree offers new spring shoots tinged with purple and white camellia-like flowers in summer (perhaps even the first year after transplanting). Multicolored fall foliage gives way in winter to distinctive flaking bark. See *Stewartia pseudocamellia*, p. 156.

B 'Black Knight' butterfly bush
(use 3)
(!) *This plant is considered invasive in the Mid-Atlantic.*
From midsummer on, spikes of fragrant purple flowers bloom on the arching shoots of this large deciduous shrub. Cut back hard each spring; fresh shoots quickly reach 5 ft. tall. See *Buddleia davidii*, p. 123.

C 'Bonica' rose (use 3)
This shrub rose forms a large mound that's covered with small, scentless, double pink flowers all summer. A reliable plant, free of common rose ailments. See *Rosa*, p. 153.

D White evergreen azalea
(use 3)
Masses of lovely flowers cover these neat, compact shrubs in mid- to late spring. The small green leaves are attractive all year. See *Rhododendron*, p. 150.

E 'Little Princess' Japanese spirea (use 1)
(!) *This plant is considered invasive in the Mid-Atlantic.*
This compact rounded shrub, wider than tall, with fine-textured, deciduous dark green leaves is a good companion for the vase-shaped butterfly bush nearby. Clusters of pink flowers last for weeks in June. See *Spiraea japonica*, p. 155.

F Southernwood (use 3)
Sweet-scented, feathery, silver-gray leaves are the attraction of this shrubby perennial, which rarely flowers. Prune it back halfway every spring to keep it compact and bushy. See *Artemisia abrotanum*, p. 120.

G White Japanese anemone
(use 5)
In late summer, this perennial displays enchanting clear white, single or double flowers held on branched stalks above dark green mounds of foliage. See *Anemone x hybrida*, p. 120.

H 'Kashmir White' geranium
(use 17)
Edging two portions of the bed, this perennial forms a low mound of beautiful, deeply lobed leaves. In early summer, white flowers with lilac veins completely cover the plant, making it look like a bouquet. If you can't find this one at your local nursery, try 'Album', a white cultivar of *Geranium sanguineum*. See *Geranium clarkei*, p. 134.

I Christmas rose (use 5)
This perennial's large pure white flowers may be a Christmas present nestled under the stewartia in December. Dark, finely cut evergreen leaves turn bronze in winter. Although the plant takes a few years to get established, it then persists happily for decades. See *Helleborus niger*, p. 135.

J 'Bath's Pink' dianthus (use 7)
Edging the end of the bed, these low-growing perennials form a mat of grassy evergreen foliage and produce clear pink carnation-like flowers that have a marvelous scent. Flowers appear in late spring; when they fade, shear the plants back halfway and new foliage will form. See *Dianthus*, p. 130.

K Foamflower (use 15)
A native woodland perennial that spreads to form an airy evergreen ground cover under the stewartia. Clumps of maple-shaped leaves are topped with soft spikes of tiny white flowers in late spring. See *Tiarella cordifolia*, p. 157.

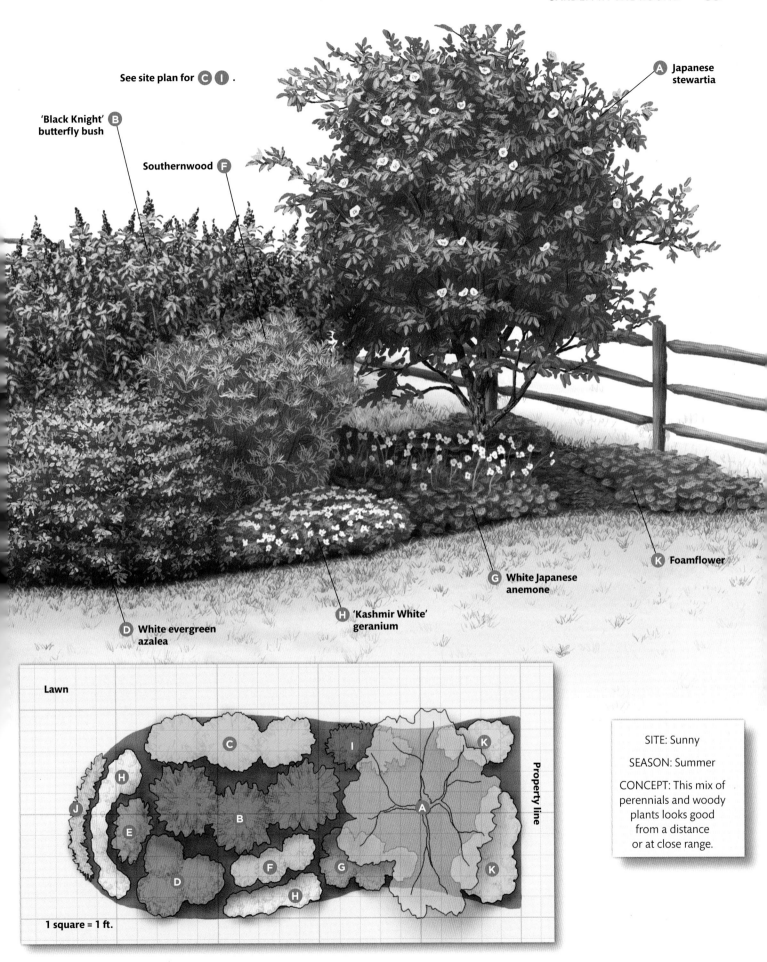

See site plan for **C I** .

A Japanese stewartia

'Black Knight' **B** butterfly bush

Southernwood **F**

D White evergreen azalea

H 'Kashmir White' geranium

G White Japanese anemone

K Foamflower

Lawn

C

I

K

H

J

B

E

A

K

F

D

G

H

Property line

1 square = 1 ft.

SITE: Sunny

SEASON: Summer

CONCEPT: This mix of perennials and woody plants looks good from a distance or at close range.

A floral peninsula

Perennials replace shrubs to give this planting a different look than the previous one. The bed is anchored by large deciduous hollies at one end and a graceful ornamental grass at the other. Linking these elements and forming a spine down the center of the bed are sizable clumps of two stiff-stalked perennials—purple coneflower and Russian sage—surrounded by an array of other colorful perennials.

This planting's foliage is varied and attractive, ranging from wispy to coarse across a spectrum of greens. But flowers are the main attraction here. Shades of blue, purple, pink, and white (with a dash of yellow) blend in various combinations as the seasons progress. Most are long-blooming; two (gaura and veronica) flower from spring through fall.

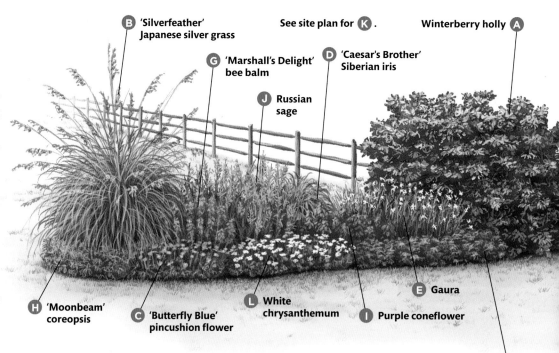

B 'Silverfeather' Japanese silver grass
See site plan for K .
Winterberry holly A
G 'Marshall's Delight' bee balm
D 'Caesar's Brother' Siberian iris
J Russian sage
H 'Moonbeam' coreopsis
C 'Butterfly Blue' pincushion flower
L White chrysanthemum
I Purple coneflower
E Gaura
'Johnson's Blue' geranium F

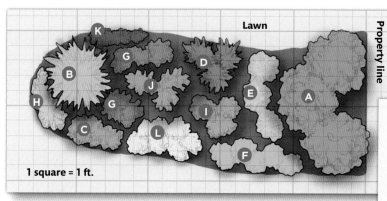

Lawn
Property line
1 square = 1 ft.

SITE: Sunny

SEASON: Fall

CONCEPT: These colorful, tough plants can take heat and drought and look good through the dog days of summer.

Plants & Projects

A Winterberry holly
(use 3 plants)
A large native deciduous shrub with bright green spineless leaves in summer and abundant red berries all winter. See *Ilex verticillata*, p. 140.

B 'Silverfeather' Japanese silver grass (use 1)
❶ *This plant is locally invasive in the Mid-Atlantic.*
Summer flowers rise several feet above the long arching leaves; silvery seed-head plumes last through winter. See *Miscanthus sinensis*, p. 145.

C 'Butterfly Blue' pincushion flower (use 5)
Neat and compact perennial that blooms from spring to frost. Flowers are a lovely shade of blue and combine handsomely with the vivid

yellow flowers of the nearby coreopsis. See *Scabiosa*, p. 154.

D 'Caesar's Brother' Siberian iris (use 3)
Perennial noted for elegant indigo blue flowers in early summer. Graceful grassy foliage earns its keep in the planting for the rest of the season. See *Iris sibirica*, p. 140.

E Gaura (use 3)
Small, starlike, white and pale pink flowers hover over an airy mass of fine foliage and slender stems from spring through fall. Cut it back partway in July to keep it bushy. See *Gaura lindheimeri*, p. 133.

F 'Johnson's Blue' geranium (use 5)
Low-growing perennial whose bright green, deeply lobed foliage is covered with 2-in.

blue flowers in late spring. See *Geranium*, p. 134.

G 'Marshall's Delight' bee balm (use 6)
A spreading perennial that forms a patch of upright stems with aromatic leaves and showy pink flowers in midsummer. See *Monarda*, p. 145.

H 'Moonbeam' coreopsis (use 5)
This perennial offers lacy dark green foliage and an abundance of pale yellow flowers from midsummer into fall. See *Coreopsis verticillata*, p. 128.

I Purple coneflower (use 3)
A perennial with big, daisylike, pink-purple blossoms held on thick stalks above a clump of coarse dark green leaves. Flowers in midsummer. See *Echinacea purpurea*, p. 130.

J Russian sage (use 3)
A vigorous shrubby perennial

sprinkled with small fragrant silvery leaves and, in late summer, tiny lavender flowers. See *Perovskia atriplicifolia*, p. 148.

K 'Sunny Border Blue' veronica (use 5)
This perennial forms a fairly large clump of thick glossy green leaves and produces slender spikes of dark purple-blue flowers all summer long. See *Veronica*, p. 157.

L White chrysanthemum (use 6)
These perennials close the season with an abundant long-lasting display of single or double flowers. Foliage looks neat all summer. Choose one of the many white-flowered cultivars. See *Dendranthema* x *grandiflorum*, p. 130.

VARIATIONS ON A THEME

Large or small, a garden you can stroll around offers multiple attractions.

This round island bed, with its creamy variegated foliage, is a striking sight, as if a cloud had drifted to land.

It takes a while to circumnavigate this island, but the journey is rewarding every step of the way.

With large shrubs, roses, grasses, perennials, and ground covers, this island packs a lot into a relatively small space.

Create a "Living Room"

ENCLOSE A PATIO WITH FOLIAGE AND FLOWERS

A patio can become a true extension of your living space with the addition of plants for privacy and pleasure. The floral and foliage motifs of the "walls" in the outdoor room shown here are three-dimensional and constantly changing. The handsome brick floor accommodates a family barbecue or a large gathering. A rounded portion extends into the yard and serves, rather like a bay window, to mingle "indoors" and "outdoors."

Scale is particularly important when planting next to the house. The small, multitrunked crape myrtles won't overwhelm the house while casting welcome shade on the patio. The room they help compose is relatively open. Perennials and grasses fill in beneath the trees but are short enough not to obstruct views or breezes through the loose screen of trees.

We've shown the design extending indefinitely into the foreground, to indicate that the patio can be made in a range of sizes. If the patio extends farther along the side of the house, you might plant additional crape myrtles along the edge that parallels the house wall. To give a more open feeling to the design, extend only the bed of grasses and perennials. You could design the patio's other end to be similar to the end shown here, or you could create an opening to accommodate traffic to and from a garage or driveway.

'Natchez' **A**
crape myrtle

'Butterfly Blue' **D**
pincushion flower

Dwarf fountain **B**
grass

'Sunny Border **H**
Blue' veronica

Plants & Projects

This design's long-blooming, easy-care plants will make any patio, old or new, a colorful spot throughout the summer and fall.

Beneath the white flowers of the crape myrtles, shades of blue and purple cool the summer days, with yellow coreopsis as a bright accent. Purple asters, rosy sedum, and the warm golden leaves of the fountain grass extend the show into fall. When it's cold, enjoy the view from the house of the crape myrtle's striking bark. Papery dry grasses are also a pretty sight under a light snow.

A **'Natchez' crape myrtle**
(use 4 plants)
These small multitrunked trees provide shade and long-blooming papery white flowers in summer, good fall color, and flaky brown bark in winter. Plant bulbs around the base of the trees for a spring display. See *Lagerstroemia indica*, p. 142.

B **Dwarf fountain grass** (use 6)
Framing the passage from patio to backyard, the arching leaves of this perennial grass turn from summer green to

autumn gold. Fluffy flower spikes wave above the foliage in late summer. See *Pennisetum alopecuroides* 'Hameln', p. 148.

C **'Autumn Joy' sedum** (use 6)
Large flat clusters of flower buds form atop the fleshy green foliage of this perennial in late summer. The flowers last for weeks, darkening from pale pink to rust, and the dry stalks remain standing in winter. See *Sedum*, p. 155.

D **'Butterfly Blue' pincushion flower** (use 14)
Tucked under the crape myrtles, these neat, compact perennials produce abundant blue flowers from May to hard frost. They make great cut flowers as well as attract butterflies. See *Scabiosa columbaria*, p. 154.

E **'Dropmore' catmint** (use 5)
This perennial's loose mounds of gray-green aromatic foliage with lavender-blue flower spikes contrast handsomely with nearby sedum. Blooms from June until frost if you shear off the spent flowers occasionally. See *Nepeta* x *faassenii*, p. 146.

F **'Moonbeam' coreopsis**
(use 12)
A delightful perennial for the edge of the patio. Pale yellow flowers cover mounds of delicate ferny foliage from mid-summer into September. See *Coreopsis verticillata*, p. 128.

G **'Purple Dome' aster**
(use 3)
On dense mounds of dark green foliage this perennial bursts into bloom in early fall, drenched in small purple flowers for a month. Its round form contrasts with the spiky veronica nearby. See *Aster novae-angliae*, p. 121.

H **'Sunny Border Blue' veronica**
(use 5)
Beautiful spikes of tiny deep blue flowers shoot up all summer from this perennial's basal clump of shiny dark green leaves. See *Veronica*, p. 157.

I **Patio**
Flagstones or pavers would look good here, too, but would make the curve more difficult to lay. See p. 172.

Plants with this symbol are considered invasive or are locally invasive, as noted. See the appropriate plant profile for suggested alternatives.

F 'Moonbeam' coreopsis

C 'Autumn Joy' sedum

E 'Dropmore' catmint

G 'Purple Dome' aster

1 square = 1 ft.

Lawn

C 'Autumn Joy' sedum

I Patio

E 'Dropmore' catmint

SITE: Sunny

SEASON: Late summer

CONCEPT: Planting provides privacy and ambiance for entertaining guests or an early-morning cup of coffee on your own.

VARIATIONS ON A THEME

These designs provide small, but comfortable, outdoor living spaces.

Like half walls, ivy-covered hedges help turn this patio into an outdoor room. Plants in interesting pots add decoration.

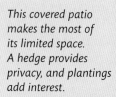

Long and narrow, this brick terrace provides a comfortable vantage point for viewing the nearby garden and will accommodate a table for four.

This covered patio makes the most of its limited space. A hedge provides privacy, and plantings add interest.

Private patio in the shade

If your patio is already blessed with a cool canopy of shade, perhaps from a large tree nearby, consider this design. Here a tall fence and small shade-tolerant trees and shrubs underplanted with shade-loving perennials create a more private, sheltered setting.

Foliage textures and colors are featured, from the delicate red leaves of the Japanese maple to the wide blue-green foliage of the hostas. Flowers in red, blue, white, and yellow brighten the patio scene from late winter to late summer.

To accommodate a longer patio, you might extend the plantings near the serviceberry and add another Japanese maple, spaced a minimum of 12 ft. from the serviceberry.

Plants & Projects

Ⓐ Serviceberry (use 1 plant)
A small multitrunked tree with something for every season: early-spring clusters of white flowers, dark purple fruits in summer, bright autumn leaves, and attractive winter branches and bark. See *Amelanchier* x *grandiflora*, p. 119.

Ⓑ 'Bloodgood' Japanese maple (use 1)
Delicately cut leaves are a dark reddish purple all season on this small deciduous tree. n leaf or bare, its graceful branches add an Oriental note. See *Acer palmatum*, p. 118.

Ⓒ Korean spice viburnum (use 1)
Leave the door open so the spicy fragrance of this deciduous shrub's white spring flowers can float into the house. See *Viburnum carlesii*, p. 158.

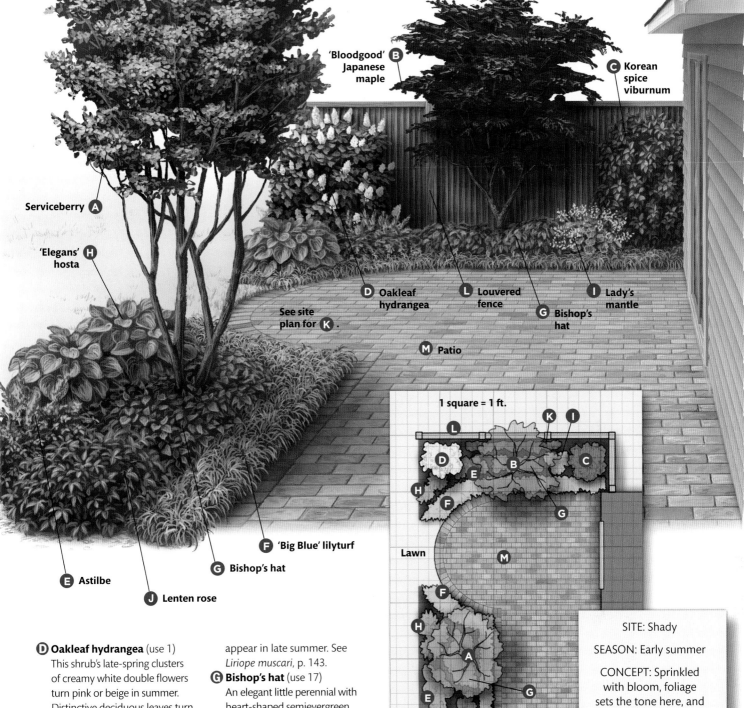

Serviceberry **(A)**

(B) 'Bloodgood' Japanese maple

(C) Korean spice viburnum

'Elegans' hosta **(H)**

(D) Oakleaf hydrangea

(L) Louvered fence

(I) Lady's mantle

(G) Bishop's hat

See site plan for **(K)** .

(M) Patio

(F) 'Big Blue' lilyturf

(G) Bishop's hat

(E) Astilbe

(J) Lenten rose

1 square = 1 ft.

Lawn

SITE: Shady

SEASON: Early summer

CONCEPT: Sprinkled with bloom, foliage sets the tone here, and a fence provides additional privacy.

(D) Oakleaf hydrangea (use 1)
This shrub's late-spring clusters of creamy white double flowers turn pink or beige in summer. Distinctive deciduous leaves turn crimson in fall. Rusty peeling bark is attractive year-round. See *Hydrangea quercifolia*, p. 138.

(E) Astilbe (use 10)
In summer, plumes of tiny flowers rise above this perennial's dark green fernlike foliage. A white- or pink-flowered cultivar will brighten the shade See *Astilbe* x *arendsii*, p. 122.

(F) 'Big Blue' lilyturf (use 24)
(!) *This plant is locally invasive in the Mid-Atlantic.*
This perennial forms a mat of grassy evergreen leaves to make a tidy edging to the patio. Spikes of small blue flowers

appear in late summer. See *Liriope muscari*, p. 143.

(G) Bishop's hat (use 17)
An elegant little perennial with heart-shaped semievergreen leaves, it spreads slowly under the trees, bearing small red, pink, white, or yellow flowers in the spring. See *Epimedium*, p. 130.

(H) 'Elegans' hosta (use 5)
The lovely broad blue leaves of this perennial make a striking contrast to the deeply cut foliage of nearby astilbes. See *Hosta sieboldiana*, p. 137.

(I) Lady's mantle (use 3)
Pleated gray-green leaves are this perennial's main attraction; early-summer chartreuse flowers are lovely, too. See *Alchemilla mollis*, p. 119.

(J) Lenten rose (use 2)
A charming harbinger of

spring, this perennial's cuplike flowers in shades of creamy white, pink, rose, or green appear in late winter above semi-evergreen foliage. See *Helleborus orientalis*, p. 135.

(K) White Japanese anemone (use 8)
Snow-white flowers on branching stalks last for weeks in September and October. This

perennial's dark foliage looks great through the summer. See *Anemone* x *hybrida*, p. 120.

(L) Louvered fence
Slanting slats of this 6-ft.-tall fence form an effective visual screen while allowing air to circulate among the plants and people on the patio. See p. 191.

See p. 82 for the following:

(M) Patio

Elegant Symmetry

MAKE A FORMAL GARDEN FOR THE BACKYARD

Formal landscaping often lends dignity to the public areas around a home (see pp. 20-23). Formality can also be rewarding in a more private setting. There, the groomed plants, geometric lines, and symmetrical layout of a formal garden can help to organize the surrounding landscape, provide an elegant area for entertaining, or simply be enjoyed for their own sake.

A boxwood hedge defines this small garden. Paths divide it into four identical quadrants arrayed around the focal point, a garden ornament set on a leafy carpet. While the layout of each quadrant is the same, the plants and color schemes differ subtly.

Formal gardens like this one look self-contained on paper, neatly packaged within rigid boundaries. But even more than other types of landscaping, actual formal gardens work well only when carefully correlated with other elements in the landscape, such as the house, garage, patio, and major plantings. A formal design is meant to play off the symmetry of these structures. Transitions, both physical and visual, between formal and more casual areas are particularly important. Plantings that screen sight lines, expanses of lawn, or level changes that separate one area from another all help formal and informal elements coexist comfortably.

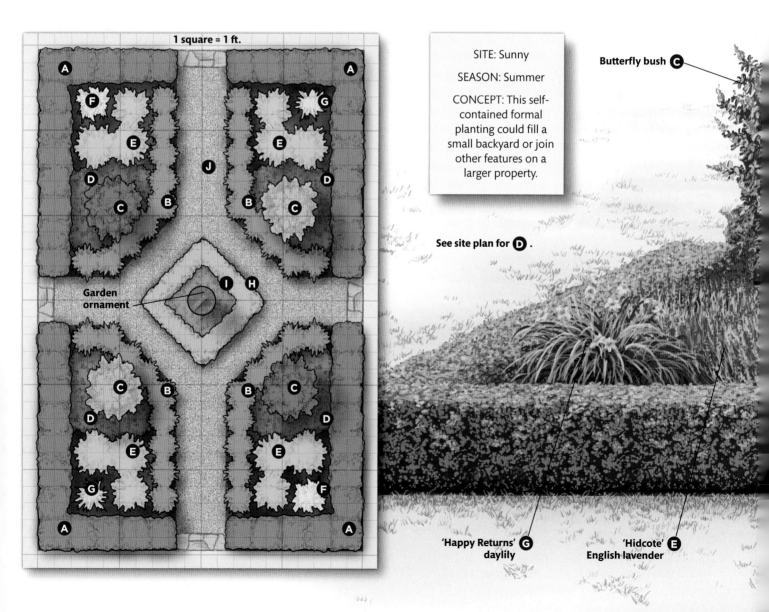

1 square = 1 ft.

Garden ornament

SITE: Sunny

SEASON: Summer

CONCEPT: This self-contained formal planting could fill a small backyard or join other features on a larger property.

Butterfly bush **C**

See site plan for **D** .

'Happy Returns' **G**
daylily

'Hidcote' **E**
English lavender

Plants & Projects

Of all gardens, a formal one most obviously reflects the vision and the efforts of its makers. Shaping plants to our specifications takes patience and persistence. It will take several years for this boxwood hedge to become fully rounded. The butterfly bushes, gray santolina, and English lavender grow faster and must be pruned hard once a year, in early spring. Shear the evergreen candytuft in June. Trim the boxwood as needed.

Ⓐ Dwarf English boxwood (use 48 plants)
Twiggy habit and fine texture of this evergreen shrub make it ideal for a rounded hedge. Shear to height and width of about 2 ft. See *Buxus sempervirens* 'Suffruticosa', p. 125.

Ⓑ 'Big Blue' lilyturf (use 36)
❗ *This plant is locally invasive in the Mid-Atlantic.*
Neat mounding clumps of this grassy evergreen perennial coalesce to form a dark green edging next to the paths, bearing blue flowers in late summer. See *Liriope muscari*, p. 143.

Ⓒ Butterfly bush (use 4)
❗ *This plant is considered invasive in the Mid-Atlantic.*
This deciduous shrub offers gray-green foliage and flowers from midsummer through fall. Use two different-colored cultivars, pairing the colors in diagonally opposed beds. See *Buddleia davidii*, p. 123.

Ⓓ Dwarf plumbago (use 48)
A deciduous perennial ground cover. Forms a carpet of small green leaves that turn maroon in fall. Small blue flowers continue from late summer through fall. See *Ceratostigma plumbaginoides*, p. 126.

Ⓔ 'Hidcote' English lavender (use 12)
This small, densely mounded semievergreen shrub has narrow silver-gray leaves and spikes of fragrant purple flowers in June. See *Lavandula angustifolia*, p. 142.

Ⓕ Blazing star (use 2)
A perennial wildflower forming tufts of grassy dark green foliage. In midsummer, tall stiff stalks bear fluffy spikes of small flowers that attract butterflies. Use a white-flowered cultivar here. See *Liatris spicata*, p. 143.

Ⓖ 'Happy Returns' daylily (use 2)
This perennial's cheerful yellow flowers nod above clumps of narrow arching foliage all summer. See *Hemerocallis*, p. 136.

Ⓗ Gray santolina (use 16)
Shear the silvery foliage of this small deciduous shrub to make a neat edging. See *Santolina chamaecyparissus*, p. 154.

Ⓘ Evergreen candytuft (use 8)
A perennial ground cover with glossy green foliage and white flowers in spring. See *Iberis sempervirens*, p. 139.

Ⓙ Paths
Neatly raked gravel contained by wooden edging complements the planting. See p. 166.

Ⓗ Gray santolina

Ⓘ Evergreen candytuft

Ⓒ Butterfly bush

Ⓑ 'Big Blue' lilyturf

Ⓙ Paths

Ⓐ Dwarf English boxwood

Ⓕ Blazing star

❗ *Plants with this symbol are considered invasive or are locally invasive, as noted. See the appropriate plant profile for suggested alternatives.*

VARIATIONS ON A THEME

These splendid designs demonstrate some of the variety and inventiveness possible in formal gardens.

Evergreen foliage and quiet symmetry give this formal garden a timeless look.

Occupying rectilinear beds cut out of cobblestone paving, an exuberant display of flowers and foliage makes a wonderful stroll garden.

Here, sheared boxwood and crimson barberry hedges create an intricate four-leaf clover pattern. Bushy lavenders provide contrast and fragrance.

A formal patio

In this design, a small table and chairs join the formal setting, providing a lovely spot for an intimate lunch or a restful hour with a favorite book.

The basic layout remains the same, but with several significant plant changes. Four slow-growing star magnolias create a sense of enclosure and will cast increasing amounts of shade as the years pass. Eventually, their dense canopies will extend to shelter the central area.

Southernwood now lines the paths; along with the lavenders, these gray-green plants contrast pleasingly with the lush green plants surrounding them. A yarrow joins a daylily and two blazing stars (one purple, one white) in bringing color to the corners. The violets and lavender treat those at the table to delicious scent in spring, early summer, and fall.

'Moonshine' **D** yarrow

SITE: Sunny

SEASON: Summer

CONCEPT: Enhance a formal setting for an intimate gathering by using small trees and scented flowers.

E Dwarf English boxwood

Plants & Projects

Ⓐ Southernwood (use 36 plants)
Train and shear this woody perennial to edge the path. The ferny gray-green foliage is fragrant. Clip hard in spring, lightly in early summer to keep it neat and bushy, about 1 ft. tall. See *Artemisia abrotanum*, p. 120.

Ⓑ Star magnolia (use 4)
A small deciduous tree, it is the first magnolia to bloom, with constellations of star-shaped white flowers lining bare branches in early spring. Dark green leaves form a dense crown, casting shade on the patio area. See *Magnolia stellata*, p. 144.

Ⓒ Sweet violet (use 48)
This perennial's dark green leaves and sweet-scented purple flowers carpet the ground beneath the trees. Blooms in early spring and again during the fall. In mild winters, leaves are evergreen. See *Viola odorata*, p. 158.

Ⓓ 'Moonshine' yarrow (use 1)
A perennial that forms a clump of tough but delicate-looking, lacy gray-green leaves. Produces flat clusters of tiny lemon yellow flowers for months in the summer. See *Achillea*, p. 118.

See p. 91 for the following:
Ⓔ Dwarf English boxwood (use 48)
Ⓕ 'Hidcote' English lavender (use 12)
Ⓖ Blazing star (use 2; one white, one purple)
Ⓗ 'Happy Returns' daylily (use 1)
Ⓘ Paths

Star magnolia **Ⓑ**

See site plan for **Ⓒ Ⓗ**.

Ⓐ Southernwood

Lawn

Table and chairs

1 square = 1 ft.

Ⓘ Paths
Ⓐ Southernwood
Ⓔ Dwarf English boxwood
Ⓕ 'Hidcote' English lavender
Ⓖ Blazing star

A Shady Hideaway

CREATE A FRAGRANT OASIS

Plants with this symbol are considered invasive or are locally invasive, as noted. See the appropriate plant profile for suggested alternatives.

A 'Emerald' American arborvitae

B Goldflame honeysuckle

Sweet autumn clematis C

M Arbor

Oakleaf hydrangea E

K 'Bath's Pink' dianthus

G Russian sage

J Bigroot geranium

H 'Sarah Bernhardt' peony

K 'Bath's Pink' dianthus

H 'Sarah Bernhardt' peony

J Bigroot geranium

'Six Hills Giant' catmint I

Flagstone paving L

If your property is long on lawn and short on shade, a bench under a leafy arbor can provide a cool respite from the heat or the cares of the day. Tucked into a corner of the property and set among attractive shrubs, vines, and perennials, the arbor shown here is a desirable destination even when the day isn't sizzling. While all the plants are lovely to look at, the main attraction of this garden is fragrance, supplied by flowers and foliage alike.

There's something in the air in every season. Late spring is most varied, with the scented flowers of lilacs, dianthus, honeysuckle, and peonies. You'll enjoy the roses all summer and the clematis in the fall. Pluck a leaf off the geraniums, Russian sage, or catmint anytime for an olfactory pick-me-up. And if you venture to the arbor in winter, the arborvitae will supply a bracing woodland fragrance.

Plants & Projects

The arbor requires more muscle than finesse to build—recruit some sturdy assistants to help out. After the vines are established on the arbor, they'll need annual pruning, as will several of the shrubs.

A 'Emerald' American arborvitae (use 2 plants) These slender evergreen shrubs at the back of the arbor create a cozy enclosure. The glossy bright green foliage has a piney fragrance. See *Thuja occidentalis*, p. 156.

B Goldflame honeysuckle (use 1) A fast-growing semievergreen vine that will cover its side of the arbor in a few years. From spring through fall, pink-and-yellow flowers produce the classic honeysuckle scent. See *Lonicera* x *heckrottii*, p. 144.

C Sweet autumn clematis (use 1) ❶ *This plant is considered invasive in the Mid-Atlantic.* This vigorous deciduous vine climbs the other side of the arbor, offering welcome shade and small white honey-scented flowers in late summer. See *Clematis terniflora*, p. 128.

D 'Miss Kim' lilac (use 2) Anchoring one end of the planting, this midsize, compact deciduous shrub has clusters of fragrant pale lilac flowers in May. Its leaves turn a pretty purple in autumn. See *Syringa patula*, p. 156.

E Oakleaf hydrangea (use 1) A four-season asset, this deciduous shrub offers handsome foliage with bright fall colors, long-lasting white flowers, and attractive peeling cinnamon-colored bark. See *Hydrangea quercifolia*, p. 138.

F 'Angel Face' rose (use 1) All summer long, a rich spicy aroma wafts from the double mauve flowers clustered on this bushy shrub. See *Rosa*, p. 153.

G Russian sage (use 3) You get an olfactory treat when you brush up against the silvery foliage of this shrubby perennial. Tiers of blue flowers cover the upright stems for weeks in late summer. See *Perovskia atriplicifolia*, p. 148.

H 'Sarah Bernhardt' peony (use 3) This old-fashioned favorite produces large, fragrant, double pink flowers in late spring. Dark glossy foliage showcases flowers and is a distinct contrast to the neighboring Russian sage. See *Paeonia*, p. 148.

I 'Six Hills Giant' catmint (use 2) Loose spikes of purple flowers rise above the soft gray, aromatic foliage of this bushy perennial off and on through the summer. See *Nepeta* x *faassenii*, p. 146.

J Bigroot geranium (use 7) Within easy reach of the bench, this perennial's semi-evergreen leaves release a musky aroma when touched. Pinkish purple flowers bloom in June. See *Geranium macrorrhizum*, p. 134.

K 'Bath's Pink' dianthus (use 3) This perennial's sweetly fragrant, clear pink flowers rise above a mat of slender evergreen leaves in late spring. See *Dianthus*, p. 130.

L Flagstone paving Flagstones lead to the bench and edge the beds as a mowing strip. See p. 166.

M Arbor With a little help, you can build this simple design in a weekend or two. See p. 190.

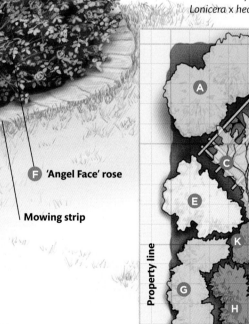

D 'Miss Kim' lilac

F 'Angel Face' rose

Mowing strip

Property line

Bench

Mowing strip

1 square = 1 ft.

SITE: Sunny

SEASON: Early summer

CONCEPT: Sheltered by vines and shrubs, relax among a potpourri of fragrant plants.

A grassy bower

In this design, the giant Chinese silver grass replaces the arborvitae as a privacy screen behind the arbor. Although you need to cut it down every year in March, this fast-growing grass will provide shade for the bench by midsummer. It's a dramatic plant with ribbonlike leaves that sway and rustle ceaselessly in the slightest breeze.

Clematis and silver fleece vines cover the arbor with purple and white flowers in summer. From the bench, you can watch butterflies flutter back and forth from the dark purple flowers of the butterfly bush to the pink yarrow and white boltonia blossoms.

Clumps of dwarf fountain grass fill the front of the bed with fine-textured foliage and bottlebrush-like flower stalks that dance in the breeze. Silvery lamb's ears makes a semievergreen edging. Bright red berries on the heavenly bamboo and the dark green needles of the dwarf mugo pine add color through the winter, complementing the tan dried grasses.

1 square = 1 ft.

Mowing strip

SITE: Sunny

SEASON: Fall

CONCEPT:
Ornamental grasses provide privacy and whispering companionship in a breeze.

Heavenly bamboo **E**

Silver fleece vine **B**

Giant Chinese silver grass **A**

Jackman clematis **C**

Arbor **L**

'Black Knight' butterfly bush **D**

'Appleblossom' yarrow **G**

Dwarf fountain grass **H**

Mowing strip

Flagstone paving **K**

'Helene von Stein' lamb's ears **J**

Mugo pine **F**

'Snowbank' boltonia **I**

'Appleblossom' yarrow **G**

Plants & Projects

Ⓐ Giant Chinese silver grass
(use 7 plants)
❶ *This plant is locally invasive in the Mid-Atlantic.*
Tall thick stalks bear wide arching leaves and seed heads that last through winter. See *Miscanthus floridulus*, p. 145.

Ⓑ Silver fleece vine (use 1)
This fast-growing deciduous vine is covered with sprays of small white flowers in fall. See *Polygonum aubertii*, p. 150.

Ⓒ Jackman clematis (use 2)
This deciduous vine will take a few years to cover its half of the arbor. Its large purple flowers appear in June and July. See *Clematis* x *jackmanii*, p. 128.

Ⓓ 'Black Knight' butterfly bush (use 1)
❶ *This plant is considered invasive in the Mid-Atlantic.*
From midsummer on, arching branches on this deciduous shrub carry long clusters of fragrant deep purple flowers. See *Buddleia davidii*, p. 123.

Ⓔ Heavenly bamboo (use 2)
❶ *This plant is considered invasive in the Mid-Atlantic.*
A narrow, erect shrub with creamy white summer flowers, colorful semievergreen foliage, and long-lasting red berries. See *Nandina domestica*, p. 416.

Ⓕ Mugo pine (use 1)
This low bushy evergreen anchors a corner of the planting. See *Pinus mugo*, p. 150.

Ⓖ 'Appleblossom' yarrow (use 5)
Clusters of long-lasting pink flowers wave above this perennial's aromatic ferny foliage. See *Achillea millefolium*, p. 118.

Ⓗ Dwarf fountain grass (use 3)
Fountains of slender leaves are topped with fluffy flowers on long stalks. Turns gold or tan in autumn. See *Pennisetum alopecuroides* 'Hameln', p. 148.

Ⓘ 'Snowbank' boltonia (use 1)
This clump-forming perennial is covered with small white asterlike flowers in fall. See *Boltonia asteroides*, p. 123.

Ⓙ 'Helene von Stein' lamb's ears (use 5)
Soft, thick, silver leaves of this perennial look like a furry throw rug at the bed's edge. See *Stachys byzantina*, p. 156.

See p. 95 for the following:

Ⓚ Flagstone paving

Ⓛ Arbor

Though it is set close to the house, this arbor has the look and feel of a secret hideaway.

VARIATIONS ON A THEME

What a treat to steal a quiet moment in a shady spot surrounded by lovely plants.

A gazebo makes a special garden retreat. As the trees leaf out, they'll create an even more private haven.

This contemplative spot is simplicity itself, with shade-loving hostas and a stone bench nestled among larger shrubs beneath a leafy canopy.

Back to Nature

CREATE A WOODED RETREAT IN YOUR BACKYARD

The open spaces and squared-up property lines in many new developments (and some old neighborhoods as well) can make a homeowner long for the seclusion and intimacy of a wooded landscape. It may come as a surprise that you can create just such a retreat on even a small property. With a relatively small number of carefully placed trees and shrubs, you can have your own backyard nature park.

Trees and shrubs take time to reach the sizable proportions we associate with a woodland. The plants in this design were chosen in part because they make an attractive setting in their early years, too. Here we show the young planting several years after installation. On the following pages you'll see the planting as it appears at maturity.

The grassy peninsula extending into the planting is an open "room" in the early years, with the juvenile trees and shrubs functioning as a large mixed border. Spring-flowering ground covers and dozens of spring bulbs make that season (shown here) particularly lively.

SITE: Sunny

SEASON: Spring

CONCEPT: Mixed planting across the back of a lot attracts birds and wildlife. It's shown here just a few years after installation.

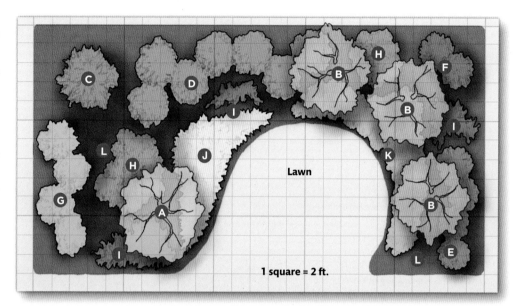

Lawn

1 square = 2 ft.

G **Mountain laurel**

C **'Nellie R. Stevens' holly**

D **Winterberry holly**

A **Black gum**

H **False indigo**

I **Christmas fern**

Plants & Projects

The young woody plants, deciduous and evergreen, provide a pleasing mix of forms, flowers, foliage, and berries throughout the year. Naturalized bulbs, clumps of perennials, ferns, and fast-spreading ground covers fill in nicely between the still-small trees and shrubs, which are spaced according to their mature growth. A deep mulch of shredded leaves or wood chips keeps weeds out of open areas and conserves moisture.

A Black gum (use 1 plant)
At the front of the planting, this handsome deciduous tree features glossy green leaves that turn a stunning bright red for weeks in fall. See *Nyssa sylvatica*, p. 147.

B Serviceberry (use 3)
Eye-catching in three seasons, this small deciduous tree has white spring flowers, edible berries that birds love, and good fall color. Commonly has several trunks. See *Amelanchier x grandiflora*, p. 119.

C 'Nellie R. Stevens' holly (use 1)
Large shrub or small tree with glossy evergreen leaves and abundant bright red berries (if a male Chinese holly is in the neighborhood). See *Ilex*, pp. 139–140.

D Winterberry holly (use 7)
A staggered line of deciduous hollies along the back of the property provides screening foliage in summer and small red berries that keep the birds happy in fall and winter. See *Ilex verticillata*, p. 140.

E Summersweet (use 4)
Fragrant, spicy-sweet white or pink flowers make this deciduous shrub a favorite stop on late-summer woodland strolls. Its glossy green foliage turns gold in autumn. See *Clethra alnifolia*, p. 128.

F European cranberry bush (use 2)
Deciduous shrub performs in four seasons. Pretty white spring flowers are followed by red fruits that ripen in late summer and last all through the winter. Maplelike leaves turn red in autumn. See *Viburnum opulus*, p. 158.

G Mountain laurel (use 4)
Dense clusters of cup-shaped white or pink flowers clothe this native evergreen shrub in May or June. See *Kalmia latifolia*, p. 141.

H False indigo (use 8)
A large perennial with distinctive blue-green foliage and an early-summer display of indigo blue flowers. Interesting dark seedpods dangle until winter cleanup. See *Baptisia australis*, p. 122.

I Christmas fern (use 33)
Easily grown fern quickly carpets the ground with glossy evergreen fronds. Spread it over areas planted with spring bulbs; the emerging ferns will hide declining bulb foliage. See Ferns: *Polystichum acrostichoides*, p. 132.

J Lily-of-the-valley (use 40)
A popular fast-spreading perennial ground cover. Its large smooth leaves are green all summer, turning gold in fall. In spring, tiny bell-like white flowers produce one of nature's most pleasing scents. See *Convallaria majalis*, p. 128.

K Sweet woodruff (use 25)
This fast-growing perennial ground cover forms a thick bushy mat with small deciduous leaves that turn from green to tan in autumn. Tiny white flowers twinkle above the foliage in spring. See *Galium odoratum*, p. 133.

L Bulbs
In spring, daffodils and squills light up the open spaces between the young plants. Plant as many as you can afford. Make a broad sweep of one kind of daffodil (yellow shown here), or mix different ones for diversity and prolonged bloom. In early spring, patches of squill produce a carpet of starlike flowers in a gorgeous shade of blue. See Bulbs: *Narcissus* and *Scilla siberica*, p. 124.

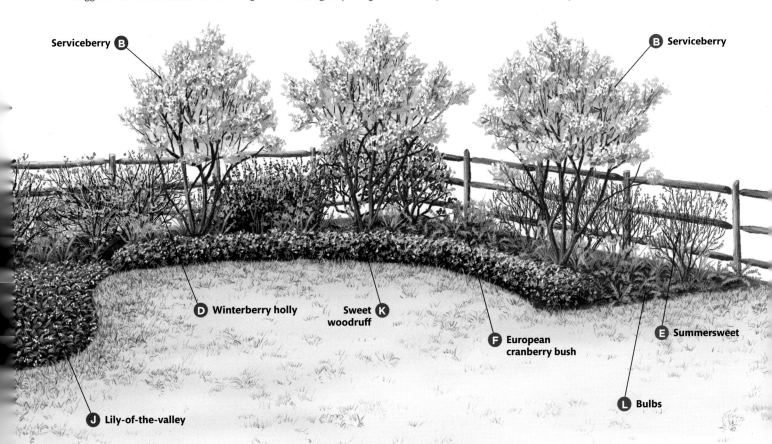

The mature woodland

Change and growth are the rule among living things, but when plants are small, it's hard to imagine what they'll look like in a dozen years. So we've done it for you.

The grassy peninsula is now a woodland meadow framed by sturdy trees rising 15 to 20 ft. Beneath them, shrubs that once seemed to stand too far apart create leafy masses 6 to 10 ft. tall, providing a luxurious sense of privacy. The woodland floor is carpeted with ground covers. Birds and small wildlife abound.

Each season pleases. In spring, flowering bulbs and ground covers are joined by masses of flowers on the serviceberries, mountain laurels, and cranberry bushes. In summer, the woodland is a cool, leafy retreat. Fall triggers a burst of color from the deciduous plants. In winter, traceries of bare branches play off the evergreen foliage of the tall 'Nellie R. Stevens' hollies and the massed mountain laurels. Berries keep birds happy in summer, fall, and winter.

See pp. 98–99 for site plan and plant descriptions.

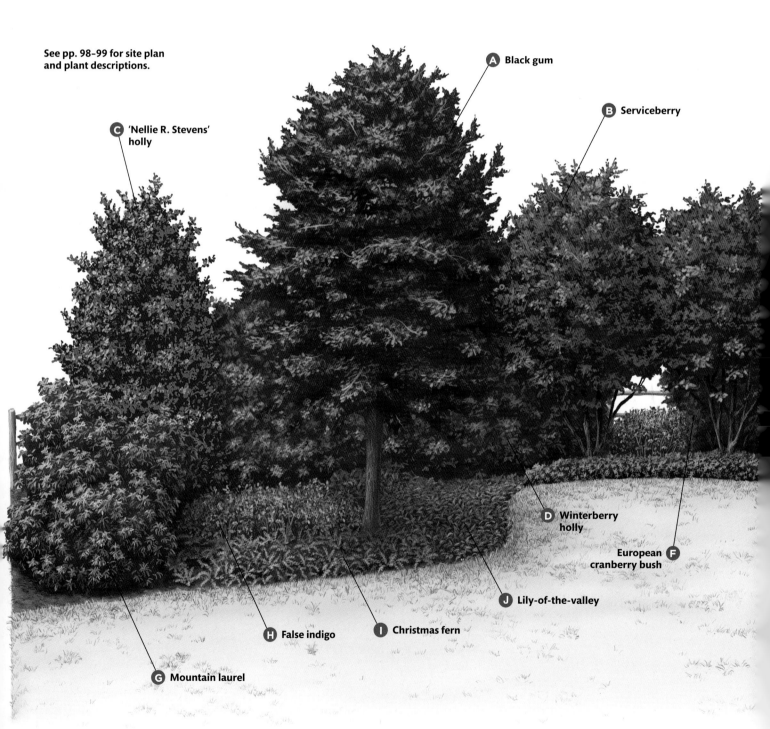

A Black gum

B Serviceberry

C 'Nellie R. Stevens' holly

D Winterberry holly

F European cranberry bush

J Lily-of-the-valley

I Christmas fern

H False indigo

G Mountain laurel

SITE: Sunny

SEASON: Fall

CONCEPT: After 12 to 15 years, the planting is a private shady woodland retreat.

VARIATIONS ON A THEME

On an acreage or a suburban lot, you can create a garden that welcomes wildlife and offers a little slice of nature.

Slender birches and an understory of shrubs make a miniature woodland.

Bounded by large shrubs, this naturalistic stroll garden harbors birds, butterflies, and bees.

B Serviceberry

E Summersweet

K Sweet woodruff

Tall grasses, Russian sage, coneflowers, and avian accommodation create a beautiful setting for watching butterflies and birds.

Splash Out

MAKE A HANDSOME WATER GARDEN IN A FEW WEEKENDS

A water garden adds a new dimension to a landscape. It can be the eye-catching focal point of the entire property, a center of outdoor entertainment, or a quiet out-of-the-way retreat. A pond can be a hub of activity—a place to garden, watch birds and wildlife, raise ornamental fish, or stage an impromptu paper-boat race. It just as easily affords an opportunity for some therapeutic inactivity; a few minutes contemplating the ripples on the water's surface makes a welcome break in a busy day.

A pond can't be easily moved, so choose your site carefully. Practical considerations are outlined on pp. 174–177 (along with instructions on installation); think about those first. Then consider how the pond and its plantings relate to the surroundings. Before plopping a pond down in the middle of the backyard, imagine how you might integrate it, visually if not physically, with nearby plantings and structures.

The plantings in this design are intended to settle the pond comfortably into an expanse of lawn. From a distance, the shrubs, ornamental grasses, and perennials that frame the pond resemble an island bed. Sitting at water's edge, however, the plantings provide enclosure, a sense of being on the island looking at its flora and fauna.

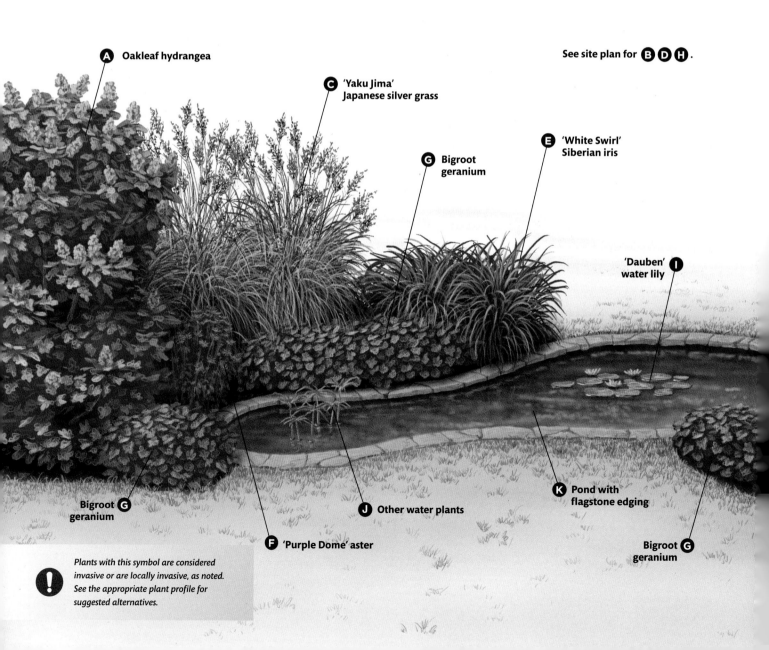

See site plan for **B D H**.

A Oakleaf hydrangea
C 'Yaku Jima' Japanese silver grass
G Bigroot geranium
E 'White Swirl' Siberian iris
I 'Dauben' water lily
G Bigroot geranium
J Other water plants
F 'Purple Dome' aster
K Pond with flagstone edging
G Bigroot geranium

Plants with this symbol are considered invasive or are locally invasive, as noted. See the appropriate plant profile for suggested alternatives.

Plants & Projects

Grass and grasslike perennials give this planting a waterside feeling. Flowers come in pinks, whites, and shades of blue and purple, including a lovely blue water lily. Saucy yellow moneywort blossoms set off the cooler colors in midsummer.

Once established, the plants take pretty good care of themselves. The pond, however, requires more attention to keep a healthy balance of water plants and fish (if you have them) in order to maintain oxygen levels and to keep algae in check. Consult local or mail-order suppliers to help you get the right mix.

A **Oakleaf hydrangea** (use 1 plant)
This deciduous shrub offers white late-spring flowers that last into summer, distinctive colorful leaves in fall, and attractive bark in winter. See *Hydrangea quercifolia*, p. 138.

B **Korean beautyberry** (use 1)
This pleasant but unobtrusive deciduous shrub bursts onto center stage in autumn, producing bright lilac-colored berries that line its arching branches like jewels strung on a necklace. See *Callicarpa dichotoma*, p. 125.

C **'Yaku Jima' Japanese silver grass** (use 4)
❶ *This plant is locally invasive in the Mid-Atlantic.*
Clumps of narrow arching leaves and, from August on, fanlike flower heads sway and flow in even a gentle breeze. Flower plumes turn white in fall; foliage is an attractive tan through the winter. See *Miscanthus sinensis*, p. 145.

D **Persian onion** (use 11)
An ornamental cousin to the familiar culinary bulb. In early summer, globes of small blue flowers perch on 3-ft. stalks above grassy leaves reminiscent of water rushes. See Bulbs: *Allium aflatunense*, p. 124.

E **'White Swirl' Siberian iris** (use 3)
This rugged perennial forms clumps of attractive grassy foliage, but its large, graceful, white early-summer flowers are the main attraction. See *Iris sibirica*, p. 140.

F **'Purple Dome' aster** (use 4)
In fall, this perennial is a mound of daisylike purple flowers, a pretty companion for the fruits on the neighboring beautyberry. Dense dark green foliage is attractive the rest of the season. See *Aster novae-angliae*, p. 121.

G **Bigroot geranium** (use 7)
A low perennial ground cover forming clumps of fragrant foliage. In late spring its pink flowers look pretty with neighboring purple onion and white iris flowers. See *Geranium macrorrhizum*, p. 134.

H **Moneywort** (use 2)
Coin-shaped leaves grow on stems that root as they run along the ground, making this perennial a good ground cover. Foliage is sprinkled with little yellow flowers for a few weeks in July. See *Lysimachia nummularia*, p. 144.

I **'Dauben' water lily** (use 1)
Pale blue flowers and green speckled leaves float on the water from summer through fall. This is a tender tropical plant, but you can grow it as an annual, then try a new cultivar next year. See *Nymphaea*, p. 146.

J **Other water plants**
You can grow a number of ornamental water plants besides water lilies. (We've shown dwarf papyrus here.) Choose from these as well as a range of plants and animals that provide oxygen, filter water, and control algae and debris. See Water plants, p. 158.

K **Pond**
This can be made in a weekend or two of energetic digging and with a commercially available pond liner edged with flagstones. See p. 174.

F 'Purple Dome' aster

C 'Yaku Jima' Japanese silver grass

Lawn

Flagstone edging

1 square = 1 ft.

SITE: Sunny

SEASON: Late summer

CONCEPT: A landscape focal point, the pond nestles among shrubs and perennials and features attractive water plants.

Mini-pond

This little pond provides the pleasures of water gardening for those without the space or energy required to install and maintain a larger pond. Within its 3-ft. diameter you can enjoy one or more water plants as well as a few fish. As for a larger pond, consult local or mail-order suppliers to help you choose a combination of plants and fish that will maintain a healthy balance.

Pond and plantings can stand alone in an expanse of lawn, but they will look their best integrated into a larger planting scheme. The plants here are small, in scale with the pool. Barberry, blue oat grass, and irises provide modest height; the rest are low ground covers. Foliage and flowers in mostly cool colors—blues, pinks, and purples—help make the little pond a restful spot.

Flagstone edging

1 square = 1 ft.

SITE: Sunny

SEASON: Spring

CONCEPT: Use a tiny pool and plantings for a courtyard garden near a patio or integrated into a larger planting.

Plants & Projects

Ⓐ **'Crimson Pygmy' Japanese barberry** (use 1 plant)
❶ *This plant is considered invasive in the Mid-Atlantic.*
This dense, low-growing, naturally rounded shrub has small burgundy leaves that turn bright red before dropping in fall. The twigs are very spiny but need no pruning. See *Berberis thunbergii*, p. 122.

Ⓑ **Blue oat grass** (use 4)
A clump-forming grass with slender blue-green leaves that last all winter. Grown for its foliage, it rarely flowers. See *Helictotrichon sempervirens*, p. 135.

Ⓒ **'Palace Purple' heuchera** (use 2)
A perennial ground cover whose dark bronze-purple leaves form a tidy mound. The foliage lasts partway into the winter. Cut it away in early spring. Blooms in summer, with dainty white flowers. See *Heuchera*, p. 136.

Ⓓ **Bloody cranesbill** (use 4)
A short, vigorous perennial ground cover whose lacy foliage and soft pink late-spring flowers reward closer inspection. See *Geranium sanguineum* var. *striatum*, p. 134.

Ⓔ **Evergreen candytuft** (use 4)
Another perennial ground cover, its low mounds of evergreen foliage blanketed with clusters of small white flowers for weeks in the spring. Candytuft will creep attractively over the stone edging. See *Iberis sempervirens*, p. 139.

Ⓕ **Water plants**
You can grow a surprising range and number of plants, including water lilies, in a small container like this. The dwarf papyrus shown here will reach 30 in. tall during the growing season, bearing airy globes of foliage on tall thin stems. It is a shade-tolerant tropical native that you can overwinter as a houseplant indoors. See Water plants, p. 158.

Ⓖ **Pond**
Use a round vinyl liner, a preformed fiberglass shell, a stock tank, or a half barrel lined with heavy plastic. Bury the container so the waterline is close to ground level. You'll have to add water often during dry weather and scoop some out after heavy rains. See p. 174.

See p. 103 for the following:

Ⓗ **'White Swirl' Siberian iris** (use 1)

❶ **Moneywort** (use 2)

Ⓒ 'Palace Purple' heuchera   Ⓓ Bloody cranesbill   ❶ Moneywort   Ⓑ Blue oat grass

Ⓗ 'White Swirl' Siberian iris   Ⓖ Pond   Ⓕ Water plants   Ⓔ Evergreen candytuft   Ⓐ 'Crimson Pygmy' Japanese barberry   Flagstone edging

VARIATIONS ON A THEME

Surrounding a pond with shrubs, grasses, and perennials transforms it from a curiosity into an integral part of a home landscape.

Here a rectilinear pool mirrors an adjacent walkway; the exuberant planting contrasts effectively with the cut-stone formality of the pool and hardscape.

The landscape around this large pond looks so natural it's hard to tell that humans had a hand in it. A closer look reveals the artifice: a border of ferns, grasses, and perennials, and a grassy bank that's been recently mowed.

Displaying a variety of foliage shapes and colors, these plants are the perfect size for a small pond in a shady spot.

Connected to a nearby patio by a path and planting, this lily pond blends seamlessly with its surroundings.

Under the Old Shade Tree

CREATE A COZY GARDEN IN A COOL SPOT

This planting is designed to help homeowners blessed with a large shade tree make the most of their good fortune. A bench is provided, of course. There's no better spot to rest on a hot summer day. But why stop there? The tree's high wide canopy provides an ideal setting for a planting of understory shrubs, perennials, and ferns. The result is a woodland garden that warrants a visit any day of the year.

The planting roughly coincides with the pool of shade cast by the tree. A selection of medium to large deciduous and evergreen shrubs extends about halfway around the perimeter. You can position these to provide privacy, screen a view from the bench, or block early-morning or late-afternoon sun. Smaller plants (ferns, hostas, and perennial ground covers) are placed nearer the path and bench, where they can be appreciated at close range.

The planting blooms for weeks in spring and early summer. White flowers cover the buckeyes, Korean spice viburnums, cherry laurels, and climbing hydrangea, which snakes up the trunk and along the limbs of the tree. As summer heats up, the little woodland is an oasis of cool foliage, brightened by the small silvery leaves of lamium, the green-and-white ivy, and the colorful, puckered leaves of the hosta. As fall shifts to winter, the tracery of bare branches in the canopy overhead is nicely balanced by evergreen foliage below.

SITE: Shady

SEASON: Summer

CONCEPT: Woodland understory plants make a lovely shade garden for sitting or strolling.

Plants & Projects

For best results, thin the tree canopy, if necessary, to produce dappled rather than deep shade. Also remove limbs to a height of 8 ft. or more to provide headroom. The tree's roots compete for moisture with anything planted nearby. The plants here do well in these drier conditions, but judicious supplemental watering and moisture-conserving mulch will improve their performance. (For more on planting under a shade tree, see p. 205.)

A Climbing hydrangea
(use 1 plant)
A vining relative of the common shrub, it has clusters of lacy white flowers in June, glossy dark green leaves, and a stout trunk with flaky cinnamon-colored bark. See *Hydrangea petiolaris*, p. 138.

B Bottlebrush buckeye (use 2)
A sizable deciduous shrub that forms a mound of large, medium green leaves. Slender spikes of white flowers stand like birthday candles above the foliage in early summer. See *Aesculus parviflora*, p. 119.

C Korean spice viburnum (use 4)
These deciduous shrubs frame the entrance to the path with dense green foliage from spring through fall. In May, pretty pink buds open into clusters of fragrant white flowers. See *Viburnum carlesii*, p. 158.

D 'Otto Luyken' cherry laurel
(use 6)
These beautiful shrubs form spreading mounds of glossy evergreen foliage. Its sweet-scented small white flowers brighten the shady scene in late spring. See *Prunus laurocerasus*, p. 150.

E Mountain laurel (use 4)
Large evergreen shrubs with shiny oblong leaves make a handsome screen. Striking clusters of cuplike white or pink flowers appear in late spring. See *Kalmia latifolia*, p. 141.

F Dwarf Hinoki cypress (use 2)
The dense curly foliage of these small slow-growing evergreen trees screens the bench. See *Chamaecyparis obtusa* 'Nana Gracilis', p. 127.

G 'Frances Williams' hosta
(use 18)
A popular perennial valued for its stately size and exotic foliage. Large, heavily textured leaves have a blue-green center and irregular green-gold edges. White flowers in mid- to late summer. See *Hosta*, p. 136.

H Japanese autumn fern (use 19)
A clump-forming fern. New fronds are a coppery color, turning glossy dark green by midsummer and lasting partway into the winter. See Ferns: *Dryopteris erythrosora*, p. 132.

I Lenten rose (use 32)
A long-lived perennial with very early, very lovely nodding flowers in shades of white to dusky pink to rose. Leaves are evergreen. See *Helleborus orientalis*, p. 135.

J 'Beacon Silver' lamium (use 25)
This perennial ground cover brightens the path with green-edged silver leaves and pink flowers in early summer. The foliage is evergreen where winters are mild. See *Lamium maculatum*, p. 142.

K European wild ginger (use 24)
A splendid ground cover for shade, this perennial spreads slowly to form a glossy evergreen carpet of elegant heart-shaped leaves. See *Asarum europaeum*, p. 121.

L 'Glacier' English ivy (use 40)
❶ *This plant is considered invasive in the Mid-Atlantic.*
A hardy, ground-covering vine. Pale evergreen leaves are mottled with white and gray in summer and turn pinkish in winter. See *Hedera helix*, p. 134.

M Path
A 4-in. layer of wood chips is serviceable and attractive in this situation. See p. 166.

'Glacier' **L**
English ivy

Korean spice **C**
viburnum

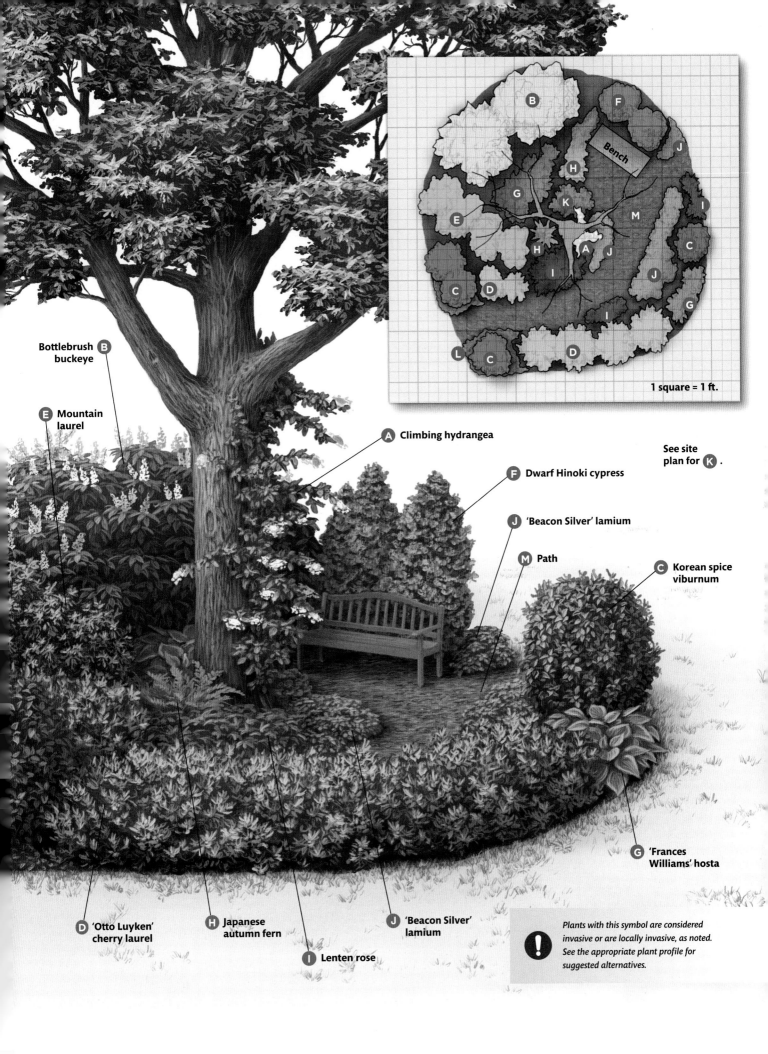

Bottlebrush **B** buckeye

E Mountain laurel

A Climbing hydrangea

F Dwarf Hinoki cypress

J 'Beacon Silver' lamium

M Path

See site plan for **K**.

C Korean spice viburnum

G 'Frances Williams' hosta

D 'Otto Luyken' cherry laurel

H Japanese autumn fern

I Lenten rose

J 'Beacon Silver' lamium

Bench

1 square = 1 ft.

Plants with this symbol are considered invasive or are locally invasive, as noted. See the appropriate plant profile for suggested alternatives.

Woodland retreat

This planting is a variation on the theme of the previous design. Here a secluded niche, tucked among large shrubs, provides a quiet spot for enjoying the shade and a lovely collection of plants.

Once again, spring is graced with a profusion of flowers. Whites are supplied by the tall Prague viburnums, rhododendrons, and creeping phlox. In the interior, yellow archangel's tiny flowers and silver leaves make a speckled carpet, while fragrant yellow azaleas invite a stroll around the perimeter.

As before, foliage takes over in summer, supported by the flowers of the bleeding hearts, buckeyes, and hostas. Evergreen shrubs, ferns, and ground covers color the winter garden. For spring, plant drifts of small early-blooming bulbs such as winter aconite and snowdrops.

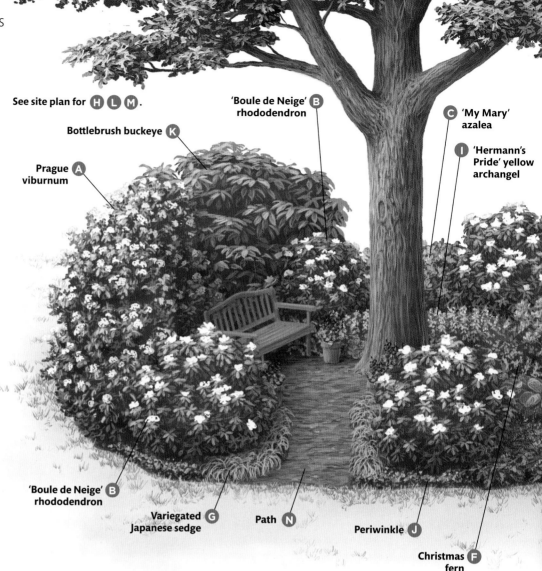

See site plan for **H** **L** **M**.

Prague viburnum **A**

Bottlebrush buckeye **K**

'Boule de Neige' rhododendron **B**

'My Mary' azalea **C**

'Hermann's Pride' yellow archangel **I**

'Boule de Neige' rhododendron **B**

Variegated Japanese sedge **G**

Path **N**

Periwinkle **J**

Christmas fern **F**

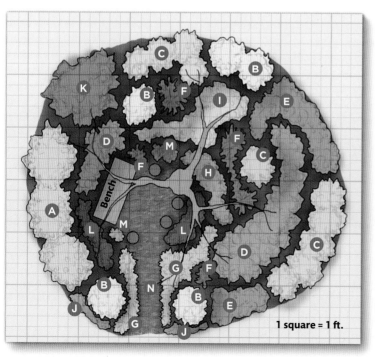

1 square = 1 ft.

Plants & Projects

A **Prague viburnum**
(use 3 plants)
A fast-growing evergreen shrub with lustrous dark green leaves, creamy white flowers in spring, and dark berries in summer. See *Viburnum* x *pragense*, p. 158.

B **'Boule de Neige' rhododendron** (use 5)
A broad evergreen shrub. In late spring, showy white flowers gleam against the glossy dark green leaves. See *Rhododendron*, p. 150.

C **'My Mary' azalea** (use 10)
A slow-growing deciduous shrub. Fragrant yellow flowers bloom profusely in spring. Good fall color, too. See *Rhododendron*, p. 150.

D **'Elegans' hosta** (use 13)
A perennial with puckered blue-gray leaves the size of dinner plates in a handsome clump much wider than tall. See *Hosta sieboldiana*, p. 137.

E **'Luxuriant' bleeding heart**
(use 18)
A perennial with beautiful ferny foliage. Rows of vivid pink flowers hang like tiny lanterns on thin curving stems from spring until midsummer. See *Dicentra*, p. 130.

F **Christmas fern** (use 45)
Use patches of this native fern as a ground cover between shrubs. Its glossy fronds are fully evergreen. See Ferns: *Polystichum acrostichoides*, p. 132.

G **Variegated Japanese sedge**
(use 37)
Evergreen clumps of grassy, gold-and-green striped foliage make a neat edging along the path. See *Carex morrowii* 'Aureo-variegata', p. 126.

SITE: Shady

SEASON: Spring

CONCEPT: Create a private woodland perch for contemplation and enjoyment of handsome plants.

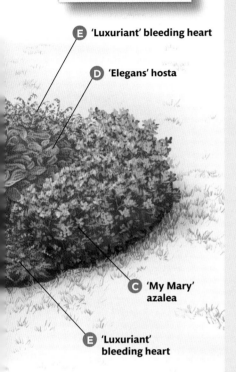

E 'Luxuriant' bleeding heart

D 'Elegans' hosta

C 'My Mary' azalea

E 'Luxuriant' bleeding heart

VARIATIONS ON A THEME

Here are some other approaches to enhancing your entry or another part of your property.

Nestled among understory ferns and shrubs, the gnarled twisty trunks of this tree are the focal point of this small shade garden.

Here, a gravel patio in a shady spot screened by large shrubs can accommodate a small gathering of friends.

Comfortably seated in the shelter of a leafy canopy, you could spend a happy hour or more just admiring the nearby plants.

H **'Bruce's White' creeping phlox** (use 22)
A low, spreading evergreen ground cover with fragrant white flowers in May. See *Phlox stolonifera*, p. 149.

I **'Hermann's Pride' yellow archangel** (use 37)
A silvery green perennial with tiny yellow spring flowers. See *Lamiastrum galeobdolon*, p. 142.

J **Periwinkle** (use 14)
❶ *This plant is considered invasive in the Mid-Atlantic.*
An evergreen ground cover with small leaves and lilac flowers in spring. See *Vinca minor*, p. 158.

See p. 106 for the following:

K **Bottlebrush buckeye** (use 1)

L **Lenten rose** (use 18)

M **European wild ginger** (use 11)

N **Path**

A Woodland Link

CREATE A SHRUB BORDER FOR NEARBY WOODS

Plants with this symbol are considered invasive or are locally invasive, as noted. See the appropriate plant profile for suggested alternatives.

'Arnold Promise' witch hazel **B**

'Sibirica' Siberian dogwood **E**

Oakleaf **G** hydrangea

The woodlands and forests of the Mid-Atlantic are treasured by all who live in the region. Many subdivisions, both new and old, incorporate woodland areas, with homes bordering landscapes of stately trees and large shrubs. (In some older neighborhoods, mature trees on adjacent lots create almost the same woodland feeling.)

The planting shown here integrates a domestic landscape with a woodland at its edge. It makes a pleasant transition between the open area of lawn, with its sunny entertainments, and the cool, secluded woods beyond. The design takes inspiration from the border of small trees and shrubs nature provides at the sunny edge of a wood, and it should have the same attraction to birds and wildlife.

Small deciduous native trees, growing to about 20 ft., mingle with shrubs varying in height from 8 ft. to 18 in., imitating natural layered growth. A curving path disappears between tall shrubs into the adjacent woods, adding a hint of mystery.

Whether viewed from the path or the distant house, the planting is attractive all year. From late winter to early summer, there is a procession of flowers in whites, yellows, and magenta, some very fragrant. Handsome foliage and a variety of berries carry through summer into fall, when this largely deciduous planting blazes with color. In winter, a few well-placed evergreens complement patterns of bare branches, including the eye-catching red stems of the dogwood.

Plants & Projects

Trees and large shrubs give the planting a solid structure. Three witch hazels form a small copse at one corner, balanced by two large viburnums at the other. Winterberry holly and the buckeye are large presences at the back of the planting, and the serviceberry anchors a casual arrangement of smaller shrubs extending to the lawn. Once the plants are established, in a year or so, just devote a weekend each spring and fall to mulching and basic pruning, then sit back and enjoy.

A **Serviceberry** (use 1 plant)
This small deciduous multitrunked tree earns its place in front with white flowers in April, purple fruits in July, and pretty fall color. See *Amelanchier* x *grandiflora*, p. 119.

B **'Arnold Promise' witch hazel** (use 3)
In early spring these deciduous multitrunked trees repay a stroll to their corner of the planting with sweet-scented yellow flowers. Leaves turn gold in fall. See *Hamamelis* x *intermedia*, p. 134.

C **Bottlebrush buckeye** (use 1)
This forms a mounded thicket with attractive large leaves, brushy white flowers in early summer, and leathery seedpods. A wide-spreading shrub, it may eventually crowd out nearby azaleas. See *Aesculus parviflora*, p. 119.

D **'Shasta' double-file viburnum** (use 3)
A stately deciduous shrub with tiers of horizontal branches whose rich green leaves turn purple in fall. Clusters of lovely white flowers in spring are followed by bright red fruits. See *Viburnum plicatum* var. *tomentosum*, p. 158.

E **'Sibirica' Siberian dogwood** (use 6)
Bright red stems in winter, white flowers in spring, bluish berries in summer, and crimson foliage in fall—this deciduous shrub has it all. See *Cornus alba*, p. 129.

F **'Sparkleberry' winterberry holly** (use 5)
An upright or vase-shaped deciduous shrub. Thousands of tiny bright red berries line the twigs in fall and winter and make a sparkling display until the birds eat them all. See *Ilex verticillata*, p. 140.

G **Oakleaf hydrangea** (use 1)
A deciduous shrub that is striking in every season: showy white flowers in spring, handsome leaves with good fall color, and attractive flaking bark for the winter months. See *Hydrangea quercifolia*, p. 138.

H **'PJM' rhododendron** (use 6)
A narrow, upright evergreen shrub with stunning clusters of magenta flowers in early spring. Small leathery leaves are green in summer, turning maroon in winter. See *Rhododendron*, p. 150.

I **'Gold Dust' azalea** (use 5)
A deciduous shrub with striking clusters of fragrant yellow flowers in spring. Fall foliage is also colorful. See *Rhododendron*: Deciduous azaleas, p. 151.

J **Pink evergreen azalea** (use 3)
An attractive small shrub with year-round presence, perfect

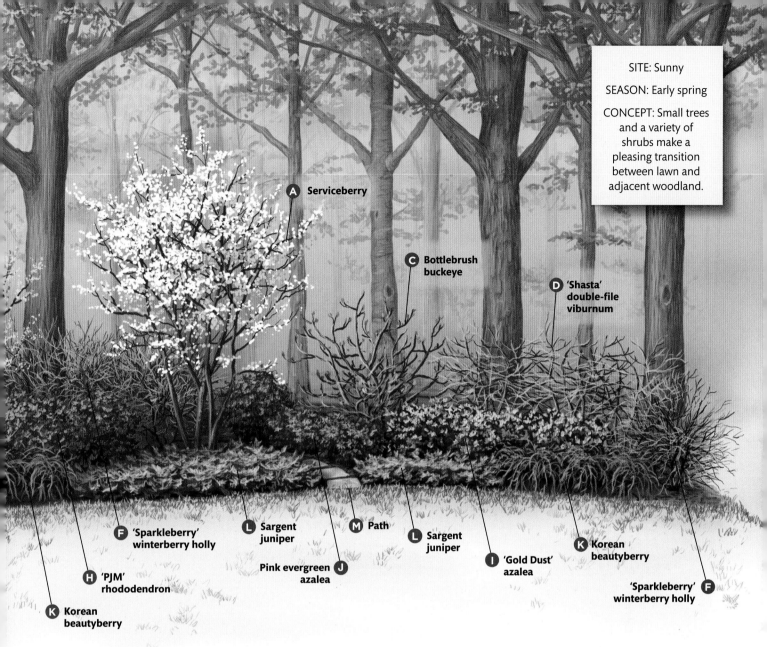

SITE: Sunny

SEASON: Early spring

CONCEPT: Small trees and a variety of shrubs make a pleasing transition between lawn and adjacent woodland.

A Serviceberry
C Bottlebrush buckeye
D 'Shasta' double-file viburnum
F 'Sparkleberry' winterberry holly
H 'PJM' rhododendron
L Sargent juniper
J Pink evergreen azalea
M Path
L Sargent juniper
I 'Gold Dust' azalea
K Korean beautyberry
F 'Sparkleberry' winterberry holly
K Korean beautyberry

for edging the path. Try 'Pink Gumpo', which has clusters of large pink flowers in spring. See *Rhododendron*, p. 150.

K Korean beautyberry (use 7) Spectacular lilac-colored berries line the arching branches of this deciduous shrub in autumn. Foliage blends into the background the rest of the season. See *Callicarpa dichotoma*, p. 125.

L Sargent juniper (use 7) This low-growing evergreen shrub forms a fine-textured green carpet edging the lawn and path at the foot of the serviceberry. See *Juniperus chinensis* var. *sargentii*, p. 141.

M Path Flagstone steppingstones, 18 in. square, curve through the planting. See p. 166.

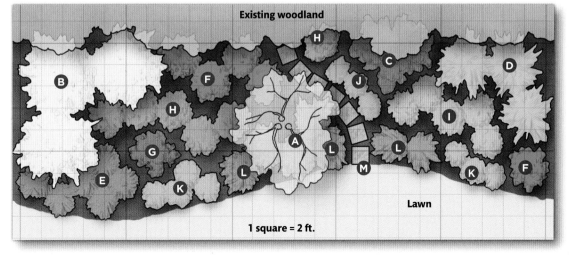

Existing woodland

Lawn

1 square = 2 ft.

Evergreens for shade

If your lot is on the shady side of a woodland or you prefer a look with more evergreen foliage, try this design. Here evergreen plants of the woodland understory replace many of the deciduous trees and shrubs in the previous planting. The layout is much the same in both designs, but the effect is very different, particularly in winter.

Tall trees and shrubs at the sides and back still guide the eye from lawn to taller woodland trees beyond. But their denser evergreen foliage encloses the planting more, focusing attention on the shrubs in the foreground. (If the "woodland" behind is just mature trees on a neighbor's property, these shrubs make an effective privacy screen.)

A fine display of spring flowers in shades of white and pink is particularly striking against the rich evergreen foliage. The deciduous serviceberry and oakleaf hydrangea provide contrasts of texture and color to the dominant evergreens in summer and fall. Colorful berries enliven the winter.

'Nellie R. Stevens' holly **A**

E Mountain laurel

Pink evergreen azalea **K**

'Moon Bay' heavenly bamboo **F**

C 'Roseum Elegans' rhododendron

G Spreading English yew

Path **L**

E Mountain laurel

Serviceberry **H**

Oakleaf hydrangea **J**

SITE: Shady

SEASON: Late spring

CONCEPT: Evergreen trees and shrubs make this shady site colorful all year.

Plants & Projects

A **'Nellie R. Stevens' holly** (use 3 plants)
This fast-growing evergreen tree or large shrub provides an excellent backdrop. For a heavy crop of bright red berries, plant a male Chinese holly nearby. See *Ilex*, p. 140.

B **Prague viburnum** (use 4)
A large evergreen shrub with shiny leaves. Mildly fragrant white flowers in spring are followed by dark red berries. See *Viburnum* x *pragense*, p. 158.

C **'Roseum Elegans' rhododendron** (use 4)
An evergreen shrub with large glossy leaves. Rosy pink flowers open in late spring at the same time as the nearby mountain laurels, providing a nice opportunity to compare blooms of these similar woodland shrubs. See *Rhododendron*, p. 150.

D **Japanese andromeda** (use 5)
This evergreen shrub produces masses of white, pink, or rosy early-spring flowers, but its foliage is just as striking, and lasts longer. In spring and early summer, new leaves emerge colored red to gold before maturing to a shiny dark green. Choose a cultivar for heightened leaf color or for flowers. See *Pieris japonica*, p. 149.

E **Mountain laurel** (use 7)
Less well known than rhododendrons, this evergreen shrub is just as beautiful, particularly in late spring when covered with large clusters of white, pink, or rosy flowers. Slender glossy leaves are green or green-gold. Grows slowly but develops interestingly

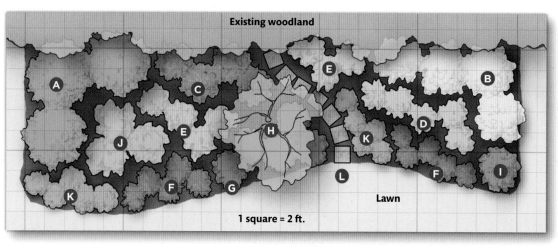

Existing woodland

Lawn

1 square = 2 ft.

B Prague viburnum

F 'Moon Bay' heavenly bamboo

D Japanese andromeda

'Sparkleberry' winterberry holly **I**

K Pink evergreen azalea

gnarled trunks and branches with age. See *Kalmia latifolia*, p. 141.

F **'Moon Bay' heavenly bamboo** (use 10)

❶ *This plant is considered invasive in the Mid-Atlantic.*
A new dwarf form of this popular evergreen shrub, only 2 ft. tall, with bright red stems and lacy foliage that is gold in spring, green in summer, and crimson in fall and winter. Always attracts attention, although it rarely if ever flowers. If unavailable, try 'Harbour Dwarf', a similar cultivar. See *Nandina domestica*, p. 146.

G **Spreading English yew** (use 5)
This evergreen shrub nestles comfortably beneath the serviceberry, forming a 2-ft.-high ground cover of dark green foliage. See *Taxus baccata* 'Repandens', p. 156.

See pp. 110–111 for the following:

H **Serviceberry** (use 1)

I **'Sparkleberry' winterberry holly** (use 1)

J **Oakleaf hydrangea** (use 3)

K **Pink evergreen azalea** (use 10)

L **Path**

VARIATIONS ON A THEME

Here are several different "approaches" to an adjacent woodland, each of them inviting to two-legged visitors and wildlife alike.

This shrub garden follows the slope into the woodland, mimicking the layered growth natural to the edge of a wood.

This path, with its carpet of tiny white flowers and odd mounding and spiky plants, makes an evocative woodland entrance for children as well as suggestive adults.

A handsome wooden fence atop a low stone wall marks a distinct boundary between a garden of low-growing shrubs and perennials and a dense wood.

Plant Profiles

Plants are the heart of the designs in this book. In this section you'll find descriptions of all the plants used in the designs, along with information on planting and maintaining them. These trees, shrubs, perennials, grasses, bulbs, and vines have all proven themselves as dependable performers in the region. They offer a wide spectrum of lovely flowers and fruits, handsome foliage, and striking forms. Most contribute something of note in at least two seasons. You can use this section as an aid when installing the designs in this book and as a reference guide to desirable plants for other home landscaping projects.

Choosing eco-friendly plants

The time and expense of installing new landscaping can do more than just make your yard look great. With the right plant selection, you have a chance to improve the outlook for migratory birds, pollinators, and other backyard wildlife, and take pleasure watching them rest, feed, nest, and raise their young in the garden you planted. While hundreds of beautiful, easy-to-grow exotic plants exist in the nursery trade, those with invasive tendencies outcompete native plants without adding habitat value for local wildlife. In large numbers, these plants damage local ecosystems. The best eco-friendly plant selections for any landscape are often the natives of the region.

Native species are those that evolved in the local area. For instance, if you live near the coast, along the piedmont, or in the mountains, consider the unique palette of plants that naturally grow there. Planting native trees, shrubs, vines, perennials, and annuals turns your property into a haven for resident wildlife and contributes essential food and shelter for migratory species. As an added bonus, these plants are almost always the least needy in terms of water, fertilizer, and pest prevention. Use at least 70 percent native plants for a diverse landscape that offers flowers, foliage, and fruits all year long.

If you want to plant natives to support wildlife, take a little time to learn about the plants and animals that originated where you live. Sometimes the most common native landscape plants are sold alongside exotic species without fanfare. Other times plants are labeled "native" that may not have originated in your particular bioregion or ecosystem. Some big nation-wide retailers may offer a few native plants at their stores, but the staff are generally not trained to know which are local natives and which are not. You'll have to know what you're looking for when you shop there. A better approach to finding suitable native plants for your yard is by shopping at an independent nursery that specifically promotes native plants. These specialists are more likely to stock a greater variety of natives and have the expertise to help you choose the best plants for your needs.

If you are not sure where to start your research, check with local nature centers, botanical gardens, your state's Department of Natural Resources, or the National Forest Service. Each of the Mid-Atlantic states has a native plant society that educates the public about, supports conservation of, and promotes the use of indigenous flora in landscaping. Their websites include lists of local nurseries that grow and sell natives:

- Delaware Native Plant Society, https://delawarenativeplants. org/2019/01/01/delaware-resources/

- Maryland Native Plant Society, https://mdflora.org/nurseries.html

- The Native Plant Society of New Jersey, https://npsnj.org/native-plants/where-to-buy-natives/

- Pennsylvania Native Plant Society, https://www.panativeplantsociety. org/native-plant-sources.html

- Virginia Native Plant Society, https://vnps.org/native-plant-nursery-list/

Native plants will provide essential food and shelter for migratory species and local wildlife.

Independent nurseries are often the best place to source native plants and get specialized guidance.

Allowing room for native plants to grow improves the health of the entire ecosystem.

Statement on invasive species

A few popular, easy-to-grow landscape plants that came from other parts of the world are not good neighbors. From our yards, their seeds are dispersed by wind or wildlife, allowing them to spring up in natural areas where they grow and spread aggressively. If the natural pressures of disease, insect damage, and animal browsing that balance native plants within the ecosystem do not affect these outsiders, invasive plant species out-compete native plants, greatly reduce the plant diversity in the area, and do not offer adequate resources for wildlife. Well known examples of problematic invasive plants include Chinese privet, multiflora rose, kudzu, and purple loosestrife.

The landscape plans in this book include a few species known to exhibit invasive qualities in parts of the Mid-Atlantic region. We have indicated the plants of greatest concern. A few strategies can help minimize the threat of potentially invasive plants. Select a non-fruiting variety of the plant in question, or diligently remove spent flowers before the seeds ripen. Another excellent option is to choose an alternative plant that can fulfill the design role in place of the invasive species—alternatives are listed within the profiles for these plants.

Clematis terniflora *is invasive in much of the Mid-Atlantic region. Use the native* Clematis virginiana, *Virgin's Bower, instead. See p. 128.*

Spiraea japonica *is a known invasive species in parts of the Mid-Atlantic region. Plant a non-invasive cultivar or be sure to remove spent flowers before seeds develop. See p. 155.*

Heavenly bamboo *is invasive and toxic to some wild birds. Choose a non-fruiting cultivar or replace with safer alternatives. See p. 146.*

Vinca minor *(periwinkle) is a known invasive plant in parts of the Mid-Atlantic region. Better to plant a non-invasive ground cover. See p. 158.*

Acer palmatum
JAPANESE MAPLE

Using the plant profiles

All of these plants are proven performers in many of the soils, climates, and other conditions commonly found in the region. But they will perform best if planted and cared for as described in the Guide to Installation. In these descriptions and recommendations, the term "garden soil" means soil that has been prepared for planting by digging or tilling and adding some organic matter, so that it's loose enough for roots and water to penetrate easily. Here also, "full sun" means a site that gets at least eight hours a day of direct sun throughout the growing season. "Partial sun" and "partial shade" both refer to sites that get direct sun for part of the day but are shaded the rest of the time by a building, fence, or tree. "Full shade" means sites that don't receive direct sunlight.

The plants are organized here alphabetically by their botanical name. While many plants are sold by common name, botanical names help ensure that you get what you want. If you're browsing, page references direct you to the designs in which the plants appear.

Acer palmatum
'Bloodgood'
JAPANESE MAPLE

Acer palmatum

JAPANESE MAPLE. A neat, small deciduous tree with delicate-looking leaves that have jagged edges. There are many kinds, with leaves that are green, bronze, or red in summer. Most turn red or scarlet in fall. 'Bloodgood' (p. 88) stays dark red all season. All need full or partial sun and rich, moist soil covered with a layer of mulch. Water deeply once a week during dry weather. Grows slowly, so buy the biggest tree you can afford to start with. Plant in spring or fall. Prune only to remove weak, damaged, or crossing limbs. Grows 10 to 20 ft. tall and wide. Pages: 59, 88.

Achillea

YARROW. A long-blooming perennial with flat clusters of small flowers on stiff stalks and finely divided gray-green leaves that have a pungent aroma. Spreads to form a patch. 'Coronation Gold' (p. 42) is a robust plant with bright gold flowers. 'Moonshine' (p. 93) is less vigorous and has lemon

Achillea 'Coronation Gold'
YARROW

Achillea millefolium 'Appleblossom'
YARROW

yellow flowers. *A. millefolium* 'Appleblossom' (pp. 44, 97) is medium-size and bears clear pink flowers. Needs full sun and garden soil. Cut off old flower stalks when the blossoms fade. Divide clumps every few years in spring or fall. Grows 2 to 3 ft. tall, spreads 3 ft. wide.

Aesculus parviflora

BOTTLEBRUSH BUCKEYE. A deciduous shrub that forms a broad, mounded clump with stout twigs, large compound leaves, and white flowers in spikes that stick up like candles in early summer. Adapts to sun or shade, garden soil. Needs no pruning or special care. May drop its leaves early after a dry summer but recovers the next year. Grows slowly but can reach 10 ft. or taller and spread 15 ft. or wider. Pages: 108, 111, 112.

Ajuga reptans

BUGLEWEED, AJUGA. ***Ajuga reptans* is locally invasive in the Mid-Atlantic.** Use with caution. A low-growing, mat-forming perennial, used as a ground cover. The smooth glossy leaves are evergreen in mild winters. Erect, 6-in. spikes densely packed with small flowers are very showy for a few weeks in May. 'Alba' (p. 47) has green foliage and white flowers. 'Bronze Beauty' (pp. 23, 53) has dark purplish bronze foliage and blue flowers. Other cultivars are good, too. Tolerates full sun in rich, moist soil. Needs partial or full shade in garden or dry soil. After flowers fade, cut them off with a string trimmer, lawn mower, or hedge shears. Spreads quickly and will invade a lawn unless you keep cutting along the edge or install a mowing strip.

Alchemilla mollis

LADY'S MANTLE. A perennial that forms clumps of gray-green leaves that are pleated like a parasol, topped with long airy sprays of lemon yellow flowers in early summer. Takes full or partial sun, garden soil. Remove flower stalks after bloom to prevent self-seeding. Cut leaves to the ground in late fall or early spring. Divide clumps every few years, in spring or right after the flowers fade. Grows about 1 ft. tall and 2 ft. wide. Pages: 73, 91.

Amelanchier x grandiflora

SERVICEBERRY. A small deciduous tree, typically grown with multiple trunks. Bears white flowers in early spring, edible blue or purplish berries in summer, bright fall foliage. Needs sun or partial

Aesculus parviflora
BOTTLEBRUSH BUCKEYE

Ajuga reptans 'Bronze Beauty'
BUGLEWEED

Alchemilla mollis
LADY'S MANTLE

Amelanchier x *grandiflora*
SERVICEBERRY

shade, garden soil. Grows fairly slowly, so buy a good-size specimen to start with. Needs little pruning: just remove any crossing branches. May grow up to 25 ft. tall, 15 ft. wide. Pages: 32, 34, 90, 101, 112, 115.

Anemone x hybrida

JAPANESE ANEMONE. A perennial with small daisylike flowers on branching stalks held well above a bushy clump of large, dark green leaves. Blooms for several weeks in late summer. 'Alba' and 'Honorine Jobert' have white flowers; other kinds have pink flowers. Needs partial shade and rich, moist soil. Cut down old stalks in the fall. Divide every few years, in the spring. Grows 3 to 4 ft. tall, 2 to 3 ft. wide. Pages: 15, 16, 84, 91.

Anemone vitifolia 'Robustissima'

PINK GRAPELEAF ANEMONE. A vigorous perennial with dark green foliage and daisylike pink flowers on branching stalks in late summer. Prefers full or partial sun, garden or fertile soil. Spreads quickly. Confine it by planting in a bottomless pot, or divide it every other year in spring. Grows 3 to 4 ft. tall. Page: 70.

Artemisia abrotanum

SOUTHERNWOOD. A shrubby perennial, woody at the base, with fragrant, gray-green, finely divided leaves. It rarely flowers. Needs full sun, garden soil. Grows slender wandlike stems 3 to 5 ft. tall if unpruned but forms a compact mound or edging if you shear it in early spring and again in summer. Pages: 84, 95.

Anemone x *hybrida*
WHITE JAPANESE ANEMONE

Anemone vitifolia 'Robustissima'
PINK GRAPELEAF ANEMONE

Artemisia abrotanum
SOUTHERNWOOD

Artemisia ludoviciana 'Valerie Finnis'
ARTEMISIA

Artemisia ludoviciana 'Valerie Finnis'

'VALERIE FINNIS' ARTEMISIA. A perennial that forms a patch of erect stems. Grown for its foliage, which is bright silvery white. Needs full sun, garden soil. Cut the stems back partway in late spring to encourage branching and to discourage blooming (the flowers aren't very attractive). Divide every second or third year, in spring or fall. Grows 2 to 3 ft. tall and wide. Page: 37.

Artemisia stelleriana 'Silver Brocade'

'SILVER BROCADE' BEACH WORMWOOD. A sprawling perennial, often used as an edging or ground cover, with deeply lobed silver-gray leaves. Flower stalks bear clusters of small yellow blossoms, but most gardeners shear these off as soon as they appear. Needs full sun, well-drained soil. If decayed spots appear on the leaves in hot humid summers, cut the stems back halfway. The plants will recover in cooler weather. Grows under 1 ft. tall, up to 2 ft. wide. Page: 44.

Asarum europaeum

EUROPEAN WILD GINGER. A low-growing perennial with glossy, heart-shaped evergreen leaves and inconspicuous flowers. Spreads slowly but gradually forms an excellent ground cover. Needs partial or full shade and rich, moist, well-drained soil. Requires no routine care. Can be divided in spring to make new plants. Grows about 6 in. tall and spreads up to 1 ft. wide. Pages: 106, 109.

Aster x frikartii 'Monch'

'MONCH' ASTER. A carefree perennial that blooms over a long season from summer to fall, bearing thousands of light purple flowers. Thrives in full sun and garden soil. Cut stems back partway in midsummer if the plant has gotten floppy. Divide every year or two in early spring. Grows 2 to 3 ft. tall and wide. Page: 66.

Aster novae-angliae 'Purple Dome'

'PURPLE DOME' NEW ENGLAND ASTER. A compact form of the popular perennial wildflower, this aster forms a dense attractive mound of dark green foliage all summer, then bears thousands of striking, dark purple, daisylike flowers for a month or so in early fall. Plant in full sun. Grows best in moist soil with plenty of loam but also adapts to ordinary garden soil. Divide the plants every year or two in early spring. Grows about 2 ft. tall and wide. Pages: 53, 74, 86,103.

Artemisia stelleriana 'Silver Brocade'
BEACH WORMWOOD

Asarum europaeum
EUROPEAN WILD GINGER

Aster x frikartii 'Monch'
ASTER

Aster novae-angliae 'Purple Dome'
NEW ENGLAND ASTER

Recommended astilbes

Astilbe x *arendsii,* Hybrid astilbe

Forms a bushy mound of foliage bearing up to a dozen or more flower stalks that are 18 to 42 in. tall. The season of bloom ranges from late June to early August. 'Bridal Veil' (3 ft. tall, midseason) and 'Deutschland' (18 in., early) have white flowers. 'Bressingham Beauty' (3 ft., midseason) and 'Rheinland' (2 ft., early) bear pink flowers. 'Fanal' (2 ft., midseason) and 'Red Sentinel' (2 ft., late) have red flowers. Pages: 28, 50, 53, 89.

A. *chinensis* var. *pumila,* Dwarf Chinese astilbe

Shorter (under 1 ft. tall) and smaller than hybrid astilbes, this spreads to form a low mat or edging. Bears plump clusters of mauve flowers in August. Page: 80.

A. *simplicifolia,* Astilbe

Looks like a hybrid astilbe, but forms a smaller mound of daintier foliage and the flower spikes are more delicate. 'Alba', with white flowers, may be hard to find, but 'Sprite', with clear pink flowers, is widely available. Under 1 ft. tall. Page: 73.

Astilbe x *arendsii*

Astilbe x *arendsii*

Astilbe chinensis var. *pumila*
DWARF CHINESE ASTILBE

Astilbe

ASTILBE. Among the best perennials for shady or partly shady sites, with fluffy plumes of white, pink, rose, red, or magenta flowers in summer and healthy, glossy, compound leaves all season. Astilbes prefer rich, moist, well-drained soil and need shade from midday sun. Cut off flower stalks when the blooms turn brown (or leave them in place, if you like the looks of the dried flowers). Cut foliage to the ground in late fall or early spring. Divide every three to five years in spring or late summer, using a sharp spade, ax, or old pruning saw to cut the tough, woody rootstock into a few large chunks. See box at left for information on specific cultivars.

Aurinia saxatilis

BASKET-OF-GOLD. One of the first perennials to bloom in spring, bearing masses of gold flowers at the time when daffodils and forsythias bloom. Gray foliage is attractive for the rest of the summer and fall. Needs full sun, well-drained garden soil. Cut stems back halfway after it blooms and again in summer if the leaves get diseased during a spell of hot humid weather. Fast-growing but short-lived, so buy replacements every few years. Grows about 6 to 8 in. tall, spreads 2 to 3 ft. wide. Page: 63.

Baptisia australis

FALSE INDIGO. A perennial prairie wildflower that's unusually carefree and long-lived. Forms a mushroom-shaped mound of blue-green foliage, topped in early summer with showy spikes of indigo blue flowers, followed by clusters of inflated seedpods lasting for months. Adapts to sun or partial shade. Plant in average garden soil. Cut stalks to the ground in winter. Needs no other care. Grows about 3 ft. tall and 3 to 6 ft. wide. Pages: 78, 99.

Berberis thunbergii 'Crimson Pygmy'

'CRIMSON PYGMY' JAPANESE BARBERRY. **All fruit-bearing cultivars of *Berberis thunbergii* are potentially invasive. Consider replacing it with dwarf ninebark, *Physocarpus opulifolius* 'Nanus', or one of its cultivars like 'Tiny Wine' ninebark.** A deciduous shrub that grows naturally into a broad, low, cushionlike mound. Valued for its shape and its foliage, which is dark maroon all summer, turning crimson in fall. Needs full sun (foliage turns green if it doesn't get enough sun) and well-drained soil. Pruning is not required, but you can sheer it if you want to. Grows about 2 ft. tall, spreads 3 to 5 ft. wide. Pages: 26, 39, 68, 104.

Aurinia saxatilis
BASKET-OF-GOLD

Baptisia australis
FALSE INDIGO

Berberis thunbergii 'Crimson Pygmy'
JAPANESE BARBERRY

Boltonia asteroides
'Snowbank'
BOLTONIA

Boltonia asteroides 'Snowbank'

'SNOWBANK' BOLTONIA. A perennial wildflower that forms an erect clump of many stems and slender leaves. Foliage is pale green and looks healthy all summer. Blooms for many weeks in fall, bearing thousands of small white asterlike blossoms. Takes full or partial sun, garden or moist soil. Cut stems back partway in late spring to reduce height of clump, if desired. Cut to the ground in winter. Divide every few years in early spring. Grows 3 to 4 ft. tall, 2 to 4 ft. wide. Pages: 49, 63, 97.

Buddleia davidii

BUTTERFLY BUSH. **Buddleia davidii is a known invasive in much of the Mid-Atlantic region. Choose a non-seeding cultivar or replace it with a non-invasive species like Itea virginica 'Henry's Garnet', or Clethra alnifolia 'Ruby Spice'.** A fast-growing deciduous shrub that blooms from midsummer through fall. Arching shoots make a vase-shaped clump. Spikes of small white, pink, lilac, blue, or purple flowers form at the end of each stem. The flowers have a sweet fragrance and really do attract butterflies. 'Black Knight' (pp. 76, 82, 97) has purple flowers. 'Pink Delight' is medium pink. 'White Profusion' (p. 35) is white. Needs full sun and well-drained soil. Cut old stems down to 1-ft. stubs in early spring to promote vigorous growth and maximum flowering. Grows 5 to 8 ft. tall and wide by the end of the summer. Page: 91.

Buddleia davidii 'White Profusion'
BUTTERFLY BUSH

Recommended bulbs

Allium aflatunense, Persian onion
Makes a big ball of lilac-blue flowers on a 3-ft. stalk in early summer. Plant bulbs 6 in. deep, 8 in. apart. Flowers may be smaller after the first year. Page: 103.

**Anemone blanda,
White Grecian windflower**
Daisylike white flowers on 4-in. stalks in April. Plant bulbs 3 in. deep, 3 in. apart. Often spreads by seed to form a patch. Page: 59.

Camassia esculenta, Camas
Loose clusters of large violet-blue flowers on 18-in. stalks in April or May. Plant 5 in. deep, 5 in. apart. Needs rich, moist soil. Page: 59.

Crocus, Crocus
Cup-shaped flowers on 4-in. stalks in March. Available in white, yellow, lilac, and purple. Plant bulbs 4 in. deep, 4 in. apart. Forms large clumps after a few years. Pages: 49, 76.

**Endymion hispanica,
Spanish bluebell**
In April, bell-shaped blue flowers dangle from 18-in. stalks. Plant bulbs 5 in. deep, 5 in. apart. Forms large clumps after a few years and also spreads by seed. Page: 32.

Eranthis hyemalis, Winter aconite
Bright golden flowers peek through the snow, nestled against fringed leafy collars. Grows 4 in. tall. Plant bulbs 3 in. deep, 3 in. apart. Difficult to start, as the bulbs are sometimes dried out, but once established, forms good clumps and also self-seeds. Page: 59.

Galanthus nivalis, Snowdrop
Bright white flowers droop from 6-in. stems in February. Plant 3 in. deep, 3 in. apart. Difficult to start, as the

Allium aflatunense
PERSIAN ONION

bulbs are sometimes dried out, but once established, forms big clumps or patches. Page: 59.

Narcissus, Daffodils, jonquils, and narcissus
Bright yellow, white, or bicolor flowers, often fragrant, on stalks 6 to 18 in. tall. Different kinds bloom in sequence from early February through late April. Plant bulbs 4 to 6 in. deep, 4 to 6 in. apart, depending on their size. Very reliable, carefree, and long-lived. Forms big clumps after a few years. Pages: 59, 76, 99.

Scilla siberica, Squill
Clusters of star-shaped flowers on 6-in. stalks last for a week or two in March or April. Usually has sky blue flowers, but there is a white version, too. Plant bulbs 3 in. deep, 3 in. apart. Very easy to grow; spreads fast. Page: 99.

Tulipa, Tulips
Large flowers in bright or pastel shades of all colors but blue, held on stalks 6 to 20 in. tall, blooming in sequence between March and early May. Plant bulbs 4 to 6 in. deep, 4 to 6 in. apart, depending on their size. Typically short-lived. May stop blooming or disappear altogether after the second or third year. Page: 59.

Narcissus
DAFFODIL

Narcissus
DAFFODIL

Tulipa
TULIP

Bulbs

The bulbs recommended in this book are all perennials that come up year after year and bloom in late winter, spring, or early summer. After they flower, their leaves continue growing until sometime in summer, when they gradually turn yellow and die down to the ground. To get started, you must buy bulbs from a garden center or catalog sometime in the fall (they usually aren't available until after Labor Day). Plant them promptly in a sunny or partly sunny bed with well-prepared soil, burying them two to three times as deep as the bulb is high. In subsequent years, all you have to do is pick off the faded flowers in spring and remove (or ignore, if you choose) the old leaves after they turn yellow in summer. Most bulbs can be divided every few years if you want to spread them to other parts of your property. Dig them up as the foliage is turning yellow, shake or pull them apart, and replant them right away. For more information on specific bulbs, see box on facing page.

Buxus

BOXWOOD. A very popular and highly prized shrub that forms a dense mass of neat, small, glossy evergreen leaves. The leaves, and also the small flowers in spring, have a distinct fragrance. Boxwood forms soft mounded shapes if left alone or can be sheared into formal globes, cones, hedges, or topiary. There are many kinds of boxwood, differing in rate of growth, size of leaf, natural habit (upright or spreading), and winter foliage color (green or bronzy). 'Green Beauty' littleleaf boxwood (*B. microphylla*; pp. 47, 49, 66) has small leaves that stay bright green in winter and forms a compact globe up to 4 ft. tall. Regular English boxwood (*B. sempervirens*; p. 32) has darker green leaves and can grow quite large, up to 20 ft. tall. Dwarf English boxwood (*B. sempervirens* 'Suffruticosa'; pp. 24, 91, 93) is similar but has smaller leaves and stays compact, usually under 3 ft. tall. Boxwoods grow slowly, so buy the largest plants you can afford. They need well-drained soil and grow best in full or partial sun. Use mulch to protect their shallow roots. Shear in early summer, if desired.

Calamagrostis x acutiflora 'Karl Foerster'

'KARL FOERSTER' FEATHER REED GRASS. A perennial grass that forms narrow, erect clumps. Leaves develop early in the season. Slender stalks topped with flower spikes that resemble pipe cleaners form in

Buxus microphylla 'Green Beauty'
LITTLELEAF BOXWOOD

Buxus sempervirens 'Suffruticosa'
BOXWOOD

midsummer. The whole plant gradually turns beige or tan by late summer, but it stands up well into the winter. Cut it all down to the ground before new growth starts in spring. Can be divided every few years if you want more plants. Otherwise leave it alone. Adapts to most soils but needs full or partial sun. Flower stalks reach 5 to 6 ft. tall; foliage spreads about 2 ft. wide. Pages: 35, 42, 74, 78.

Callicarpa dichotoma

KOREAN BEAUTYBERRY. A deciduous shrub grown for its bright lilac-colored berries, which line the stems in fall. Easy to grow if sited in full sun and fertile, moist, well-drained soil. Cut old stems close to the ground in early spring. Grows 3 to 4 ft. tall and wide by the end of the summer. Pages: 103, 111.

Calamagrostis acutiflora 'Karl Foerster'
FEATHER REED GRASS

Callicarpa dichotoma
KOREAN BEAUTYBERRY

Campanula carpatica 'Blue Clips'
CARPATHIAN BELLFLOWER

Carex morrowii 'Aureo-variegata'
VARIEGATED JAPANESE SEDGE

Caryopteris x *clandonensis*
'Longwood Blue'
BLUEBEARD

Ceratostigma plumbaginoides
DWARF PLUMBAGO

Cercis canadensis
REDBUD

Campanula carpatica 'Blue Clips'

'BLUE CLIPS' CARPATHIAN BELLFLOWER. A short, compact perennial that blooms for most of the summer, with sky blue flowers and medium green foliage. Prefers full sun and well-drained soil. Divide clumps every few years in spring. Grows about 1 ft. tall and wide. Pages: 63, 76.

Carex morrowii 'Aureo-variegata'

VARIEGATED JAPANESE SEDGE. An evergreen perennial that looks like a tuft of grass with green-and-gold leaves. Neat and attractive all year round. Needs partial shade and moist, fertile soil. Care is minimal—trim off any tattered foliage in early spring. Can be divided every few years if you want to make more plants. Grows about 1 ft. tall, 1 to 2 ft. wide. Pages: 29, 36, 73, 108.

Caryopteris x clandonensis

BLUEBEARD, BLUE MIST SHRUB. A small deciduous shrub that blooms for weeks in late summer. Bright or dark blue flowers contrast with the soft gray foliage. 'Longwood Blue' is a popular cultivar with medium blue flowers. Other cultivars are good substitutes. Needs full sun and well-drained soil. Thrives in a warm dry spot. Cut it down close to the ground each spring for compact growth and maximum bloom. Will grow 2 to 3 ft. wide by fall. Pages: 26, 47, 65, 78.

Ceratostigma plumbaginoides

DWARF PLUMBAGO. A perennial ground cover with indigo blue flowers in summer and fall and dark green foliage that turns maroon or crimson in fall. Deciduous in winter and late to emerge in spring, it looks good with early-spring bulbs. Adapts to full or partial sun, garden soil. Cut old stems to the ground in early spring. Stays under 1 ft. tall, spreads 2 to 3 ft. wide. Pages: 60, 71, 91.

Cercis canadensis

REDBUD. A small deciduous tree native to the Mid-Atlantic region. Clusters of bright pink-purple flowers line the twigs in midspring, before the leaves unfold. Heart-shaped leaves are medium green all summer and turn gold in fall. Tolerates partial shade and grows in any well-drained soil. Available with single or multiple trunks. Grows quickly, so it's reasonable to start with a small plant. Prune every summer, removing limbs that hang too low and dead twigs that accumulate inside the crown. May reach 20 to 25 ft. tall and wide. Page: 73.

eic simplex 'White Pearl'

Chamaecyparis obtusa 'Nana Gracilis'

DWARF HINOKI CYPRESS. A slow-growing conifer with graceful, glossy, emerald green foliage. Grows naturally into a narrow cone and doesn't need any pruning or shearing. Prefers partial sun and moist, well-drained soil. Buy the largest plant you can afford. It may someday reach 8 ft. or taller and spread 3 to 4 ft. wide. Pages: 53, 59, 60, 78, 106.

Chionanthus virginicus

FRINGE TREE. A deciduous small tree or large shrub. Usually has multiple trunks and forms a rounded or domed crown. Blooms profusely in late spring, with loose clusters of fragrant white flowers dangling from every branch. Needs full or partial sun and garden soil. Normally sold in small sizes, since larger plants don't transplant well. Grows slowly, so use low-growing perennials, bulbs, or annuals to fill the space around it for the first few years. Eventually reaches 20 ft. tall and wide. Pages: 39, 41, 78.

Chrysanthemum nipponicum

NIPPON OR MONTAUK DAISY. An unusual daisy that blooms in late fall. Forms a shrubby clump of sturdy stems clothed with thick glossy leaves all summer. Full sun, garden soil. Doesn't branch on its own, but you can shear off the tips of the stems a few times in spring and summer if you want to make the plant bushier. Cut all stems to the ground in winter. Grows 2 to 3 ft. tall and wide. Once established, should not be divided or moved. Page: 65.

Chrysanthemum x superbum

SHASTA DAISY. A popular perennial with large daisy blossoms borne on long stalks, good for bouquets as well as in the garden. Forms a low mat of glossy foliage. 'Becky' (p. 65) is a vigorous plant that grows at least 3 ft. tall and wide and blooms all summer despite heat and humidity. 'Silver Princess' (pp. 41, 65) is only 1 ft. tall and wide, and blooms for a shorter period in June and July. Needs full sun, garden soil. Divide every year or two in early spring.

Cimicifuga simplex 'White Pearl'

'WHITE PEARL' BUGBANE. An uncommon but excellent garden perennial that blooms in early fall, with wandlike sprays of white flowers held above clumps of dark green compound leaves. Prefers partial shade and moist, fertile soil. Needs no routine care and can go years without being divided. Grows about 3 ft. tall, 2 to 3 ft. wide. Page: 80.

Chamaecyparis obtusa 'Nana Gracilis'
DWARF HINOKI CYPRESS

Chionanthus virginicus
FRINGE TREE

Chrysanthemum nipponicum
NIPPON DAISY

Chrysanthemum x superbum 'Becky'
SHASTA DAISY

Cimicifuga simplex 'White Pearl'
BUGBANE

Recommended clematis

Clematis x *jackmanii*, Jackman clematis
Large violet-purple flowers in summer. Prune all stems under 1 ft. tall in spring, just as the buds start to swell. Pages: 66, 97.

C. tangutica, Golden clematis
Small yellow flowers bloom throughout the summer, followed by fluffy, silvery seed heads that last throughout the fall and into the winter. Prune in early spring, removing older shoots and cutting others back partway. Page: 66.

C. terniflora, Sweet autumn clematis
Clematis terniflora is invasive in much of the Mid-Atlantic region. Use the native *Clematis virginiana*, Virgin's Bower, instead. It is very similar in appearance and growth habit. Small, starry, fragrant white flowers in August and September. More vigorous than most clematis, it can climb 25 ft. or higher. Prune in early spring, cutting back partway or close to the ground, depending on how far you want it to climb. Often sold under the name *C. paniculata*. Pages: 78, 95.

'Henryi' clematis
Single white flowers 4 in. wide in June and again in late summer. Remove only dead twigs in spring, then cut all stems back to about 3 ft. after the first flowering. 'Candida' is a good substitute for 'Henryi', similar in all regards. Page: 47.

Clematis x *jackmanii*
JACKMAN CLEMATIS

Clematis tangutica
GOLDEN CLEMATIS

Clematis virginiana
VIRGIN'S BOWER

Clematis
CLEMATIS. A deciduous vine that climbs or sprawls, forming a tangle of leafy stems adorned with masses of flowers, which can be tiny or large. See box at left for more information on specific kinds. Clematis needs partial or full sun and good garden soil. If your soil is acid, add a cup or so of ground limestone to the planting area and mix it thoroughly into the soil. Plant clematis in spring. Unlike most plants, clematis needs a hole deep enough to cover the root ball and base of the stem with about 2 in. of soil. Cut the stem back to the lowest set of healthy leaves to encourage the plant to branch out near the base. Guide the new stems into position and use twist-ties or other fasteners to secure them as soon as they have grown long enough to reach the trellis, wire, or other support. Prune annually according to the specific directions in the box at left. It takes most clematis a few years to cover a fence or trellis 6 to 8 ft. tall.

Clethra alnifolia
SUMMERSWEET. A deciduous shrub with very sweet-scented white or pink flowers in the heat of August. Glossy dark foliage looks fresh all summer and turns gold in fall. Very adaptable—tolerates sun or shade, garden or damp soil. Prune each year in early spring, cutting some of the older stems to ground level and cutting new stems back by one-third. Some plants may send up suckers around the base and gradually form a patch. Grows 6 to 10 ft. tall and wide. Pages: 32, 36, 99.

Convallaria majalis
LILY-OF-THE-VALLEY. A perennial that spreads to form a patch, with large smooth leaves held in a vertical position. Very fragrant white flowers appear in spring. Prefers a shady site with garden or moist soil. Makes a good ground cover, although in hot dry years the leaves may wither early, leaving the ground bare until the next spring. Needs no routine care. Can be (but doesn't have to be) divided every few years in spring or summer. Grows about 8 in. tall, spreads indefinitely. Page: 99.

Coreopsis verticillata 'Moonbeam'
'MOONBEAM' COREOPSIS. Even this slower-growing cultivar can escape cultivation and become problematic, especially in the milder southeastern part of the Mid-Atlantic region. Use all English Ivy cultivars with caution. Consider replacing it with climbing *Parthenocissus quinquefolia*, Virginia

Creeper, or non-climbing *Pachysandra terminalis*, Japanese Spurge. A long-blooming perennial that bears hundreds of small, lemon yellow, daisylike blossoms from July into September. The short, needlelike leaves are very dark green. Spreads to form a low patch but isn't invasive. A perfect plant for the front of a border. Needs full sun but grows well in any garden soil. Grows about 2 ft. tall and wide. With age the center may die back. If so, divide and replant. Pages: 26, 74, 84, 86.

Cornus alba

SIBERIAN DOGWOOD. A deciduous shrub with stems that turn bright red in winter, white flowers in spring, pale blue berries in late summer, and crimson foliage in fall. It forms a vase-shaped clump with many erect or arching stems. 'Elegantissima' (p. 80) has variegated green-and-white leaves. 'Sibirica' (p. 110) has green foliage and bright coral-red stems. Needs full or partial sun, garden or moist soil. Cut all the stems down close to the ground every few years (or every year, if you want to) in early spring. After a few weeks, the plant will send up vigorous new shoots. These young shoots develop the brightest-colored bark. Grows 6 to 8 ft. tall and 8 to 12 ft. wide.

Cornus kousa

KOUSA DOGWOOD. A small deciduous tree with large white flowers in early summer, edible plump red fruits in late summer, crimson fall foliage, and attractive flaking bark in winter. Choose a single- or multiple-trunk specimen at the nursery. Small sizes transplant better than large specimens do. Plant in early spring or fall, not in the heat of summer. Needs full or partial sun and garden soil. Prune in midsummer, right after it blooms, only to remove weak, crossing, or lower limbs. The Kousa dogwood, which came from China, seems resistant to the fungal disease that attacks our North American flowering dogwood. Grows up to 25 ft. tall and wide. Pages: 71, 78.

Clethra alnifolia
SUMMERSWEET

Convallaria majalis
LILY-OF-THE-VALLEY

Coreopsis verticillata 'Moonbeam'

Cornus alba 'Elegantissima'
VARIEGATED SIBERIAN DOGWOOD

Cornus alba 'Sibirica'
SIBERIAN DOGWOOD

Cornus kousa
KOUSA DOGWOOD

Daphne x *burkwoodii*
'Carol Mackie'
DAPHNE

Dendranthema x *grandiflorum* 'Sheffield'
CHRYSANTHEMUM

Dianthus 'Bath's Pink'

Daphne x burkwoodii 'Carol Mackie'

'CAROL MACKIE' DAPHNE. A small, slow-growing, rounded shrub with lovely variegated green-and-cream foliage that looks good all year, plus clusters of deliciously fragrant pale flowers in spring. Needs well-drained soil and prefers partial shade. Try not to disturb the thick roots when planting it, and be sure not to plant it too deep. Once established, needs no pruning or routine care. Gradually reaches 3 ft. tall, 3 to 5 ft. wide. Pages: 50, 66, 68, 73.

Dendranthema x grandiflorum

HARDY GARDEN CHRYSANTHEMUM. A perennial that blooms for many weeks in late summer and fall, with single or double blossoms in many sizes and colors. Soft, gray-green, aromatic foliage is quietly attractive throughout the summer. 'Sheffield' (p. 74) has single pink flowers. (Nurseries often sell

hardy garden chrysanthemums under their former name, *Chrysanthemum* x *morifolium*.) Needs full sun and garden soil. Buy plants in spring for best results; the blooming plants commonly sold in the fall may not have time to get established in your garden before winter sets in. Leave bloom stalks in place over the winter as a natural mulch to protect the roots from temperature changes. Cut down the stalks in early spring. A few weeks later, divide the clump and replant the most vigorous-looking shoots. Height and spread vary, but most garden mums grow between 1 and 3 ft. tall and wide. Page: 84.

Dianthus

DIANTHUS, PINK. A low-growing perennial with very fragrant flowers like small carnations. They bloom in late spring and early summer. The grassy, blue-green, evergreen foliage forms a dense mat. 'Aqua' (p. 42) has pure white flowers. 'Bath's Pink' (pp. 41, 82, 95) has clear pink flowers. Both need full sun and well-drained soil. After they bloom, shear off the flower stalks and cut the leaves back halfway. Fresh new foliage will soon develop. Divide every few years in early spring. Foliage grows 4 to 6 in. tall and spreads 1 to 3 ft. wide. Flower stalks are about 1 ft. tall.

Dicentra 'Luxuriant'

'LUXURIANT' BLEEDING HEART. A perennial that forms a rounded clump of soft-textured lacy foliage, topped with bright pink flowers that dangle from delicate stalks. Needs partial shade and fertile, moist, well-drained soil. Cut off flower stalks after it blooms. Divide every few years in spring or fall. Grows 2 to 3 ft. tall and wide. Page: 108.

Echinacea purpurea

PURPLE CONEFLOWER. A prairie wildflower that thrives in gardens and blooms for several weeks in mid- to late summer. Large pink daisylike blossoms are held on stiff branching stalks above a basal mound of dark green foliage. Needs full sun and garden soil. Cut back flower stalks if you choose, or let the seed heads ripen for winter interest. May self-sow but isn't weedy. Older plants can be divided in early spring. Grows about 3 ft. tall, 2 ft. wide. Pages: 35, 44, 76, 84.

Epimedium

BISHOP'S HAT. A slow-growing but long-lived perennial with very attractive foliage that is

Dicentra 'Luxuriant'
BLEEDING HEART

Echinacea purpurea
PURPLE CONEFLOWER

evergreen in mild winters. There are many kinds, all with similar foliage but with red, pink, yellow, or white blossoms. The flowers are small but add interest in spring. Needs partial or full shade, garden soil. Adapts well to the dry soil under trees. Shear off discolored or damaged leaves in early spring. Can be divided every few years. Grows about 1 ft. tall, spreads indefinitely and makes a good ground cover. Page: 89.

Euonymus kiautschovicus 'Manhattan'

'MANHATTAN' EUONYMUS. An evergreen shrub with thick, glossy, rounded, medium green leaves and small but showy pink-and-orange fruits that ripen in the fall. Tolerates sun or shade, any well-drained soil. Grows naturally as an upright shrub, reaching about 6 ft. tall and 4 ft. wide, but can be sheared, pruned, or trained as you choose. Leaves will discolor and may drop in severe winters. Page: 23.

Epimedium
BISHOP'S HAT

Euonymus kiautschovicus
'Manhattan'

Recommended ferns

Athyrium goeringianum 'Pictum', Japanese painted fern

A colorful fern that forms rosettes of fine-cut fronds marked in shades of green, silver, and maroon. They look almost iridescent. Deciduous. Grows about 1 ft. tall, 2 ft. wide. Page: 50.

Dryopteris erythrosora, Japanese autumn fern

A fern that forms erect clumps of glossy fronds that start out coppery-colored, then turn dark green. Evergreen in mild winters but freezes to the ground in cold ones. Grows 2 to 3 ft. tall, 1 ft. wide. Pages: 50, 80, 106.

Osmunda claytoniana, Interrupted fern

A handsome native fern that tolerates dry soil better than most ferns do. The clumps look like large badminton shuttlecocks. Fronds have a bare spot midway up but are leafy on top. Deciduous. Grows 3 to 4 ft. tall, 2 ft. wide. Page: 60.

Polystichum acrostichoides, Christmas fern

A native fern with glossy evergreen fronds. New fronds are held upright in summer but flop down on the ground in winter. Grows about 2 ft. tall and wide. Pages: 32, 99, 108.

Athyrium goeringianum 'Pictum'
JAPANESE PAINTED FERN

Dryopteris erythrosora
JAPANESE AUTUMN FERN

Osmunda claytoniana
INTERRUPTED FERN

Polystichum acrostichoides
CHRISTMAS FERN

Ferns

Ferns are carefree, long-lived perennials for shady sites. Despite their delicate appearance, they're among the most durable and trouble-free plants you can grow. Almost all ferns need shade from the midday and afternoon sun. Most tolerate garden soil but grow better in soil that's been amended with extra organic matter. You can divide them every few years in early spring if you want more plants, or leave them alone for decades. They need no routine care. See box opposite for more information on specific ferns.

Festuca ovina var. *glauca*

BLUE FESCUE GRASS. A neat, compact grass that forms a dense tuft of very slender, blue-green leaves. Narrow flower spikes appear in early summer and soon turn tan. 'Sea Urchin' (pp. 59, 60, 68) is a popular cultivar with especially blue-colored foliage. Needs full sun and well-drained soil. Must be cut down at least once a year. If you cut the clump down to the ground in midsummer, fresh new foliage appears in the fall and lasts all winter. Or you can leave the old foliage and flower stalks in place and wait until late winter to cut it all down. Divide every few years in early spring. Grows about 1 ft. tall and wide.

Forsythia viridissima 'Bronxensis'

'BRONXENSIS' GREENSTEM FORSYTHIA. A low-growing, densely branched shrub with neat, glossy, bright green foliage. Blooms later and less abundantly than common forsythia. Needs full or partial sun, garden soil. Grows slowly, so start with the biggest plants you can find. Needs little if any pruning. Usually stays under 1 ft. tall but spreads 3 to 4 ft. wide. Pages: 39, 71.

Galium odoratum

SWEET WOODRUFF. A deciduous perennial ground cover that spreads quickly, needs no care, and lasts for decades. Fine-textured foliage is bright green throughout the growing season, then turns beige or tan in late fall. Thousands of tiny white flowers sparkle above the fresh new foliage in spring. Adapts to most soils, prefers partial or full shade. Shear or mow close to the ground in early spring and rake away the old foliage. Easily divided in spring or fall to make more plants. Buy just a few plants to start with and you'll have all the plants you want in a year or two. Grows about 6 in. tall, spreads indefinitely. Pages: 80, 99.

Gaura lindheimeri

GAURA. A perennial wildflower that forms a loose clump of graceful arching stems and bears pale pink and white flowers from spring through fall. Needs full sun and well-drained soil. Too much shade or moisture makes the stems floppy. Cut to the ground in winter. Grows 3 ft. tall and wide. Pages: 78, 84.

Festuca ovina var. *glauca* 'Sea Urchin'
BLUE FESCUE GRASS

Forsythia viridissima 'Bronxensis'
GREENSTEM FORSYTHIA

Galium odoratum
SWEET WOODRUFF

Gaura lindheimeri
GAURA

Recommended geraniums

Geranium clarkei, 'Kashmir White' geranium

Forms a loose mound of finely cut leaves, with white flowers in early summer. Grows about 18 in. tall and wide. Page: 82.

G. endressii, 'Wargrave Pink' geranium

Forms a large sprawling mound of rich green foliage topped with pink flowers. Blooms heavily for a few weeks in early summer, with scattered flowers off and on until fall. Grows 18 in. tall, 2 to 3 ft. wide. Page: 47.

G. 'Johnson's Blue', 'Johnson's Blue' geranium

Forms a large sprawling mound, wider than tall, with medium-size leaves and blue-purple flowers in late spring and early summer. Grows about 1 ft. tall, 2 ft. wide. Page: 84.

G. macrorrhizum, Bigroot geranium

A short, compact plant that forms bushy clumps of fragrant semievergreen foliage, with magenta or pink flowers in late spring. Makes a good ground cover for partial shade and dry soil. Grows up to 1 ft. tall, 18 to 24 in. wide. Pages: 60, 95, 103.

G. sanguineum var. striatum, Bloody cranesbill

A variable plant that can form a low mound or mat of small, very fine-cut leaves, topped with pale pink flowers in late spring or early summer. This plant is often sold under the name 'Lancastriense'. Stays under 1 ft. tall but can spread 2 ft. wide. Page: 104.

Geranium endressii 'Wargrave Pink'
GERANIUM

Geranium macrorrhizum
BIGROOT GERANIUM

Geranium sanguineum var. *striatum*
BLOODY CRANESBILL

Geranium

GERANIUM, CRANESBILL. Unlike the common geraniums that are grown as bedding plants and in pots, these are hardy perennials that form a compact or sprawling mound of attractive leaves with jagged edges and bloom in spring or early summer, with clusters of flowers in various shades of pink, purple, blue-purple, and white. Sun or partial shade, well-drained garden soil. Cut off flower stalks when the blossoms fade. If plants look tattered or get floppy in midsummer, cut them back partway and they will bush out again. Otherwise wait until late fall and cut them to the ground. See box at left for more information on specific kinds.

Hakonechloa macra 'Aureola'

GOLD-VARIEGATED HAKONECHLOA. A slow-growing grass that forms a clump of thin arching leaves with lengthwise green-and-yellow stripes. Needs partial shade and rich, moist, well-drained soil. Cut old leaves to the ground in early spring. Grows about 1 ft. tall, 2 to 3 ft. wide. Pages: 36, 78.

Hamamelis x intermedia 'Arnold Promise'

'ARNOLD PROMISE' WITCH HAZEL. A deciduous small tree or large shrub, often grown with multiple trunks. Clusters of small but very sweet-scented yellow flowers line the twigs in early spring and last for several weeks. Foliage turns gold in late fall. Prefers partial shade and moist, well-drained soil. Grows fairly slowly, so buy the biggest plant you can find to start with. Prune in early summer, if needed to control size. Eventually reaches 20 ft. tall and wide. Pages: 80, 110.

Hamamelis vernalis

VERNAL OR OZARK WITCH HAZEL. A vase-shaped deciduous shrub with tiny, sweet-scented, reddish or gold flowers in very early spring, weeks earlier than 'Arnold Promise'. Foliage turns gold in fall. Adapts to sun or shade and garden or moist soil. Prune in early summer. Grows up to 10 ft. tall and wide. Page: 32.

Hedera helix 'Glacier'

'GLACIER' ENGLISH IVY. **Even this slower-growing cultivar can escape cultivation and become problematic, especially in the milder southeastern part of the Mid-Atlantic region. Use all English Ivy cultivars with caution. Consider replacing it with climbing *Parthenocissus quinquefolia*, Virginia Creeper, or non-climbing *Pachysandra terminalis*, Japanese Spurge. An** evergreen vine that can creep along the ground or climb a fence or tree. 'Glacier' grows much more slowly than common English ivy and won't take over your garden. It has small leaves that are mottled with green, gray, and white. Prefers partial or full shade and moist, well-drained soil. Rarely climbs above 6 ft. Page: 106.

Helictotrichon sempervirens

BLUE OAT GRASS. A clump-forming grass with thin, wiry, pale blue, evergreen leaves. Blooms sparsely, with thin flower spikes that turn beige or tan. Needs full sun and well-drained or dry soil. Do not cut down in spring. Simply comb your fingers through the clump to pull out any loose, dead leaves. Old clumps may die out in the middle; if so, divide them in early spring. Grows 18 to 24 in. tall and wide. Pages: 31, 68, 104.

Helleborus

HELLEBORE. A clump-forming perennial with dark leathery leaves and round flowers that bloom for many weeks in both late winter and early spring. *H. foetidus*, stinking hellebore (p. 55), has clusters of pale green flowers about an inch wide in early spring. *H. niger*, Christmas rose (pp. 31, 82), has white flowers 3 to 4 in. wide that open some years as early as Christmas. *H. orientalis*, Lenten rose (pp. 28, 59, 60, 89, 106, 109), has pink, rosy, white, or greenish flowers 2 to 3 in. wide in early spring. All need partial shade and rich, well-drained soil. Hellebores are slow-growing, but they self-sow, gradually spreading to form a patch. Once established, all are carefree and long-lived. Groom once a year by cutting off any dead leaves when the flower buds appear. Established clumps are typically about 18 in. tall, 18 to 24 in. wide.

Hakonechloa macra 'Aureola'
GOLD-VARIEGATED HAKONECHLOA

Hamamelis vernalis
VERNAL WITCH HAZEL

Hedera helix 'Glacier'
ENGLISH IVY

Helictotrichon sempervirens
BLUE OAT GRASS

Helleborus foetidus
STINKING HELLEBORE

Helleborus orientalis
LENTEN ROSE

Hemerocallis
DAYLILY

Hemerocallis
DAYLILY

Hemerocallis 'Stella d'Oro'
DAYLILY

Hemerocallis

DAYLILY. Some of the most reliable and popular perennials, with large lilylike flowers in summer, held above dense clumps or patches of grassy arching leaves. The common roadside daylily has orange flowers for about two weeks in July, but cultivated kinds come in many other colors and bloom for a longer season. 'Happy Returns' (yellow flowers; pp. 66, 91, 93) and 'Stella d'Oro' (gold-orange flowers; pp. 35, 41) bloom from early June until October and are compact plants 18 to 24 in. tall. 'Gentle Shepherd' has large, nearly white flowers in midsummer on stalks 30 in. tall. 'Hyperion' (p. 60) has sweet-scented, pale yellow flowers in midsummer on stalks 40 in. tall. All prefer full sun and garden soil. Cut off flower stalks after blooming is finished. Divide every few years in late summer. When planting, space shorter daylilies about 1 ft. apart, taller kinds 2 ft. apart. Pages: 47, 60.

Heuchera micrantha 'Palace Purple'

'PALACE PURPLE' HEUCHERA. A clumping perennial with dark bronzy purple leaves, shaped like maple leaves with long stalks. It also forms sprays of tiny white flowers in summer. Looks best in partial shade, because the leaves tend to scorch or fade if exposed to too much sun. Prefers moist, well-drained soil. Cut old leaves to the ground in early spring. Divide every few years, and contrary to normal rules, replant the divisions 1 to 2 in. deeper than they were growing before. Grows about 1 ft. tall and wide. Pages: 36, 50, 78, 104.

Hosta

HOSTA. A long-lived, carefree, shade-tolerant perennial with beautiful leaves in a wide variety of colors and sizes. See box opposite for more information on specific hostas. Plants form dome-shaped clumps or spreading patches of foliage that look good from spring to fall and die down in winter. Lavender, purple, or white flowers appear on slender stalks in mid- to late summer. 'Royal Standard' hostas tolerate full sun, but others grow better in partial or full shade. All need fertile, moist, well-drained garden soil. Cut off flower stalks before seedpods ripen. Clumps can be divided in early spring if you want to make more plants; otherwise leave them alone.

Heuchera 'Palace Purple'
HEUCHERA

Recommended hostas

'Francee' hosta
Leaves are medium green, edged with a neat white stripe. Forms a leafy mound under 2 ft. tall, 2 to 3 ft. wide. Pages: 36, 80.

'Frances Williams' hosta
Large, round, puckered leaves are blue-green in the center with yellow around the edge. Forms a large specimen over 2 ft. tall, 3 to 6 ft. wide. Page: 106.

'Halcyon' hosta
Leaves are solid-colored powder blue in spring, darker blue-green in summer. Forms low mounds about 1 ft. tall and 2 ft. wide. Page: 50.

Hosta fortunei 'Aureo-marginata', Gold-edged hosta
Leaves are dark green, edged with gold. Forms a leafy mound under 2 ft. tall, 2 to 3 ft. wide. Page: 36.

H. sieboldiana 'Elegans'
Large, puckered leaves are blue-gray. Forms a large specimen 2 to 3 ft. tall, 4 to 6 ft. wide. Pages: 28, 89, 108.

'Krossa Regal' hosta
Leaves are medium blue-gray. Grows taller than most hostas. Forms vase-shaped clumps 3 ft. tall, 2 ft. wide, with flower stalks 5 to 6 ft. tall. Page: 36.

'Royal Standard' hosta
Leaves are medium green. Large white flowers have a sweet aroma. Forms a leafy mound under 2 ft. tall, about 3 ft. wide. Pages: 50, 59, 60, 71.

Hosta 'Francee'

Hosta 'Frances Williams'

Hosta 'Halcyon'

Hosta 'Aureo-marginata'

Hosta 'Krossa Regal'

Hosta 'Royal Standard'

Hydrangea macrophylla
GARDEN HYDRANGEA

Hydrangea quercifolia
OAKLEAF HYDRANGEA

Hydrangea petiolaris
CLIMBING HYDRANGEA

Hypericum 'Hidcote'

Hydrangea macrophylla

GARDEN HYDRANGEA. A medium-size deciduous shrub with large round leaves and very showy clusters of papery-textured blue, pink, or white flowers. 'Nikko Blue' is a popular cultivar with blue flowers. Adapts to full or partial sun. Needs fertile, moist, well-drained soil. Stalks grow one year, bloom the next year. Cut stalks that have bloomed to the ground in fall. Remove only damaged or frozen shoots in spring. May freeze to the ground in subzero weather. It will recover but won't bloom the following summer. Grows 4 to 6 ft. tall, spreads 5 to 8 ft. wide. Page: 50.

Hydrangea petiolaris

CLIMBING HYDRANGEA. A long-lived vine that has a thick trunk with peeling bark, large glossy leaves that open in early spring and don't drop until late fall, and lacy clusters of white flowers in early summer. Clings to a tree or wall and climbs by itself. Tolerates sun or shade; prefers moist, well-drained soil. Grows slowly for the first few years, then climbs several feet a year, eventually reaching 40 ft. or more. Needs no pruning, but you can cut it back if it goes too far. Pages: 50, 80, 106.

Hydrangea quercifolia

OAKLEAF HYDRANGEA. A deciduous shrub that forms a large clump of thick erect stems. Flowers open white in late spring and turn pink or beige in summer. Leaves turn maroon or crimson in fall. 'Snowflake' and 'Snow Queen' have especially large and showy flowers. Adapts to sun or shade, garden or dry soil. Prune in early spring, removing only weak, damaged, or frozen shoots. Grows up to 8 ft. tall, 6 ft. wide. Pages: 89, 95, 103, 110, 113.

Hypericum

HYPERICUM. A small shrub, usually treated like a perennial. Neat pairs of oval leaves line the arching stems. Golden flowers bloom throughout the summer. *H. calycinum* grows about 1 ft. tall and 2 ft. wide and has flowers 2 in. wide. 'Hidcote' is a larger plant, up to 3 ft. tall and wide, with flowers up to 3 in. wide. Adapts to most soils, in sun or partial shade. Prune close to the ground in early spring; it regrows quickly. Needs no other care. Pages: 55, 57.

Iberis sempervirens

EVERGREEN CANDYTUFT. A bushy perennial that forms a low or sprawling mound of slender, glossy evergreen foliage, topped for several weeks in spring with clusters of bright white flowers. 'Snowflake' is a popular cultivar with larger-than-average flowers. 'Autumn Beauty' blooms in spring and again in fall. Needs full or partial sun and does best in well-drained soil. Shear off the top half of the plants after they bloom. This will encourage fuller growth. Needs no other care. Don't try to divide it; buy new plants if you want more. Stays under 1 ft. tall, spreads 2 to 3 ft. wide. Pages: 44, 47, 49, 91, 104.

Iberis sempervirens
EVERGREEN CANDYTUFT

Recommended evergreen hollies

Ilex x *attenuata* 'Foster #2'
FOSTER HOLLY

Ilex crenata 'Steeds'
JAPANESE HOLLY

Ilex x *meserveae*
'Blue Prince'
HOLLY

Ilex x *attenuata* 'Foster #2', Foster holly

A slim, columnar or conical tree with narrow shiny leaves and lots of red berries. Grows up to 25 ft. tall, 10 to 15 ft. wide. Where temperatures fall much below zero, substitute an arborvitae (*Thuja occidentalis*), an evergreen conifer of similar size and shape. Pages: 22, 25, 57.

I. crenata, 'Steeds' Japanese holly

A compact, upright-growing shrub with small dark leaves and no berries. If it is unavailable, 'Chesapeake' is a good substitute. If unpruned, grows about 6 ft. tall, 3 ft. wide. Pages: 55, 57.

I. x *meserveae*, 'Blue Prince' holly

A pyramidal shrub with glossy, spiny, very dark blue-green leaves and stout purple-black twigs. 'Blue Stallion' is a good substitute. If

unpruned, grows up to 15 ft. tall and wide. Pages: 31, 32.

I. x *meserveae*, 'Blue Princess' holly

Resembles 'Blue Prince' (by which it is pollinated) but has heavy crops of bright red berries. 'Blue Maid' is a good substitute. If unpruned, grows up to 15 ft. tall and wide. Pages: 23, 28, 31.

'Nellie R. Stevens' holly

A conical tree or large shrub with medium green leaves and bright red berries. Fast-growing, reaching up to 25 ft. tall and 15 ft. wide. Not hardy where temperatures fall much below zero. In cold areas, substitute 'Jersey Princess' American holly (*I. opaca*). Pages: 99, 112.

Ilex opaca
'Nellie R. Stevens'
HOLLY

Ilex

EVERGREEN HOLLY. A versatile group of evergreen shrubs and trees used for foundation plantings, hedges, and specimens. The stiff-textured leaves can be small or large, smooth or spiny, dull or glossy. Holly plants are either male or female. If a suitable male is planted within a few hundred yards, females bear heavy crops of small round berries that ripen in fall and last through the next spring. See box on page 139 for more information on specific hollies. All tolerate sun or shade and need well-drained garden soil. Prune or shear at any season to keep them at the desired size.

Ilex verticillata

WINTERBERRY HOLLY. A deciduous shrub with many twiggy stems and soft spineless leaves. Female plants such as 'Sparkleberry' (pp. 84, 110), 'Sunset', and 'Winter Red' bear clusters of small, bright red berries that ripen in early fall and last all winter. To get berries, there has to be a male plant such as 'Apollo', 'Early Male', or 'Southern Gentleman' within 200 yd. Adapts to sun or shade, garden or damp soil. Rather slow-growing, so start with the largest, fullest plants you can find. Prune only to remove dead or damaged shoots. Eventually reaches 8 to 12 ft. high, depending on cultivar and site, and usually spreads wider than tall. Pages: 84, 99.

Iris sibirica

SIBERIAN IRIS. A perennial that forms an arching clump of tall slender leaves. Blooms for a few weeks in early summer. 'Caesar's Brother' (pp. 53, 84) has dark blue-purple flowers. 'White Swirl' (pp. 62, 103, 104) has white flowers. Other kinds are pale blue or yellow. Needs full or partial sun and moist, fertile, well-drained soil. Remove flower stalks after the blooms fade, or let the seedpods develop if you like their looks. Divide large clumps every few years in late summer. Grows 2 to 3 ft. tall.

Ilex verticillata 'Sparkleberry' WINTERBERRY HOLLY

Ilex verticillata WINTERBERRY HOLLY

Iris sibirica 'Caesar's Brother' SIBERIAN IRIS

Iris sibirica 'White Swirl' SIBERIAN IRIS

Jasminum nudiflorum
WINTER JASMINE

Juniperus chinensis var. *sargentii*
SARGENT JUNIPER

Juniperus sabina
'Tamariscifolia'
TAMARIX JUNIPER

Jasminum nudiflorum

WINTER JASMINE. A sprawling shrub with slender green twigs and pale yellow forsythia-like flowers in late winter and early spring. Small leaves may or may not drop off in winter. Needs full or partial sun and well-drained soil. Prune every year in early summer, cutting back long straggly stems. After several years, cut all the stems close to the ground to promote fresh new growth. Usually less than 4 ft. tall, it may spread up to 8 ft. wide if it is left unpruned. Page: 73.

Juniperus chinensis var. sargentii

SARGENT JUNIPER. A low evergreen shrub, usually grown as a ground cover, that forms a patch of short, upright stems. Foliage is fine-textured and needlelike. Regular Sargent juniper has dark green foliage. 'Glauca' has a blue-green color. Needs full sun, well-drained soil. Carefree. Grows 1 to 2 ft. tall, spreads to 3 ft. or more. Page: 111.

Juniperus sabina 'Tamariscifolia'

TAMARIX JUNIPER. Evergreen shrub that forms a low mound of fine-textured blue-green foliage. Spreads sideways, grows fast, and makes a good ground cover. Needs full sun, well-drained soil. Subject to disease in humid conditions but usually not sold in areas where disease is a serious problem. If unavailable, other creeping junipers are good substitutes. Grows 1 ft. tall, spreads to 4 ft. or more. Page: 39.

Juniperus squamata 'Blue Star'

'BLUE STAR' JUNIPER. A small, slow-growing evergreen shrub that makes an irregular mound of sparkling

Juniperus squamata 'Blue Star'
JUNIPER

Kalmia latifolia
MOUNTAIN LAUREL

blue, prickly-textured foliage. Needs full sun, well-drained soil. Reaches 1 to 2 ft. tall, 2 to 4 ft. wide after several years. Page: 68.

Kalmia latifolia

MOUNTAIN LAUREL. A native shrub with smooth evergreen leaves and very showy clusters of white, pale pink, or rosy flowers in late spring. Slow-growing at first but faster in subsequent years. Adapts to shade but blooms much more profusely in partial or full sun. Needs moist, well-drained soil. Snap off flower clusters after the petals drop. At the same time, do any pruning needed to direct the shape of the plant. Reaches 10 ft. tall and wide after many years. Pages: 99, 106, 112.

Lagerstroemia indica

CRAPE MYRTLE. A deciduous small tree or large shrub, usually grown with multiple trunks. Blooms for many weeks in the heat of summer, with large clusters of papery-textured pink, rose, or white flowers at the top of each stem. Leaves typically turn red, orange, or purplish in fall. Flaking trunk bark is attractive in winter. 'Hopi' (p. 66) has pink flowers and grows about 10 ft. tall. 'Natchez' (pp. 30, 86) has white flowers and can reach 20 to 25 ft. tall. Needs full sun and well-drained soil. Prune in spring, removing weak, broken, and frozen shoots. May freeze to the ground in subzero winters. If it does so, cut it down in spring and wait for it to grow back again.

Lamiastrum galeobdolon 'Hermann's Pride'

'HERMANN'S PRIDE' YELLOW ARCHANGEL. A short perennial that usually forms clumps but may spread into a patch. Grown mostly for its silver-and-green foliage but also has pretty yellow flowers in late spring. Prefers partial shade; adapts to garden or moist soil. Use hedge shears to cut it back halfway after it blooms. Cut it back again in late summer if it starts looking shabby. Divide every few years in spring or fall. Grows about 1 ft. tall and 1 to 2 ft. wide. Page: 109.

Lamium maculatum 'Beacon Silver'

'BEACON SILVER' LAMIUM. A creeping perennial that forms a low mat of foliage that is attractive from early spring until late fall. Heart-shaped leaves are silver with a thin green band around the edge. It is an excellent ground cover. Clusters of lilac-pink flowers bloom in early summer. 'White Nancy' has similar foliage but white flowers. Prefers partial shade and moist soil but does well in garden soil. Cut off flower stalks after it blooms. Divide every few years in spring or fall. Under 6 in. tall but spreads to 2 ft. or wider. Page: 106.

Lavandula angustifolia

ENGLISH LAVENDER. A small shrub, evergreen in mild climates. Freezes back partway and is treated more like a perennial where winters are cold. Forms a bushy mound of fragrant silver-gray foliage, topped in early summer with countless long-stalked spikes of very fragrant flowers. 'Hidcote' (pp. 91, 93) has dark purple flowers. 'Munstead' (pp. 57, 65) has pale lavender flowers. Needs full sun and well-drained soil. Shear off the tops of the

Lagerstroemia indica 'Natchez'
CRAPE MYRTLE

Lagerstroemia indica 'Hopi'
CRAPE MYRTLE

Lamiastrum galeobdolon 'Hermann's Pride'   YELLOW ARCHANGEL

Lamium maculatum 'Beacon Silver'   LAMIUM

Lavandula angustifolia 'Munstead'
ENGLISH LAVENDER

Liatris spicata 'Kobold'
BLAZING STAR

plants in midspring, removing any frozen stems. Shear flower stalks to the height of the foliage when the petals fade. If regularly sheared, grows about 1 to 2 ft. tall, 2 to 3 ft. wide.

Liatris spicata

BLAZING STAR. A perennial prairie wildflower that blooms in midsummer, with dense spikes of small flowers on tall stiff stalks, arising from a clump or tuft of grassy dark green foliage. The flowers attract butterflies. Needs full sun; adapts to most soils. 'Floristan White' has white flowers. 'Kobold' has purple flowers. Cut off the flower stalks after bloom. Needs no other care. Grows 2 to 3 ft. tall, 1 ft. wide. Pages: 91, 93.

Liriope muscari

LILYTURF. **Liriope muscari is emerging as a localized invasive species. Reduce invasive tendencies by trimming the flower stalks after flowering and before the berries ripen. Consider alternatives like *Carex flaccosperma* or *Iris cristata* before planting.** A perennial that forms clumps of grasslike evergreen leaves and bears spikes of small flowers in late summer. 'Big Blue' (blue flowers; pp. 23, 26, 31, 32, 55, 89, 91) and 'Majestic' (purple flowers; pp. 49, 60) have dark green foliage. 'Variegata' (pp. 26, 29, 50) has lilac flowers and leaves edged with narrow stripes that start out golden yellow and fade to creamy white. Prefers partial sun or shade, garden soil. Mow or shear off old foliage in early spring. Can be divided every few years to make more plants. Clumps grow 1 to 2 ft. tall and wide.

Liriope muscari 'Variegata' VARIEGATED LILYTURF

Liriope muscari 'Big Blue' LILYTURF

Lysimachia nummularia
MONEYWORT

Magnolia stellata
STAR MAGNOLIA

Lonicera x heckrottii
GOLDFLAME HONEYSUCKLE

Magnolia virginiana
SWEET BAY MAGNOLIA

Lonicera x heckrottii

GOLDFLAME HONEYSUCKLE. A woody vine that grows fast enough to make an impressive display in just a few years but is not aggressive and will not take over your garden. Leafs out in early spring, grows all summer, and doesn't freeze back until early winter. Blooms heavily in late spring and fall, off and on all summer, with clusters of pink-and-yellow flowers that smell sweet on warm nights. Needs full or partial sun, garden soil. Prune young plants hard, repeating two or three times the first year if needed to encourage lots of branching near the base. Prune older plants once a year in late winter, removing dead wood and trimming too-long stems. Climbs to 10 ft. or higher. Pages: 68, 95.

Lysimachia nummularia

MONEYWORT. A creeping, clinging perennial that forms a carpet of round green leaves. Cheerful yellow flowers last for a month or so in June and July. Tolerates full sun if the soil is moist but also does well in full shade. Grows especially well by water. Start with one and divide it later if you want more plants. Spreads up to 1 ft. per year. Pages: 103, 104.

Magnolia stellata

STAR MAGNOLIA. A deciduous small tree or shrub that's covered with fresh white flowers in early spring, before the leaves appear. Typically forms a dense, rounded or oval crown. Plant in spring, being careful not to break the roots, which are rather brittle. Plant in full or partial sun, garden soil. Needs little pruning, but you can remove weak or crossing limbs in early summer. Grows up to 20 ft. tall and wide. Pages: 55, 93.

Magnolia virginiana

SWEET BAY MAGNOLIA. A medium-size tree or large shrub with fragrant white flowers in early summer. Glossy leaves with silver bottoms look neat all summer and hang on until late fall or even throughout the winter. Plant in spring, being careful not to break the roots. Adapts to sun or shade, garden or damp soil. Prune in midsummer if needed, cutting back any new shoots that grow too long and lanky, to make a fatter, fuller plant. Grows 20 to 30 ft. tall, 10 to 20 ft. wide. Pages: 24, 57.

Malus sargentii

SARGENT CRAB APPLE. A deciduous shrub or small tree with fragrant white flowers in late spring and small, shiny red fruits in fall and winter. (Birds find the bitter-tasting fruits more palatable than humans do.) Forms a low, broad, twiggy crown. Needs full sun, garden soil. Prune when young to establish a single or multiple trunk and a framework of wide-spreading limbs. Older plants need little if any annual pruning. Grows 6 to 10 ft. tall, 10 to 15 ft. wide. Page: 68.

Malva alcea 'Fastigiata'

HOLLYHOCK MALLOW. A perennial that blooms abundantly in midsummer, with dozens of erect flower stalks bearing hundreds of clear pink, hollyhock-like flowers. In spring and fall, it's a low mound of medium green foliage. Needs full or partial sun, garden soil. Cut flower stalks to the ground after it blooms. Often self-sows but isn't weedy. Grows 3 to 4 ft. tall, 2 ft. wide. Page: 78.

Malus sargentii
SARGENT CRAB APPLE

Miscanthus

JAPANESE SILVER GRASS, MISCANTHUS. *Miscanthus sinense* is locally invasive in the Mid-Atlantic region. Remove flower stalks before seed set, or replace with a non-invasive ornamental grass, like *Panicum virgatum*, Switchgrass. or *Schizachyrium scoparium*, Little Bluestem. A showy grass that forms vase-shaped or rounded clumps of long arching leaves. Blooms in late summer or fall on stalks up to 6 ft. tall; fluffy seed heads last through the winter. 'Autumn Light' (p. 74) has green leaves ½ in. wide and blooms in September. 'Silverfeather' (p. 84) has similar leaves but starts blooming a few weeks earlier and has very silvery plumes. 'Morning Light' (pp. 26, 35) has silvery leaves ⅛ in. wide and blooms in October. 'Yaku Jima' (p. 103) looks like 'Morning Light' but is a smaller plant and blooms in August. All of these cultivars of *M. sinensis* are excellent plants, and if you can't find one, use another. *M. floridulus*, giant Chinese silver grass (p. 97), grows up to 8 ft. tall with leaves 1 to 2 in. wide and blooms in October. All miscanthus need full sun and garden soil. Cut old leaves and flower stalks close to the ground in late winter or early spring. Divide clumps in early spring every few years.

Monarda didyma

BEE BALM, MONARDA. A spreading perennial that forms a patch of erect stems topped with moplike clusters of bright-colored flowers that attract hummingbirds. Blooms for several weeks in midsummer. Common bee balm has scarlet flowers. 'Sunset' (p. 49) and 'Mahogany' have darker

Malva alcea 'Fastigiata'
HOLLYHOCK MALLOW

Miscanthus sinensis 'Morning Light'
JAPANESE SILVER GRASS

Monarda 'Marshall's Delight'
BEE BALM

red flowers. 'Marshall's Delight' (p. 84), a hybrid, has pink flowers. Sun or shade and fertile, moist, well-drained soil. Cut old stalks to the ground in fall. Divide every few years in early spring.

Myrica pensylvanica

BAYBERRY. A deciduous native shrub with an irregular, mounded profile. Spreads to form a patch. Fragrant leaves develop late in spring but are glossy green all summer, turn maroon or purple in fall, and last partway into the winter. Small, waxy, silver-gray berries form along the stems of female plants. Adapts to almost any soil, in sun or shade. Doesn't need pruning or regular care but can be pruned if you choose. Unpruned, it may grow 8 to 10 ft. tall and wide. Page: 36.

Myrica pensylvanica
BAYBERRY

Nandina domestica

HEAVENLY BAMBOO. **Heavenly bamboo is invasive and toxic to some wild birds. Choose a non-fruiting cultivar, like 'Sienna Sunrise' or 'Gulfstream'. Or replace with safer alternatives like** *Aralia spinosa*, **Devil's Walking Stick, or** *Itea virginica*, **Virginia Sweetspire.** An evergreen shrub that forms a clump of slender, erect stems. Fine-textured compound leaves change color with the seasons, from gold to green to red. Fluffy clusters of white flowers in summer are followed by red berries that last for months. Common nandina grows 4 to 6 ft. tall, 2 to 3 ft. wide. 'Moon Bay' (p. 113) is one of several new nonflowering dwarf forms, only 2 ft. tall and wide. Adapts to most soils, in sun or shade. Prune old, weak, or damaged stems off at ground level. May freeze back in severe winters. If so, cut off frozen stems in spring and it will recover. Pages: 28, 31, 57, 59, 60, 97.

Nandina domestica
'Gulfstream'
HEAVENLY BAMBOO

Nepeta x faassenii

CATMINT. A perennial that forms a bushy mound of soft gray foliage topped with clusters of small violet-blue flowers. Blooms most in early summer but continues or repeats throughout the season. Full sun, garden soil. Shear plants back halfway after the first blooming to keep them tidy and to promote new growth. Cut to the ground in late fall or winter. May self-sow. 'Dropmore' (pp. 42, 44, 65, 74, 86) grows about 2 ft. tall and wide; if it is unavailable, 'Blue Wonder' is a good substitute. 'Six Hills Giant' (p. 95) grows 3 ft. tall and wide.

Nymphaea

WATER LILY. The most popular plant for pools and ponds, available mostly from specialty nurseries. There are two main groups of water lilies. Hardy water lilies survive outdoors from year to year and bloom in midsummer. Tropical water lilies need warm water and bloom over a longer season from summer through fall. Because they freeze in the winter, tropical water lilies are usually treated like annuals and overwintered indoors or replaced each spring. Both kinds are available in dwarf-size plants, suitable for small pools, with fragrant or scentless flowers in shades of white, yellow, and pink. Tropicals such as the 'Dauben' water lily (p. 103), which is pale blue, also come in shades of blue and purple. All water lilies need full sun. Plant

Nepeta x faassenii 'Dropmore'
CATMINT

Nepeta x faassenii 'Six Hills Giant'
CATMINT

Nandina domestica 'Moon Bay'
HEAVENLY BAMBOO

Nymphaea 'Dauben'
WATER LILY

Nyssa sylvatica
BLACK GUM

the roots in a container of heavy, rich, garden soil, and set it in the pool so about 6 in. of water covers the soil. (See p. 173 for more on planting.)

Nyssa sylvatica

BLACK GUM. A large deciduous tree with neat, glossy leaves that turn bright crimson in fall. Also bears small fruits that attract birds. Plant in full sun, garden or damp soil. Needs only routine pruning to establish its shape when young. Mature trees reach 30 to 60 ft. tall, 20 to 30 ft. wide. Page: 99.

Ophiopogon planiscapus

BLACK MONDO GRASS. A small, slow-growing perennial with grassy evergreen foliage in an unusual shade of purple-black. Spreads gradually to form a patch. Prefers partial sun and moist, well-drained soil. Cut the leaves back partway in early spring to remove any damaged tips. Needs no other care. Under 1 ft. tall. Page: 29.

Pachysandra terminalis

PACHYSANDRA. A tough, adaptable ground cover with glossy evergreen leaves. Creeps slowly to form dense patches. Prefers partial or full shade, well-drained soil. Does well under and around trees and shrubs. Plant rooted cuttings in spring or fall, spaced four cuttings per square foot. Mulch between the plants, hand-weed for the first year or two, and you'll never have to tend it again. Grows about 8 in. tall. Page: 50.

Ophiopogon planiscapus
BLACK MONDO GRASS

Pachysandra terminalis
PACHYSANDRA

Paeonia 'Sarah Bernhardt'
PEONY

Pennisetum alopecuroides 'Hameln'
DWARF FOUNTAIN GRASS

Perovskia atriplicifolia
RUSSIAN SAGE

Paeonia

PEONY. A long-lived perennial that forms a bushy clump of many stems, with spectacular large, fragrant white, pink, or rosy flowers in late spring and dark glossy foliage that turns purple or gold before it dies down in fall. The kinds that have single flowers (p. 78) tend to stand up better. Double-flowered types such as 'Festiva Maxima' (white flowers; p. 65) and 'Sarah Bernhardt' (pink; pp. 53, 95) may need staking to support the heavy blossoms. Requires full sun and deep, well-drained, fertile soil. Plant in late summer, and position the thick rootstock so the pink buds are no more than 1 in. deep. (If the rootstocks are planted too deep, peonies may not bloom.) Established clumps are typically 2 to 3 ft. tall, 3 to 4 ft. wide.

Pennisetum alopecuroides 'Hameln'

DWARF FOUNTAIN GRASS. A grass that forms a hassocklike clump of arching leaves, green in summer and gold or tan in fall. Blooms over a long season from midsummer to fall, with fluffy spikes on arching stalks. Needs full sun, garden soil. Cut old leaves to the ground in late winter, or sooner if storms knock them down. Clumps can go many years without being divided. Grows 2 ft. tall, 3 ft. wide. Pages: 63, 76, 86, 97.

Perovskia atriplicifolia

RUSSIAN SAGE. A shrubby perennial that forms an open, vase-shaped clump of straight, fairly stiff stems with sparse silver-gray foliage and abundant lavender-blue flowers. Blooms for weeks in late summer. Needs full sun and well-drained soil. Cut old stems down to 6-in. stubs in spring. Grows 3 to 5 ft. tall and wide by fall. Pages: 41, 66, 74, 84, 95.

Philadelphus x *virginalis* 'Miniature Snowflake'

'MINIATURE SNOWFLAKE' MOCK ORANGE. A new compact form of a favorite old-fashioned shrub, with masses of very fragrant, double white flowers in late spring. Deciduous leaves are green in summer, with little fall color. Needs full or partial sun, well-drained soil. Prune after it blooms, only if needed to correct shape. Grows only 3 ft. tall and wide. Page: 53.

Phlox paniculata 'David'

'DAVID' GARDEN PHLOX. A perennial with clusters of fragrant white flowers in late summer. Forms a

Philadelphus x *virginalis* 'Miniature Snowflake'
MOCK ORANGE

Phlox paniculata 'David'
GARDEN PHLOX

Phlox stolonifera 'Bruce's White'
CREEPING PHLOX

clump or patch of erect stalks with healthy foliage that stays green all summer. Needs full or partial sun; rich, moist soil is best, but adapts to garden soil. Cut off flowers after they fade. Divide clumps every few years in spring. Grows 3 to 4 ft. tall, 2 to 3 ft. wide. Pages: 49, 65.

Phlox 'Rosalinde'

'ROSALINDE' MEADOW PHLOX. A perennial with big clusters of fragrant pink flowers in midsummer. Forms a clump or patch of erect stalks with healthy foliage that stays green all summer. Needs full or partial sun; rich, moist soil is best, but adapts to garden soil. Cut off flowers after they fade. Divide clumps every few years in spring. Grows 2 to 3 ft. tall, 2 ft. wide. Page: 63.

Phlox stolonifera 'Bruce's White'

'BRUCE'S WHITE' CREEPING PHLOX. A low perennial with creeping stems, small evergreen leaves, and clusters of fragrant white flowers in spring. Spreads fairly quickly to form a patch or ground cover. If it is unavailable, the blue-flowered 'Blue Ridge' is a good substitute. Needs partial or full shade and fertile, moist, well-drained soil. Grows only a few inches tall, but it can spread quickly, 1 to 2 ft. in a year. Page: 109.

Pieris japonica

JAPANESE ANDROMEDA. An evergreen shrub with neat, glossy foliage; beadlike flower buds that are conspicuous all winter; and drooping clusters of white or pink blooms in spring. Even young plants bloom abundantly. The new leaves that

Pieris 'Brouwer's Beauty'
JAPANESE ANDROMEDA

form in spring and early summer are often bright gold or red and contrast beautifully with the older green leaves. There are many fine cultivars. 'Mountain Fire' (p. 50) has bright red new growth. 'Spring Snow' (p. 32) bears lovely white flowers. 'Brouwer's Beauty', a hybrid (p. 73), has white flowers held in a horizontal position. All need partial shade, preferably afternoon shade, and rich, moist, well-drained soil. Slow-growing, so buy the biggest plants you can find. Be sure to slit and tease apart the roots of container-grown andromedas when you plant them. Prune in early summer, removing spent flowers and trimming any wayward shoots. Most cultivars eventually reach 4 to 8 ft. tall and wide; some get larger. Page: 112.

Pieris japonica 'Mountain Fire'
JAPANESE ANDROMEDA

Pinus mugo
MUGO PINE

Prunus laurocerasus 'Otto Luyken'
CHERRY LAUREL

Polygonum aubertii
SILVER FLEECE VINE

Pinus mugo

MUGO PINE. A slow-growing pine that forms an irregular shrubby mound, not a conical tree. Needles are dark green. Needs full sun and well-drained soil. Doesn't require pruning, but you can shear it in early summer if you want to, cutting new growth back by less than one-half. Typically grows just a few inches a year, but some plants are faster than others. Usually stays under 3 to 6 ft. tall and 5 to 10 ft. wide for many years. Page: 97.

Polygonum aubertii

SILVER FLEECE VINE. A carefree, fast-growing vine that quickly covers a fence or trellis. Blooms in midsummer, with sprays of small white flowers at the tip of each shoot. Adapts to most soils, in sun or partial shade. Cut old stems partway or all the way down to the ground in early spring. Can climb or spread 25 ft. or more. Page: 97.

Prunus laurocerasus 'Otto Luyken'

'OTTO LUYKEN' CHERRY LAUREL. An adaptable evergreen shrub, that is often used for foundation plantings. Glossy leathery leaves are dark green. Spikes of heavy-scented white flowers stick up like birthday candles in late spring. Adapts to sun or shade; prefers moist, well-drained soil but tolerates dry sites. Stays compact even if you don't prune it and looks fine if you leave it alone, but can be pruned at any time of year if you prefer a tidy, formal look. If unpruned, grows about 4 ft. tall, 6 to 8 ft. wide. Pages: 26, 31, 60, 106.

Rhododendron

RHODODENDRON, AZALEA. An especially diverse and popular group of shrubs with very showy flowers between early spring and early summer. The leaves can be small or large, deciduous or evergreen. The plants can be short, medium, or tall, with spreading, mounded, or erect habits. All rhododendrons and azaleas do best with partial shade, and they need fertile, moist, well-drained soil. Mix a 3-in. layer of peat moss into the soil when you prepare a bed for these plants.

Plant rhododendrons and azaleas in spring or early fall. Be sure not to plant them too deep—the top of the root ball should be level with, or a little higher than, the surrounding soil. Azaleas are usually sold in containers. When planting them it's very important that you make a few deep cuts down the root ball and tease apart some of the roots; otherwise azaleas typically do not root well into the surrounding soil. Treat container-grown rhododendrons the same way. Large rhododendron plants are often sold balled-and-burlapped; their roots were cut when the plants were dug and need no further attention. The roots will grow out through the burlap in time.

Recommended rhododendrons and azaleas

'Boule de Neige' rhododendron
Pure white flowers in late spring on a compact, rounded shrub about 5 ft. tall and wide. Large evergreen leaves. Pages: 71, 108.

'Nova Zembla' rhododendron
Dark red flowers in late spring on an upright shrub about 5 ft. tall and wide. Large evergreen leaves. Page: 28.

'PJM' rhododendron
Magenta flowers in very early spring on an upright shrub about 4 ft. tall and 3 ft. wide. Small evergreen leaves turn maroon in winter. Pages: 32, 110.

'Roseum Elegans' rhododendron
Pink or pinkish purple flowers in late spring on an upright shrub about 6 ft. tall and wide. Large evergreen leaves. Page: 112.

Deciduous azaleas
Masses of flowers on erect shrubs, usually 4 to 8 ft. tall, with leaves that turn bright colors before dropping in fall. There are scores of excellent cultivars with rose, pink, white, yellow, or two-tone flowers, often sweet-scented. The bloom season ranges from April to July; individual plants bloom for about two weeks. 'Gold Dust' (p. 110), 'Golden Lights', and 'My Mary' (p. 108) all have lovely fragrant yellow flowers. Ask your nursery for advice if you'd like a different color.

Evergreen azaleas
Masses of flowers in mid- to late spring on compact shrubs, usually 2 to 4 ft. tall, with small evergreen leaves. Can be sheared to produce a neat massed effect. Unsheared, they form irregular billowing mounds. 'Nancy of Robin Hill' and 'Pink Gumpo' are outstanding varieties with pink flowers. Pages: 28, 111, 113. 'Aiokoku', 'Gumpo White', and 'Helen Curtis' are some of the best white-flowered azaleas. Pages: 25, 30, 32, 50, 53, 82.

Rhododendron 'Boule de Neige' (left); assorted azaleas (right)

Rhododendron 'PJM'

Rhododendron 'Roseum Elegans'

'Pink Gumpo' EVERGREEN AZALEA (left); WHITE EVERGREEN AZALEA (right)

Recommended roses

Rosa 'Angel Face'

Rosa 'Betty Prior'

'Angel Face' rose

A bushy shrub about 3 ft. tall with fragrant lilac-colored blossoms throughout the summer. Flowers are about 3 in. wide, double, in small clusters. Page: 95.

'Betty Prior' rose

A broad, open shrub 4 to 6 ft. tall with spicy-scented single flowers from late spring until late fall. Flowers are dark pink in cool weather, fading in the heat of summer. Page: 68.

'Bonica' rose

A broad bush up to 5 ft. tall and wide with clusters of small double pink flowers all summer. Flowers are scentless. Page: 82.

'Carefree Beauty' shrub rose

A rounded shrub about 3 to 4 ft. tall and wide with mildly fragrant, coral-pink double flowers all summer and into the fall. Page: 76.

'Golden Showers' rose

A "climbing" rose with long canes that can be tied to a fence, trellis, or arbor. Grows 8 to 10 ft. tall. Blooms all summer, with large, fragrant, double golden yellow flowers. Pages: 49, 66.

'The Fairy' rose

A low, spreading shrub with small shiny leaves and masses of small, scentless, light pink flowers from early summer until hard frost. Page: 65.

Rosa 'Golden Showers'

Rosa 'Bonica'

Rosa 'The Fairy'

(*Rhododendron*, Con't.)

Use a layer of mulch to keep the soil cool and damp around your azaleas and rhododendrons, and water the plants during any dry spell for the first few years. If the site is exposed to winter sun and wind, protect evergreen azaleas and rhododendrons for the first few winters by spraying the leaves with an antitranspirant such as Wilt-Pruf™ in late fall or by erecting a burlap cage or plywood A-frame around the plants. Plants on sheltered sites and plants that have had a few years to get established do not need winter protection. Prune or shear off the flower stalks as soon as the petals fade to prevent seeds from forming and to neaten the plants. Prune or shear to control the size and shape of the plant at the same time (usually in early summer). See box on page 151 for more information on specific varieties.

Rosa

ROSE. Fast-growing deciduous shrubs with glossy compound leaves, thorny stems or canes, and very showy, often fragrant flowers. For descriptions of specific roses see box on the facing page. In the spring, many garden centers stock bare-root roses, with the roots wrapped in a plastic bag and packed in a cardboard box. These are a good investment if you buy them right after they arrive in the stores and plant them promptly, but their quality deteriorates with every day in the box. Nurseries may sell bare-root roses in the spring, but they usually grow the plants in containers. If you buy a potted rose, you can plant it anytime from spring to fall.

All roses grow best in full sun and fertile, well-drained soil topped with a few inches of mulch. Once established, the roses recommended in this book require no more care than many other shrubs. Prune them once a year in spring before new growth starts. Remove any extremely skinny or weak stems, plus a few of the oldest stems (you can tell by looking at their bark, which is tan or gray instead of green), by cutting them off at the ground. Cut back remaining stems to a healthy bud. Throughout the summer, cut off flower clusters as the petals drop, cutting back to a healthy leaf.

These roses have good resistance to various fungal diseases, but may have problems some years when the weather is especially sultry. To control fungus, mix ¼ cup baking soda plus a few drops of salad oil in 1 gal. of water and spray the rose foliage until it's dripping wet. Repeat every 10 days.

Aphids—soft-bodied insects the size of a pinhead—may attack the new growth on roses but do no serious damage. You can wash them away with plain or soapy water. Japanese beetles are a major problem in some areas, and unfortunately there isn't much you can do but go out every morning and knock them into a pail of hot soapy water, where they drown. Other beetle-control methods such as traps and sprays all have significant drawbacks. Swarms of beetles eat rosebuds, blossoms, and foliage in July and August but are fairly uncommon in June or from September onward, so early and late blossoms may be untouched.

Rudbeckia fulgida 'Goldsturm'

'GOLDSTURM' CONEFLOWER. An improved form of a popular perennial wildflower, bearing hundreds of cheerful black-eyed Susan flowers for several weeks in late summer. Forms a robust clump, with large dark green leaves at the base and stiff, erect, branching flower stalks. Adapts to most soils but needs full or partial sun. Cut down the flower stalks in fall or spring, as you choose. Divide every few years in early spring. Grows 2 to 3 ft. tall and wide. Page: 41.

Rudbeckia fulgida 'Goldsturm'
CONEFLOWER

Salvia x *superba* 'East Friesland'
SALVIA

Salvia x *superba* 'May Night'
SALVIA

Santolina chamaecyparissus
GRAY SANTOLINA

Salvia x superba

SALVIA. A long-blooming perennial that forms a patch of dark green foliage topped with countless flower spikes. 'East Friesland' (pp. 26, 76) has reddish purple flowers. 'May Night' (pp. 35, 63) has dark indigo-purple flowers. Both start blooming in May and continue off and on through summer and fall. Prefers full sun and well-drained soil. Shear or trim off the old flower stalks from time to time to keep the plant blooming. Divide every few years in spring or fall. Grows 18 to 24 in. tall, spreads 2 ft. wide.

Santolina chamaecyparissus

GRAY SANTOLINA. A bushy little shrub with soft, fragrant, fine-textured, silver-gray foliage. Often sheared to make an edging or a formal specimen. If unsheared, it bears round yellow blossoms in midsummer. Needs full sun and well-drained soil. Prune every year in early spring, before new growth starts, cutting the old stems back halfway to the ground. Leaves may rot in hot humid weather; if that happens, cut the plant back or pull it out and replace it with a new plant. Grows 1 to 2 ft. tall, 2 to 3 ft. wide. Page: 91.

Scabiosa columbaria 'Butterfly Blue'

'BUTTERFLY BLUE' PINCUSHION FLOWER. A compact perennial that forms a neat clump of bright green foliage and blooms all season from May until hard frost. The round, sky blue flowers attract butterflies, and make good cut flowers, too. Needs full sun and well-drained soil. Keep picking off the old flowers

Scabiosa columbaria 'Butterfly Blue'
PINCUSHION FLOWER

as they fade. Divide every few years in early spring. Grows about 1 ft. tall and wide. Pages: 74, 84, 86

Sedum 'Autumn Joy'

'AUTUMN JOY' SEDUM. A perennial that forms a vase-shaped clump of thick stems lined with large, fleshy, gray-green leaves. Broad flat clusters of buds form at the top of each stem in late summer and gradually change from creamy white to pink to rust as the flowers open and mature. Needs full sun and garden soil. Cut stems back partway in early summer to keep them from flopping over and to make the clump bushier. In late fall or spring, cut old stems to the ground. Divide clump every few years in early spring. Grows about 2 ft. tall and 2 to 3 ft. wide. Pages: 26, 47, 63, 86.

Sedum 'Vera Jameson'

'VERA JAMESON' SEDUM. A perennial that forms a low mound with many stems. The chubby rounded leaves are an unusual dusty purple color. Clusters of rosy pink flowers top each stem in August. Needs full or partial sun and garden soil. Cut old stems down in fall or spring, as you choose. Divide clumps every few years in spring. Grows about 1 ft. tall and wide. Pages: 42, 53, 74, 76.

Spiraea

SPIREA. **Spiraea japonica is a known invasive species in parts of the Mid-Atlantic region. Plant a non-invasive cultivar like 'Crispa', 'Dart's Red', or 'Neon Flash', otherwise be sure to remove spent flowers before seeds develop. Better still, choose non-invasive alternatives like Physocarpus opulifolius, Ceanothus americanus, or Fothergilla gardenii.** A small to medium-size deciduous shrub with a neat rounded habit, fine-textured foliage, and round clusters of pretty pink or white flowers. *S.* x *bumalda* 'Anthony Waterer' (pp. 39, 41) grows about 2 ft. tall and 3 ft. wide, with dark pink flowers for several weeks in July and early August. *S. japonica* 'Little Princess' (pp. 43, 71, 82) grows about 3 ft. tall and 2 ft. wide, with medium-pink flowers in June and July. *S. nipponica* 'Snowmound' (p. 76) grows about 4 ft. tall and wide, with clear white flowers in May. Spireas thrive in garden soil with full or partial sun. Shear off the tops of the stems after the flowers fade. After several years, spireas often get uneven or straggly-looking. When that happens, cut the bush to the ground in early spring and it will grow back good as new.

Sedum 'Autumn Joy'

Sedum 'Vera Jameson'

Spiraea japonica 'Crispa'
JAPANESE SPIREA

Spiraea japonica 'Neon Flash'
JAPANESE SPIREA

Spiraea japonica 'Dart's Red'
JAPANESE SPIREA

Stachys byzantina
'Helene von Stein'
LAMB'S EARS

Thuja occidentalis
'Emerald'
AMERICAN ARBORVITAE

Stewartia pseudocamellia
JAPANESE STEWARTIA

SYRINGA PATULA 'Miss Kim'
LILAC

Stachys byzantina

LAMB'S EARS. A mat-forming perennial whose large oval leaves are densely covered with soft white fuzz. Typically the leaves are 3 to 4 in. long, and the plant spreads about 18 in. wide. 'Helene von Stein' (sometimes called 'Big Ears'; pp. 26, 97) is a special cultivar with leaves 6 to 8 in. long; it spreads about 3 ft. wide. Blooms in early summer, with small purple flowers on thick stalks about 1 ft. tall. Needs full or partial sun and garden soil. Cut off the bloom stalks when the flowers fade, or as soon as they appear if you don't like their looks. Use a soft rake to clean away the old leaves in early spring. Divide clumps every few years. Page: 47.

Stewartia pseudocamellia

JAPANESE STEWARTIA. A medium-size deciduous tree with white flowers in midsummer, colorful fall foliage, and flaking bark that's conspicuous in winter. Prefers fertile, moist, well-drained soil and partial or full sun. Buy a container-grown tree and plant it in spring so it has a full season to get established. Usually sold in small sizes, which transplant best. It grows quickly and may bloom the first year. Prune and train it carefully, making sure the main trunks and limbs diverge at wide angles. Once established, Japanese stewartia needs little pruning and no routine care. Grows 30 to 40 ft. tall, about 20 ft. wide. Pages: 82, 83.

Syringa patula 'Miss Kim'

'MISS KIM' LILAC. A better-than-average lilac, with graceful clusters of wonderfully fragrant lilac-blue flowers in May plus a compact habit and disease-resistant leaves that turn purple before dropping in fall. Needs full sun for maximum bloom and prefers garden soil. After the flowers drop, prune off the clusters of developing seedpods and cut back any too-long limbs. Needs little other pruning. If it gets straggly after several years, cut the whole bush to the ground in early summer to renew it. Grows about 5 ft. tall and wide. Pages: 65, 95.

Taxus

YEW. Evergreen shrubs and trees with flat sprays of dark green, needlelike foliage. Yews tolerate repeated pruning and are often sheared into formal or geometric shapes and used for specimens, hedges, and foundation plantings. Some kinds are naturally compact and don't need to be sheared. Female yews produce red berries, which are attractive but poisonous. Yews adapt to full sun, partial sun, or shade but must have well-drained soil. They are sold in containers or balled-and-burlapped. Large plants are readily available and transplant well, if you want fast results. To maintain a formal look, shear back the new growth in early summer, before it has hardened. For a natural look, prune individual branches as needed to maintain the desired shape. See box on the facing page for information on particular yews.

Thuja occidentalis 'Emerald'

'EMERALD' AMERICAN ARBORVITAE. A slender evergreen shrub with glossy green, scalelike foliage that releases a pleasant aroma when touched. Keeps its color all winter. Needs full or partial sun, garden or moist but well-drained soil. Plant in spring or fall. Fairly slow-growing, so buy the biggest plant you can find. Needs no routine care. Eventually grows about 15 ft. tall, 6 ft. wide. Page: 95.

Tiarella cordifolia
FOAMFLOWER

Tiarella cordifolia

FOAMFLOWER. A perennial woodland wildflower that spreads quickly to form a dense low patch of evergreen foliage, covered with spikes of dainty white flowers in late spring. Prefers partial shade and moist, well-drained soil. Divide every few years in spring or fall if you want to make more plants or if the patch has gotten crowded and stopped flowering. Grows about 8 in. tall, at least 2 ft. wide. Pages: 32, 80, 82.

Veronica

VERONICA, SPEEDWELL. Perennials that bloom all summer, bearing many slender spikes crowded with tiny flowers above a basal mat of glossy green leaves. 'Goodness Grows' (p. 74) has light lavender-blue flowers and grows 1 ft. tall. 'Sunny Border Blue' (pp. 63, 74, 84, 86) has dark blue-purple flowers and grows 2 ft. tall. They do best with afternoon shade and garden soil. Keep cutting off the old flower stalks. Divide every few years in early spring.

Veronica 'Sunny Border Blue'

Recommended yews

Taxus baccata 'Repandens', Spreading English yew

A low-growing, wide-spreading yew with unusually large needles that stay dark green all year. Grows about 2 ft. tall, 6 to 8 ft. wide after many years. Pages: 41, 113.

T. cuspidata 'Nana', Dwarf Japanese yew

A compact yew, wider than tall, with bright green needles all year. Slow-growing. Reaches 3 to 4 ft. tall, 4 to 5 ft. wide after several years. If unavailable, substitute 'Densiformis' hybrid yew. Page: 23.

T. x *media* 'Densiformis', 'Densiformis' hybrid yew

A fast-growing but compact yew that reaches about 3 to 4 ft. tall, 4 to 6 ft. wide. Foliage looks bunchy and more irregular, less neat than that of some yews. Although dark green in summer, it turns bronzy in cold weather. Page: 24.

T. x *media* 'Hatfield', 'Hatfield' hybrid yew

An upright yew that forms a broad pyramid or cone, reaching 10 to 12 ft. tall and wide. Slow-growing. Foliage stays green all year. Pages: 22, 24.

T. x *media* 'Hicksii', 'Hicksii' hybrid yew

A narrow, upright-growing yew with many leaders. Fast-growing and good for hedges 4 to 8 ft. tall. (Grows up to 20 ft. if unpruned.) Stays green all year. Page: 55.

Taxus baccata 'Repandens'
SPREADING ENGLISH YEW

Taxus cuspidata 'Nana'
DWARF JAPANESE YEW

Taxus x *media* 'Densiformis'
HYBRID YEW

Taxus x *media* 'Hicksii'
HYBRID YEW

Viburnum carlesii
KOREAN SPICE VIBURNUM

Viburnum carlesii

KOREAN SPICE VIBURNUM. A deciduous shrub with stiff twigs and a dense habit. Clusters of pretty pink buds open into spicy-scented white flowers in May. Leaves are plain green all summer and fall. Blooms best in full sun and moist, well-drained soil. Fairly slow-growing, so start with the biggest one you can buy. Prune in early summer, right after it blooms, to shape a neat sphere. Grows 6 ft. tall and wide. Pages: 26, 88, 106.

Viburnum opulus

EUROPEAN CRANBERRY BUSH. A large deciduous shrub with upright growth, maplelike leaves that turn reddish in fall, lacy clusters of white flowers in May, and bright red berries that last from late summer into the winter. Prefers full sun and fertile, moist, well-drained soil. Grows fairly quickly, reaching up to 12 ft. tall and wide. Prune in early spring, cutting old, crooked, or damaged stems to the ground. If aphids attack the new growth, wash them off with a spray of soapy water. Page: 99.

Viburnum opulus
EUROPEAN CRANBERRY BUSH

Viburnum plicatum var. *tomentosum* 'Shasta'
DOUBLE-FILE VIBURNUM

Viburnum plicatum var. tomentosum 'Shasta'

'SHASTA' DOUBLE-FILE VIBURNUM. A deciduous shrub with wide-spreading limbs lined with large white flowers in late spring, dark berries in summer, and crinkled green leaves that turn purplish in fall. Prefers partial shade and moist soil. Grows rather slowly, reaching 6 ft. tall and 10 to 12 ft. wide. Needs little if any pruning. Page: 110.

Viburnum x pragense

PRAGUE VIBURNUM. A large upright or vase-shaped shrub with small glossy evergreen leaves, white flowers in spring, and dark red-black berries in summer. Grows fairly quickly and adapts to sun or partial shade, garden or moist soil. Needs little pruning—just remove weak, dead, or damaged stems in early spring. Grows up to 10 ft. tall and wide. Pages: 108, 112.

Vinca minor

PERIWINKLE. **Vinca minor is a known invasive plant in parts of the Mid-Atlantic region. Better to plant a non-invasive ground cover like *Mitchella repens* (Partridge Berry), *Antennaria plantaginifolia* (Pussytoes), or *Phlox divaricata* (Wild Sweet William).** An evergreen ground cover with small, glossy, leathery, dark green leaves. Gradually forms a thick mass of foliage about 6 in. tall. Blooms in late spring, with round lilac flowers. Adapts to most soils, in partial sun or shade. Once established, needs absolutely no care. Pages: 57, 109.

Viola odorata

SWEET VIOLET. A low-growing perennial that spreads by seeds and runners to make a patch or ground cover. Dark green, heart-shaped leaves are evergreen in mild winters. Blooms in late fall and again in early spring, with wonderfully fragrant purple flowers that perfume the whole garden. Adapts to most soils, in sun or shade. Invasive, but too short (under 4 in.) to be much of a threat. Pull up runners and seedlings that stray into a path or lawn. Page: 93.

Water plants

Most big garden centers have a small collection of water plants. Mail-order water-garden specialists offer several dozen kinds. Most water plants are fast-growing, even weedy, so you need only one of each kind to start with. The plants

Phlox divaricata
WILD SWEET WILLIAM

Viola odorata
SWEET VIOLET

Yucca filamentosa

named here are all tender to frost, but you can overwinter them indoors in a pot or aquarium. There are three main groups of water plants: marginal, floating, and oxygenating. Choose one or more of each for an interesting and balanced effect. Marginal, or emergent, plants grow well in containers covered with 2 in. or more of water; their leaves and flower stalks stick up into the air. For example, dwarf papyrus (*Cyperus haspan*) is a popular marginal with leaves that branch out like umbrella spokes; it grows 18 in. tall. Floating plants have leaves that rest on the water and roots that dangle down into it. Water lettuce (*Pistia stratiotes*) is a floater that forms saucer-size rosettes of iridescent pale green leaves. Oxygenating, or submerged, plants grow underwater; they help keep the water clear and provide oxygen, food, and shelter for fish. Anacharis (*Elodea canadensis*) is a popular oxygenator with tiny, dark green leaves. (For water lilies, see *Nymphaea*.) Pages: 103, 104.

Weigela florida 'Minuet'

'MINUET' WEIGELA. A small deciduous shrub with unusual purple-green foliage and clusters of purple-red flowers in early summer. Needs full or partial sun (foliage turns green without enough sun) and garden soil. Prune by cutting back the ends of the stems after it blooms and by cutting some of the older stems (they have rougher-textured bark) to the ground in early spring. Grows quickly but doesn't exceed 3 ft. tall and wide. Page: 53.

Yucca filamentosa

YUCCA. An unusual shrub with daggerlike leaves, 2 ft. long, that stick out in all directions from a short thick trunk. Leaves are evergreen but get droopy in cold weather. Blooms in June, with bunches of large white flowers on stiff stalks 4 to 6 ft. tall. The woody seedpods are decorative, too. Needs full or partial sun, garden soil. Cut down the old flower stalks whenever you choose, and peel dead leaves from around the base of the plant in spring. Once established, it lives for decades and can't be moved, but you can dig up the baby plants that form around the base and transplant them. Page: 74.

Guide *to* Installation

In this section, we introduce the hard but rewarding work of landscaping. Here you'll find information on all the tasks you need to install any of the designs in this book, organized in the order in which you'd most likely tackle them. Clearly written text and numerous illustrations help you learn how to plan the job; clear the site; construct paths, patios, ponds, fences, arbors, and trellises; prepare the planting beds; and install and maintain the plantings. Roll up your sleeves and dig in. In just a few weekends, you can create a landscape feature that will provide years of enjoyment.

Organizing Your Project

If your gardening experience is limited to mowing the lawn, pruning the bushes, and growing some flowers and vegetables, the thought of starting from scratch and installing a whole new landscape feature might be intimidating. But in fact, adding one of the designs in this book to your property is completely within reach, if you approach it the right way. The key is to divide the project into a series of steps and take them one at a time. This is how professional landscapers work. It's efficient and orderly, and it makes even big jobs seem manageable.

On this and the facing page, we'll explain how to think your way through a landscaping project and anticipate the various steps. Subsequent topics in this section describe how to do each part of the job. Detailed instructions and illustrations cover all the techniques you'll need to install any design from start to finish.

The step-by-step approach
Choose a design and adapt it to your site. The designs in this book address parts of the home landscape. In the most attractive and effective home landscapes, all the various parts work together. Don't be afraid to change the shape of beds; alter the number, kinds, and positions of plants; or revise paths and structures to bring them into harmony with their surroundings.

To see the relationships with your existing landscape, you can draw the design on a scaled plan of your property. Or you can work on the site itself, placing wooden stakes, pots, tricycles, or whatever is handy to represent plants and structures. With a little imagination, either method will allow you to visualize basic relationships.

Lay out the design on site. Once you've decided what you want to do, you'll need to lay out the paths and structures and outline the beds. Some people are comfortable laying out a design "freehand," pacing off distances and relying on their eye to judge sizes and relative positions. Others prefer to transfer the grid from the plan full size onto the site in order to place elements precisely. (Garden lime, a grainy white powder available at nurseries, can be used like chalk on a blackboard to "draw" a grid or outlines of planting beds.)

Clear the site. (See pp. 164–165.) Sometimes you have to work around existing features—a nice big tree, a building or fence, a sidewalk—but it's

DIGGING POSTHOLES

AMENDING SOIL

usually easiest to start a new landscaping project if you clear as much as possible, down to ground level. That means removing unwanted structures or pavement and killing, cutting down, or uprooting all the plants. Needless to say, this can generate a lot of debris, and you'll need to figure out how to dispose of it all. Still, it's often worth the trouble to make a fresh start.

Build the "hardscape." (See pp. 166-195.) "Hardscape" means anything you build as part of a landscape—a fence, trellis, arbor, retaining wall, walkway, edging, outdoor lighting, or whatever. If you're going to do any building, do it first, and finish the construction before you start any planting. That way you won't have to worry about stepping on any of the plants, and they won't be in the way as you work.

Prepare the soil. (See pp. 196-197.) On most properties, it's uncommon to find soil that's as good as it should be for growing plants. Typically, the soil around a house is shallow, compacted, and infertile. It may be rocky or contain buried debris. Some plants tolerate such poor conditions, but they don't thrive. To grow healthy, attractive plants, you need to improve the quality of the soil throughout the entire area that you're planning to plant.

Do the planting and add mulch. (See pp. 200-205.) Putting plants in the ground usually goes quite quickly and gives instant gratification. Spreading mulch over the soil makes the area look neat and "finished" even while the plants are still small.

Maintain the planting. (See pp. 205-217.) Most plantings need regular watering and occasional weeding for the first year or two. After that, depending on the design you've chosen, you'll have to do some routine maintenance—pruning, shaping, cutting back, and cleaning up— to keep the plants looking their best. This may take as little as a few hours a year or as much as an hour or two every week throughout the growing season.

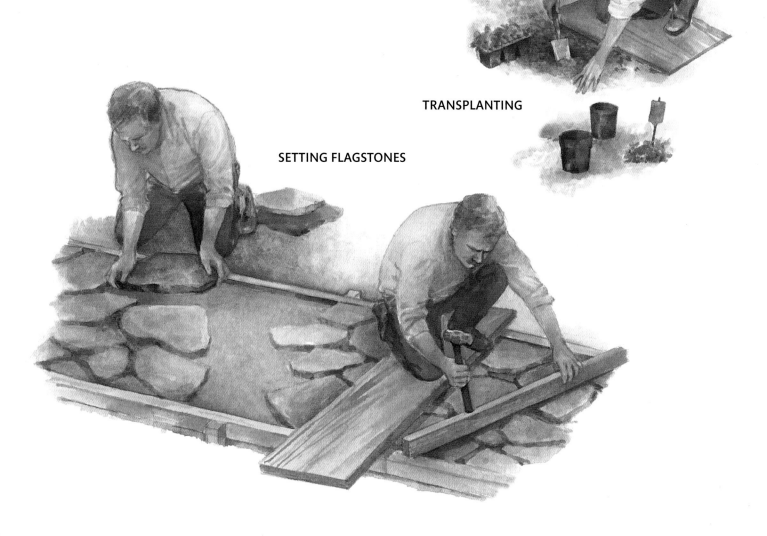

TRANSPLANTING

SETTING FLAGSTONES

Clearing the Site

The site you've chosen for a landscaping project may or may not have any man-made objects (fences, old pavement, trash, etc.) to be removed, but it will almost certainly be covered with plants.

Before you start cutting plants down, try to find someone—a friend or neighbor who enjoys gardening—to identify these plants for you. As you walk around together, make a sketch that shows which plants are where, and attach labels to the plants, too. Determine if there are any desirable plants worth saving—mature shade trees that you should work around, shapely shrubs that aren't too big to dig up and relocate or give away, worthwhile perennials and ground covers that you could divide and replant, healthy sod that you could lay elsewhere. Likewise, decide which plants have to go—diseased or crooked trees, straggly or overgrown shrubs, weedy brush, invasive ground covers, tattered lawn.

You can clear small areas yourself, bundling the brush for pickup and tossing soft-stemmed plants on the compost pile, but if you have lots of woody brush or any trees to remove, you might want to hire someone else to do the job. A crew armed with power tools can turn a thicket into a pile of wood chips in just a few hours. Have them pull out the roots and grind the stumps, too. Save the chips; they're good for surfacing paths or you can use them as mulch.

Working around a tree

If there are any large, healthy trees on your site, be careful as you work around them. It's okay to prune off some of a tree's limbs, as shown on the facing page, but respect its trunk and its roots. Never cut or wound the bark on the trunk (don't nail things to a tree), as that exposes the tree to disease organisms. Don't pile soil or mulch against the trunk, since that keeps the bark wet and can make it rot.

Killing perennial weeds

Some common weeds that sprout back from perennial roots or runners are bedstraw, bindweed, blackberry and other briers, ground ivy, poison ivy, quack grass, and sorrel. Garden plants that can become weedy include ajuga, akebia, bamboo, bishop's weed, English ivy, Japanese honeysuckle, Japanese knotweed, lily-of-the-valley, loosestrife, sundrops, and tansy. Once they get established, perennial weeds are hard to eliminate. You can't just cut off the tops, because they keep sprouting back. You have to dig the weeds out, smother them with mulch, or kill them with an herbicide, and it's better to do this before rather than after you plant a bed.

Smothering weeds

This technique is easier than digging, particularly for eradicating large infestations, but much slower. First mow or cut the tops of the weeds as close to the ground as possible ❶. Then cover the area with sections from the newspaper, overlapped like shingles ❷, or flattened-out cardboard boxes and top with a layer of mulch, such as straw, grass clippings, tree leaves, wood chips, or other organic material spread several inches deep ❸.

Smothering works by excluding light, which stops photosynthesis. If any shoots reach up through the covering and produce green leaves, pull them out immediately. Wait a few months, until you're sure the weeds are dead, before you dig into the smothered area and plant there.

SMOTHERING WEEDS

❶ **Smothering kills weeds by depriving them of light. Cut the tops off close to the ground.**

❷ **Cover with thick newspaper or cardboard.**

❸ **Top with several inches of mulch. Wait a few months to be sure weeds are dead, then till rotted newspaper and mulch into the soil.**

Digging. In many cases, you can do a pretty good job of removing a perennial weed if you dig carefully where the stems enter the ground, find the roots, and follow them as far as possible through the soil, pulling out every bit of root that you find. Some plant roots go deeper than you can dig, and most plants will sprout back from the small bits that you miss, but these leftover sprouts are easy to pull.

Spraying. Herbicides are easy, fast, and effective weed killers when chosen and applied with care. Look for those that break down quickly into more benign substances, and make sure the weed you're trying to kill is listed on the product label. Apply all herbicides exactly as directed by the manufacturer. After spraying, you usually have to wait from one to four weeks for the weed to die completely, and some weeds need to be sprayed a second or third time before they give up. Some weeds just "melt away" when they die, but if there are tough or woody stems and roots, you'll need to dig them up and discard them.

Replacing turf

If the area where you're planning to add a landscape feature is currently part of the lawn, you have a fairly easy task ahead. How to proceed depends on the condition of the turf and on what you want to put in its place. If the turf is healthy, you can "recycle" it to replace, repair, or extend the lawn elsewhere.

The drawing below shows a technique for removing relatively small areas of strong healthy turf for replanting. First, with a sharp shovel, cut it into squares or strips about 1 to 3 ft. square (these small pieces are easy to lift) ❶. Then slice a few inches deep under each square and lift the squares, roots and all, like brownies from a pan ❷. Quickly transplant the squares to a previously prepared site; water them well until the roots are established.

If you don't need the turf, or if it's straggly or weedy, leave it in place and kill the grass. Spraying with an herbicide kills most grasses within one to two weeks. Or cover it with a tarp or a sheet of black plastic for two to four weeks during the heat of summer (it takes longer in cool weather). Then dig or till the bed, shredding the turf, roots and all, and mixing it into the soil.

Removing large limbs

If there are large trees on your property now, you may want to remove some of the lower limbs so light can reach your plantings. Major pruning of large trees is a job for a professional arborist, but you can remove limbs smaller than 4 in. in diameter and less than 10 ft. above the ground yourself with a simple bow saw or pole saw.

Use the three-step procedure shown below to remove large limbs safely. First, saw partway through the bottom of the limb, approximately 1 ft. out from the trunk ❶. This keeps the bark from tearing down the trunk when the limb falls. Then make a corresponding cut down through the top of the limb ❷—be prepared to get out of the way when the limb drops. Finally, remove the stub ❸. Undercut it slightly or hold it as you finish the cut, so it doesn't fall away and peel bark off the trunk. Note that the cut is not flush with the trunk but is just outside the thick area at the limb's base, called the branch collar. Leaving the branch collar helps the wound heal quickly and naturally. Wound dressing is considered unnecessary today.

MOVING TURF

❶ With a sharp shovel, cut healthy turf into squares or strips of manageable size.

❷ Slice a few inches deep under each square, lift it, and place as soon as possible in a new spot.

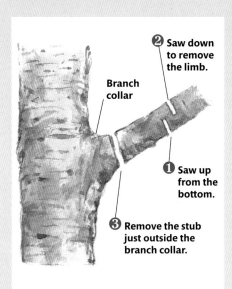

❷ Saw down to remove the limb.

Branch collar

❶ Saw up from the bottom.

❸ Remove the stub just outside the branch collar.

Making Paths and Walkways

Every landscape needs paths and walkways if for no other reason than to keep your feet dry as you move from one place to another. A path can also divide and define the spaces in the landscape, orchestrate the way the landscape is viewed, and even be a key element enhancing its beauty.

Whether it is a graceful curving garden path or a utilitarian slab leading to the garage, a walk has two main functional requirements: durability and safety. It should hold up through seasonal changes. It should provide a well-drained surface that is easy to walk on and to maintain.

A path's function helps determine its surface and its character. In general, heavily trafficked walkways leading to a door, garage, or shed need hard, smooth (but not slick) surfaces and should take you where you want to go fairly directly. A path to a backyard play area could be a strip of soft wood bark, easy on the knees of impatient children. A relaxed stroll in the garden might require only a hop-scotch collection of flat stones meandering from one prized plant to another.

Before laying out a walk or path, spend some time observing existing traffic patterns. If your path makes use of a route people already take (particularly children), they'll be more likely to stay on the path and off the lawn or flowers. Avoid areas that are slow to drain. When determining width, consider whether the path must accommodate rototillers or several strollers walking abreast, or just provide access for plant maintenance.

Dry-laid paths

You can make a path simply by laying bricks or spreading wood chips on top of bare earth. While quick and easy, this method has serious drawbacks. Laid on the surface, with no edging to contain them, loose materials are soon scattered, and solid materials are easily jostled out of place. If the earth base doesn't drain very well, the path will be a swamp or sheet of ice after rain or snowmelt. And in cold-winter areas, repeated expansion and contraction of the soil will heave bricks or flagstones out of alignment, making the path unsightly and dangerous.

The method we recommend—laying surface material on an excavated sand-and-gravel base—minimizes these problems. The sand and gravel improve drainage and provide a cushion against the freeze-thaw movement of the soil. Excavation can place the path surface at ground level, where the surrounding soil or an installed edging can contain loose materials and prevent hard materials from shifting.

All styles, from a "natural" wood-bark path to a formal cut-stone entry walk, and all the materials discussed here can be laid on an excavated base of gravel and sand.

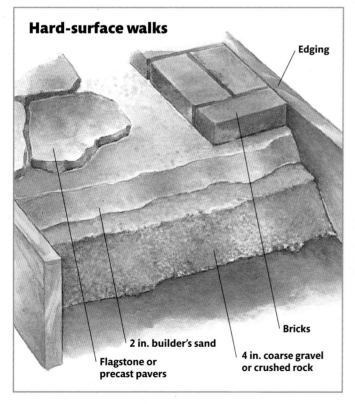

Hard-surface walks

Edging

Flagstone or precast pavers

2 in. builder's sand

Bricks

4 in. coarse gravel or crushed rock

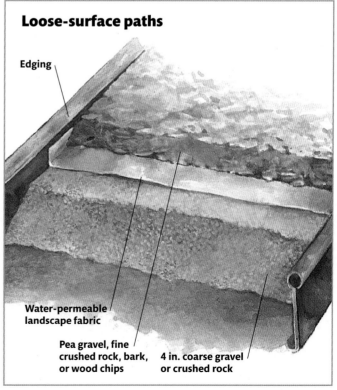

Loose-surface paths

Edging

Water-permeable landscape fabric

Pea gravel, fine crushed rock, bark, or wood chips

4 in. coarse gravel or crushed rock

Choosing a surface

Walkways and paths can be made of either hard or soft material. Your choice of material will depend on the walkway's function, your budget, and your personal preferences.

Soft materials, including bark, wood chips, pine needles, and loose gravel, are best for informal and low-traffic areas. Inexpensive and simple to install, they settle, scatter, or decompose and must be replenished or replaced every few years.

Hard materials, such as brick, flagstone, and concrete pavers, are more expensive and time-consuming to install, but they are permanent, requiring only occasional maintenance. (Compacted crushed stone can also make a hard-surface walk.) Durable and handsome, they're ideal for high-traffic, "high-profile" areas.

Bark, wood chips, and pine needles

Perfect for a "natural" look or a quick temporary path, these loose materials can be laid directly on the soil or, if drainage is poor, on a gravel bed. Bagged materials from a nursery or garden center will be cleaner, more uniform, and considerably more expensive than bulk supplies bought by the cubic yard. Check with local tree services to find the best prices on bulk material.

Gravel and crushed rock

Loose rounded gravel gives a bit underfoot, creating a "soft" but messy path. The angular facets of crushed stone eventually compact into a "hard" and tidier path that can, if the surrounding soil is firm enough, be laid without an edging. Gravel and stone type and color vary from area to area. Buy materials by the ton or cubic yard.

Concrete pavers

Precast concrete pavers are versatile, readily available, and often the least expensive hard-surface material. They come in a range of colors and shapes, including interlocking patterns. Precast edgings are also available. Most home and garden centers carry a variety of precast pavers, which are sold by the piece.

PRECAST PAVERS

Brick

Widely available in a range of sizes, colors, and textures, brick complements many design styles. When carefully laid on a well-prepared sand-and-gravel base, brick provides an even, safe, and long-lasting surface. Buy paving brick instead of the softer "facing" brick, which may break up after a few freeze-thaw cycles. (If you buy used brick, pick the hardest.) Avoid glazed brick; the glaze traps moisture and salts, which will damage the brick.

RUNNING BOND

TWO-BRICK BASKET WEAVE

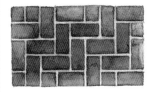

HERRINGBONE

DIAGONAL HERRINGBONE

Flagstone

"Flagstone" is a generic term for stratified stone that can be split to form pavers. Limestone, sandstone, and bluestone are common paving materials. The surfaces of marble and slate are usually too smooth to make safe paving. Cut into squares or rectangles, flagstone can be laid as individual steppingstones or in interesting patterns. Flagstones come in a range of colors, textures, and sizes. Flags for walks should be at least 2 in. thick. Purchased by weight, surface area, or pallet load, flagstones are usually the most expensive paving choice.

CUT FLAGSTONE

CUT AND IRREGULAR FLAGSTONE

IRREGULAR FLAGSTONE

Drainage

Few things are worse than a path dotted with puddles or icy patches. To prevent these from forming, the soil around and beneath the path should drain well. The path's location and construction should ensure that rainwater and snowmelt do not collect on the surface. Drainage also affects frost heaving. In cold-winter areas, the soil expands and contracts as the water in it freezes and thaws. As the soil moves, so do path and walkway materials laid on it. The effect is minimal on loose materials such as wood chips or gravel, but frost heaving can shift brick and stone significantly.

Before you locate a path, observe runoff and drainage on your property during and after heavy rains or snowmelt. Avoid routing a path where water courses, collects, or is slow to drain.

While both loose and hard paving can sometimes be successfully laid directly on well-drained soil, laying surface materials on a base of gravel and sand will help improve drainage and minimize frost heaving. In most situations, a 4-in. gravel bed topped with 2 in. of sand will be sufficient. Water moves through these materials quickly, and they "cushion" the surface materials from the expansion and contraction of the underlying soil. Very poorly drained soils may require more gravel, an additional layer of coarse rock beneath the gravel, or even drain tiles—if you suspect your site has serious drainage problems, consult a specialist for advice.

Finally, keep water from pooling on a walk by making its surface higher in the center than at the edges. The center of a 4-ft.-wide walk should be at least ½ in. higher than its edges. If you're using a drag board to level the sand base, curve its lower edge to create this "crown." Otherwise crown the surface by eye.

Edgings

All walk surfaces need to be contained in some fashion along their edges. Where soil is firm or tightly knit by turf, neatly cut walls of the excavation can serve as edging. An installed edging often provides more effective containment, particularly if the walk surface is above grade. It also prevents damage to bricks or stones on the edges of paths. Walkway edgings are commonly made of 1- or 2-in.-thick lumber, thicker landscaping timbers, brick, or stone.

Wood edging

Wood should be rot-resistant redwood, cedar, or cypress or pressure-treated for ground-contact use. If you're working in loose soils, fix a deep wooden edging to support stakes with double-headed nails. When the path is laid, pull the nails, and fill and tamp behind the edging. Then drive the stakes below grade. In firmer soils, or if the edging material is not wide enough, install it on top of the gravel base. Position the top of the edging at the height of the path. Dimension lumber 1 in. thick is pliable enough to bend around gradual curves.

Treated dimensional lumber with support stakes

Landscape timbers with crossties laid on gravel base

Brick and stone edging

In firm soil, a row of bricks laid on edge and perpendicular to the length of the path adds stability. For a more substantial edging, stand bricks on end on the excavated soil surface, add the gravel base, and tamp earth around the base of the bricks on the outside of the excavation. Stone edgings laid on end can be set in the same way. "End-up" brick or stone edgings are easy to install on curved walks.

Bricks on edge, laid on gravel base

Bricks on end, laid on soil

Preparing the base

Having decided on location and materials, you can get down to business. The initial steps of layout and base preparation are much the same for all surface materials.

Layout

Lay out straight sections with stakes and string, turning 90-degree corners with batter boards (see p. 183). You can plot curves with stakes and "fair" the curve with a garden hose, or outline the curve with hose alone, marking it with lime or sand ❶.

Excavation

The excavation depth depends on how much sand-and-gravel base your soil's drainage calls for, the thickness of the surface material, and its position above or below grade ❷. Mark the depth on a stake or stick and use this to check depth as you dig. Walking surfaces are most comfortable if they are reasonably level across their width. Check the bottom of the excavation with a level as you dig. If the walk cuts across a slope, you'll need to remove soil from the high side and use it to fill the low side to produce a level surface. If you've added soil or if the subsoil is loose, compact it by tamping.

Edging installation

Some edgings can be installed immediately after excavation; others are placed on top of the gravel portion of the base ❸. (See the sidebar "Edgings" on the facing page.) If the soil's drainage permits, you can lay soft materials now on the excavated, tamped, and edged soil base. To control weeds, and to keep bark, chips, or pine needles from mixing with the subsoil, spread water-permeable landscape fabric over the gravel or the excavated base.

Laying the base

Now add gravel (if required), rake it level, and compact it ❹. Use gravel up to 1 in. in diameter or ¼- to ¾-in. crushed stone, which drains and compacts well. You can rent a hand tamper (a heavy metal plate on the end of a pole) or a machine compactor if you have a large area to compact.

If you're making a loose-gravel or crushed-stone walk, add the surface material on top of the base gravel. (See "Loose materials" page 170.) For walks of brick, stone, or pavers, add a 2-in. layer of builder's sand, not the finer sand masons use for mixing mortar.

Rake the sand smooth with the back of a level-head rake. You can level the sand with a wooden drag board, also called a screed ❺. Nail together two 1x4s or notch a 1x6 to place the lower edge at the desired height of the sand, and run the board along the path edging. To settle the sand, dampen it thoroughly with a hose set on fine spray. Fill any low spots, rake or drag the surface level, then dampen it again.

PREPARING THE BASE

❶ Lay out the path with stakes, string, garden hose, and lime.

❷ Dig out path between layout string and lime lines.

❸ Install the edging.

❹ Rake out gravel base.

Lay out free-form curved sections with garden hose and mark with lime.

Mark straight sections with 1x2 stakes and string.

Drag board

Edging

❺ Level sand base with a drag board.

Laying the surface

Whether you're laying a loose or hard material, take time to plan your work. Provide access for delivery trucks, and have material deposited as close to the worksite as possible.

Loose materials

Install water-permeable landscape fabric over the gravel base to prevent gravel from mixing with the surface material. Spread bark or wood chips 2 to 4 in. deep. For a pine-needle surface, spread 2 in. of needles on top of several inches of bark or chips. Spread loose pea gravel about 2 in. deep. For a harder, more uniform surface, add ½ in. of fine crushed stone on top of the gravel. You can let traffic compact crushed- rock surfaces, or compact them by hand or with a machine.

Bricks and precast pavers

Take time to figure out the pattern and spacing of the bricks or pavers by laying them out on the lawn or driveway, rather than disturbing your carefully prepared sand base. When you're satisfied, begin in a corner, laying the bricks or pavers gently on the sand so the base remains even ❶. Lay full bricks first; then cut bricks to fit as needed at the edges. To produce uniform joints, which give a professional appearance, space bricks with a piece of wood cut to the joint width. You can also maintain alignment with a straightedge or with a string stretched across the path

between nails or stakes. Move the string as the work proceeds.

As you complete a row or section, bed the bricks or pavers into the sand base with several firm raps of a rubber mallet or a hammer on a scrap 2x4. Check with a level or straightedge to make sure the surface is even ❷. (You'll have to do this by feel or eye across the width of a crowned path.) Lift low bricks or pavers carefully and fill beneath them with sand; then reset them. Don't stand on the walk until you've filled the joints.

When you've finished a section, sweep fine, dry mason's sand into the joints, working across the surface of the path in all directions ❸. Wet thoroughly with a fine spray and let dry; then sweep in more sand if necessary. If you want a "living" walk, sweep a loam-sand mixture into the joints and plant small, tough, ground-hugging plants, such as thyme, in them.

Rare is the brick walk that can be laid without cutting something to fit. To cut brick, mark the line of the cut with a dark pencil all around the brick. With the brick resting firmly on sand or soil, score the entire line by rapping a wide mason's chisel called a "brickset" with a heavy wooden mallet or a soft-headed steel hammer as shown on the facing page. Place the brickset in the scored line across one face and give it a sharp blow with the hammer to cut the brick.

If you have a lot of bricks to cut, or if you want greater accuracy, consider renting a masonry saw. Whether you work by hand or machine, always wear safety glasses.

LOOSE MATERIALS

Cover gravel base with water-permeable landscape fabric and add 2 to 4 in. of bark or wood chips.

BRICKS AND PRECAST PAVERS

To turn square corners, align the edging board with a carpenter's square.

❶ Begin laying in a corner.

❷ Check the surface with a level or straightedge. Fill under low bricks; tamp down high ones. Use a plank to distribute your weight if you must work on the path.

❸ Sweep fine, dry sand into the joints to fix the bricks or pavers in place.

Steppingstones

A steppingstone walk set in turf creates a charming effect and is very simple to lay. You can use cut or irregular flagstones or fieldstone, which is irregular in thickness as well as in outline. Arrange the stones on the turf; then set them one by one. Cut into the turf around the stone with a sharp flat shovel or trowel, and remove the stone; then dig out the sod with the shovel. Placing stones at or below grade will keep them away from mower blades. Fill low spots beneath the stone with earth or sand so the stone doesn't move when stepped on.

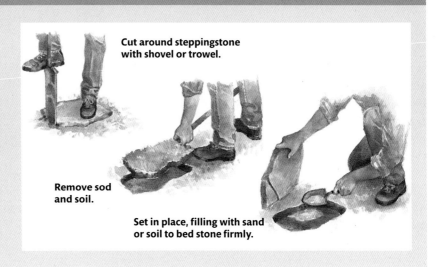

Cut around steppingstone with shovel or trowel.

Remove sod and soil.

Set in place, filling with sand or soil to bed stone firmly.

Cutting bricks

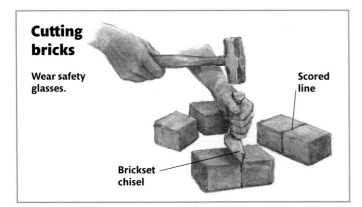

Wear safety glasses.

Scored line

Brickset chisel

Cutting flagstones

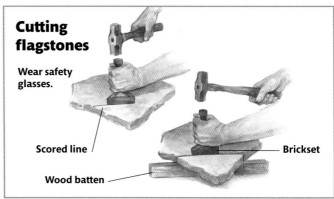

Wear safety glasses.

Scored line

Brickset

Wood batten

Flagstones

Install cut stones of uniform thickness as described for bricks and pavers. Working out patterns beforehand is particularly important—stones are too heavy to move around more than necessary. To produce a level surface with cut or irregular stones of varying thickness, you'll need to add or remove sand for each stone. Set the stone carefully on sand; then move it back and forth to work it into place ❶. Lay a level or straightedge over three or four stones to check the surface's evenness ❷. When a section is complete, fill the joints with sand or with sand and loam as described for bricks and pavers.

You can cut flagstone with a technique similar to that used for bricks. Score the line of the cut on the top surface with a brickset and hammer. Prop the stone on a piece of scrap wood, positioning the line of cut slightly beyond the edge of the wood. Securing the bottom edge of the stone with your foot, place the brickset on the scored line and strike sharply to make the cut.

FLAGSTONES

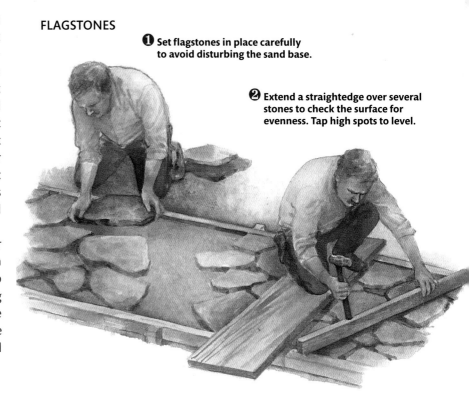

❶ Set flagstones in place carefully to avoid disturbing the sand base.

❷ Extend a straightedge over several stones to check the surface for evenness. Tap high spots to level.

Laying a Patio

You can make a simple patio using the same techniques and materials we have discussed for paths. To ensure good drainage, an even surface, and durability, lay hard surfaces such as brick, flagstone, and pavers on a well-prepared base of gravel, sand, and compacted soil. (Crushed-rock and gravel surfaces likewise benefit from a sound base.) Make sure the surface drains away from any adjacent structure (house or garage); a drop-off of ¼ in. per foot is usually adequate. If the patio isn't near a structure, make it higher in the center to avoid puddles.

Establish the outline of the patio as described for paths; then excavate the area roughly to accommodate 4 in. of gravel, 2 in. of sand, and the thickness of the paving surface. (Check with a local nursery or landscape contractor to find out if local conditions require alterations in the type or amounts of base material.) Now grade the rough excavation to provide drainage, using a simple 4-ft. grid of wooden stakes as shown in the drawings.

Drive the first row of stakes next to the house (or in the center of a freestanding patio), leveling them with a 4-ft. builder's level or a smaller level resting on a straight 2x4. The tops of these stakes should be at the height of the top of the sand base (finish grade of the patio less the thickness of the surface material) ❶. Working from this row of stakes, establish another row about 4 to 5 ft. from the first. Make the tops of these stakes 1 in. lower than those of the first row, using a level and spacer

LAYING A SIMPLE PATIO

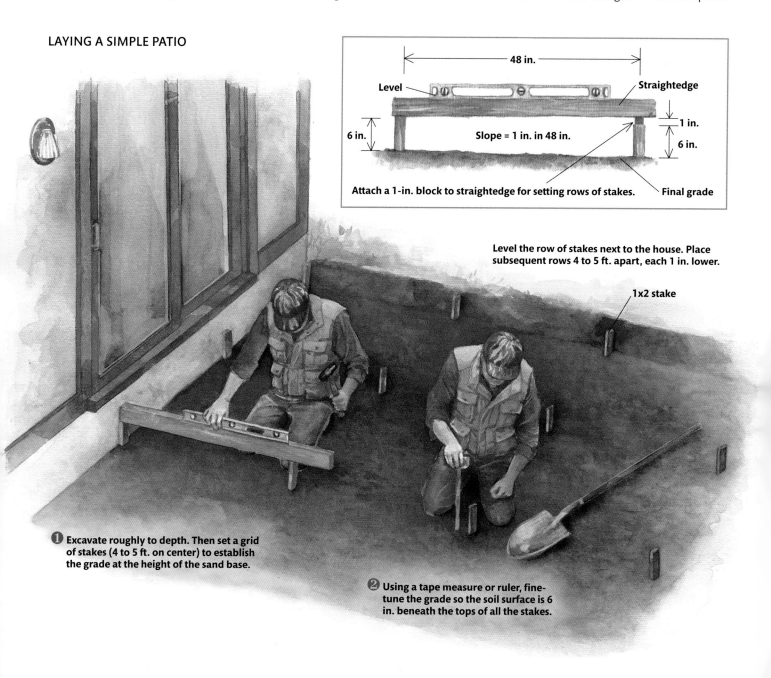

48 in.

Level   Straightedge

6 in.   Slope = 1 in. in 48 in.   1 in.

6 in.

Attach a 1-in. block to straightedge for setting rows of stakes.   Final grade

Level the row of stakes next to the house. Place subsequent rows 4 to 5 ft. apart, each 1 in. lower.

1x2 stake

❶ Excavate roughly to depth. Then set a grid of stakes (4 to 5 ft. on center) to establish the grade at the height of the sand base.

❷ Using a tape measure or ruler, fine-tune the grade so the soil surface is 6 in. beneath the tops of all the stakes.

block, as shown in the box below. Continue adding rows of stakes, each 1 in. lower than the previous row, until the entire area is staked. Then, with a tape measure or ruler and a shovel, fine-tune the grading by removing or adding soil until the excavated surface is 6 in. (the thickness of the gravel-sand base) below the tops of all the stakes ❷.

When installing the sand-and-gravel base, you'll want to maintain the drainage grade you've just established and produce an even surface for the paving material. If you have a good eye or a very small patio, you can do this by sight. Otherwise, you can use the stakes to install a series of 1x3 or 1x4 "leveling boards," as shown in the drawing below. (Before adding gravel, you may want to cover the soil with water-permeable landscape fabric to keep perennial weeds from growing; just cut slits to accommodate the stakes.)

Add a few inches of gravel ❸. Then set leveling boards along each row of stakes, with the boards' top edges even with the top of the stakes ❹. Drive additional stakes to sandwich the boards in place (don't use nails). Distribute the remaining inch or so of gravel and compact it by hand or machine, then the 2 in. of sand. Dragging a straight 2x4 across two adjacent rows of leveling boards will produce a precise grade and an even surface ❺. Wet the sand and fill low spots that settle.

You can install the patio surface as previously described for paths, removing the leveling boards as the bricks or pavers reach them ❻. Disturbing the sand surface as little as possible, slide the boards out from between the stakes and drive the stakes an inch or so beneath the level of the sand. Cover the stakes and fill the gaps left by the boards with sand, tamped down carefully. Then continue laying the surface. Finally, sweep fine sand into the joints.

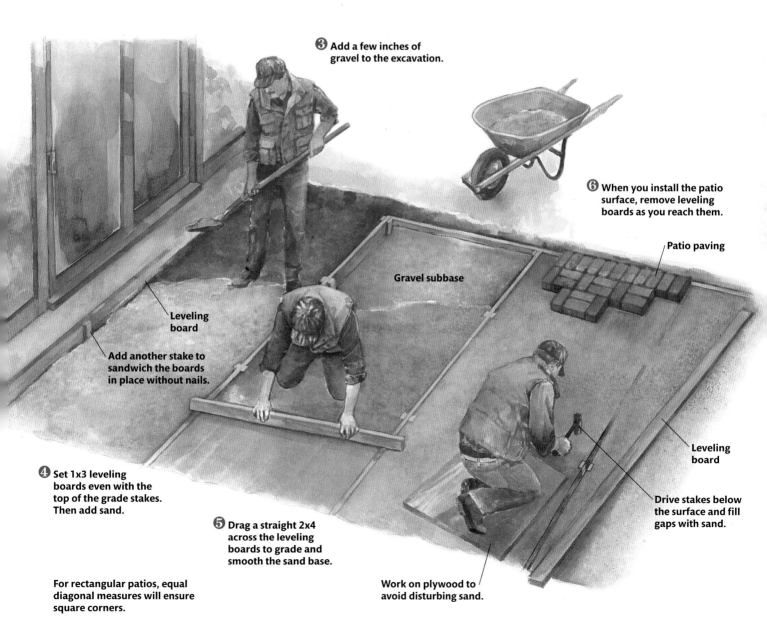

❸ **Add a few inches of gravel to the excavation.**

❻ **When you install the patio surface, remove leveling boards as you reach them.**

Patio paving

Gravel subbase

Leveling board

Add another stake to sandwich the boards in place without nails.

Leveling board

❹ **Set 1x3 leveling boards even with the top of the grade stakes. Then add sand.**

❺ **Drag a straight 2x4 across the leveling boards to grade and smooth the sand base.**

Drive stakes below the surface and fill gaps with sand.

For rectangular patios, equal diagonal measures will ensure square corners.

Work on plywood to avoid disturbing sand.

Installing a Pond

It wasn't so long ago that a garden pond like the one in this book required yards of concrete, an expert mason, and deep pockets. Today's strong, lightweight, and long-lasting synthetic liners and rigid fiberglass shells have put garden pools in reach of every homeowner. Installation does require some hard labor, but little expertise: just dig a hole, spread the liner or seat the shell, install edging, and plant. We'll discuss installation of a linered pond in the main text; see below for installing a smaller, fiberglass pool.

Liner notes

More and more nurseries and garden centers are carrying flexible pond liners; you can also buy them from mail-order suppliers specializing in water gardens. Synthetic rubber liners are longer lasting but more expensive than PVC liners. (Both are much cheaper than rigid fiberglass shells.) Buy only liners specifically made for garden ponds—don't use ordinary plastic sheeting. Many people feel that black liners look best; blue liners tend to make the pond look like a swimming pool.

Before you dig

First, make sure you comply with any rules your town may have about water features. Then keep the following ideas in mind when locating your pond. Avoid trees whose shade keeps sun-loving water plants from thriving; whose roots make digging a chore; and whose flowers, leaves, and seeds clog the water, making it unsightly and inhospitable to plants or fish. Avoid the low spot on your property; otherwise your pond will be a catch basin for runoff. Select a level spot; the immediate vicinity of the pond must be level, and starting out that way saves a lot of work. (Remember that you can use excavated soil to help level the site.)

Using graph paper, enlarge the outline of the pond provided on the site plan on p. 105, altering it as you wish. If you change the size or depth of the pond, or are interested in growing a wider variety of water plants or in adding fish, remember that a healthy pond must achieve a balance between the plants and fish and the volume, depth, and temperature of the water. Even if you're not altering size or pond plants and fish, it's a good idea to consult with a knowledgeable person at a nursery or pet store specializing in water-garden plants and animals.

Calculate the liner width by adding twice the maximum depth of the pool plus an additional 2 ft. to the width. Use the same formula to calculate the length. So, for a pond 2 ft. deep, 6 ft. wide, and 17 ft. long, the liner width would be 4 ft. plus 6 ft. plus 2 ft. (or 12 ft.). The length would be 4 ft. plus 17 ft. plus 2 ft. (or 23 ft.).

Excavation

If your soil isn't too compacted or rocky, a good-size pond can be excavated with a shovel or two in a weekend ❶. (Energetic teenagers are a marvelous pool-building resource.) If the site isn't level, you can grade it using a stake-and-level system like the one described on pp. 172–173 for grading the patio.

Outline the pond's shape with garden lime, establishing the curves freehand with a garden hose or by staking out a large grid and plotting from the graph-paper plan. The pond has two levels. The broad end, at 2 ft. deep, accommodates water lilies and other plants requiring deeper water as well as fish. Make the narrow end 12 to 16 in. deep for plants requiring shallower submersion. (You can put plant pots on stacks of bricks or other platforms to

Small fiberglass pool

A 3-ft.-diameter fiberglass shell 12 to 24 in. deep is ideal for the small round pool on p. 104. (A plastic garbage can or half barrel would work, too.)

Dig a hole about 6 in. wider on all sides than the shell; its depth should equal that of the shell plus 1 in. for a sand base, plus the thickness of the fieldstone edging. Compact the bottom of the hole and spread the sand; then lower the shell into place. Add temporary wedges or props level the shell. Slowly fill the shell with water, backfilling around it with sand or sifted soil, keeping pace with the rising water. Excavate a wide relief for the edging stones, laying them on as firm a base, slightly overhanging the rim of the shell.

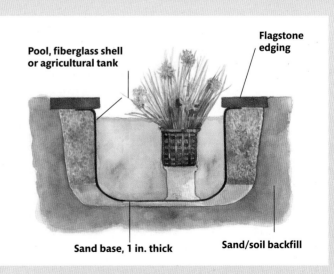

Pool, fiberglass shell or agricultural tank

Flagstone edging

Sand base, 1 in. thick

Sand/soil backfill

vary heights as necessary.) The walls will be less likely to crumble as you dig and the liner will install more easily if you slope them in about 3 to 4 in. for each foot of depth. Make the walls smooth, removing roots, rocks, and other sharp protrusions.

Excavate a shallow relief about 1 ft. wide around the perimeter to contain the liner overlap and stone edging. (The depth of the relief should accommodate the thickness of the edging stones.) Somewhere along the perimeter, create an overflow channel to take runoff after a heavy rain. This can simply be a 1- to 2-in. depression a foot or so wide spanned by one of the edging stones. Lengths of PVC pipe placed side by side beneath the stone (as shown in the drawing on p. 176)

will keep the liner in place. The overflow channel can open onto a lower area of lawn or garden adjacent to the pond or to a rock-filled dry well.

Fitting the liner

When the hole is complete, cushion the surfaces to protect the liner ❷. Here we show an inch-thick layer of sand on the bottom surfaces and carpet underlayment on the sloping walls. Fiberglass batting insulation also works well, as do old blankets or even heavy landscaping fabric.

Stretch the liner across the hole, letting it sag naturally to touch the walls and bottom but keeping it taut enough so it does

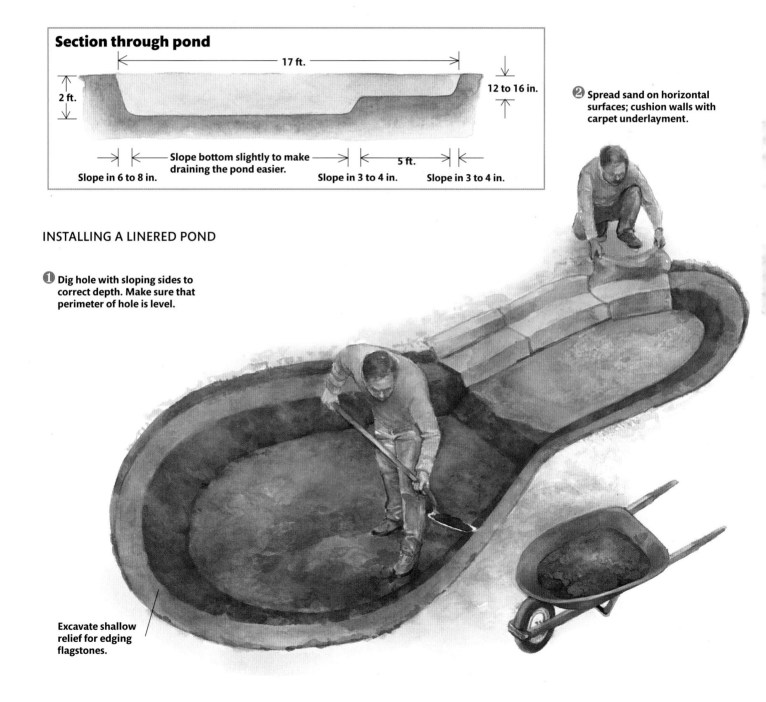

Section through pond

17 ft.

2 ft.

12 to 16 in.

Slope in 6 to 8 in.

Slope bottom slightly to make draining the pond easier.

5 ft.

Slope in 3 to 4 in.

Slope in 3 to 4 in.

❷ Spread sand on horizontal surfaces; cushion walls with carpet underlayment.

INSTALLING A LINERED POND

❶ Dig hole with sloping sides to correct depth. Make sure that perimeter of hole is level.

Excavate shallow relief for edging flagstones.

not bunch up. Weight its edges with bricks or stones; then fill it with water ❸. The water's weight will push the liner against the walls; the stones will prevent it from blowing around. As it fills, tuck and smooth out as many creases as you can; the weight of the water makes this difficult to do after the pond is full. If you stand in the pond to do so, take care not to damage the liner. Don't be alarmed if you can't smooth all the creases. Stop filling

when the water is 2 in. below the rim of the pond, and cut the liner to fit into the overlap relief ❹. Hold it in place with a few long nails or large "staples" made from coat hangers while you install the edging.

Edging the pond

Finding and fitting flagstones so there aren't wide gaps between them is the most time-consuming part of this task. Cantilevering the stones an inch or two over the water will hide the liner somewhat.

The stones can be laid directly on the liner, as shown ❺. Add sand under the liner to level the surface where necessary so that the stones don't rock. Such treatment will withstand the occasional gingerly traffic of pond and plant maintenance but not the wear and tear of young children or large dogs regularly running across the edging. (The liner won't go long without damage if used as a wading pool.) If you anticipate heavier traffic, you can bed the stones in 2 to 3 in. of mortar. It's prudent to consult with a landscape contractor about whether your intended use and soil require some sort of footing for mortared stones.

Elevation detail of pond overflow

Flagstone edging, 12 in. or more wide

Cover pipe with flagstone.

Pond liner

To overflow area

PVC pipe, 1- or 2-in.-dia., about 12 in. long

1-in. layer of sand (horizontal surfaces)

Garden bed or lawn

Carpet underlayment (walls)

---

❺ **Fit and lay flagstone edging. Add sand beneath the liner or stones where necessary to create a firm bed. Brush sand into joints when edging is complete.**

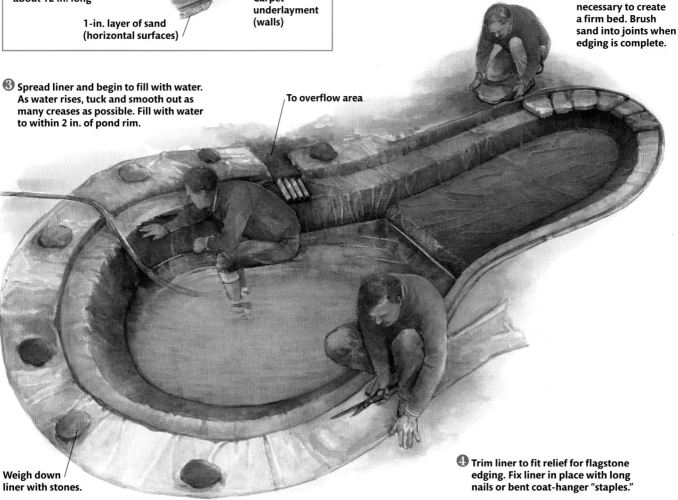

❸ **Spread liner and begin to fill with water. As water rises, tuck and smooth out as many creases as possible. Fill with water to within 2 in. of pond rim.**

To overflow area

Weigh down liner with stones.

❹ **Trim liner to fit relief for flagstone edging. Fix liner in place with long nails or bent coat-hanger "staples."**

Water work

Unless you are a very tidy builder, the water you used to fit the liner will be too dirty to leave in the pond. Siphon or pump out the water, clean the liner, and refill the pond. If you're adding fish to the pond, you'll need to let the water stand for a week or so to allow any chlorine (which is deadly to fish) to dissipate. Check with local pet stores to find out if your water contains chemicals that require commercial conditioners to make the water safe for fish.

A filtration system helps to balance the water chemistry and oxygenate the water so that fish and plants may thrive. If you purchase a pond kit, the right-sized components will be included, but when building from scratch you'll need to be sure to source the right equipment for your project.

Components of a pond filtration system include a debris skimmer, a biological filter, tubing and connectors, and a pond pump, rated in Gallons Per Hour (GPH), that can circulate all of the water once per hour.

To calculate the minimum pump size, use this formula: average length (in feet) x average width x average depth x 7.48 = Gallons of water in the pond. Using the previous example, the pond measured 17 feet long x 6 feet wide x 2 feet deep, or 204 cubic feet of water x 7.48 gallons per cubic foot = 1,525.92 gallons of water in the pond. So, we would need a pump and filtration system with a rating of greater than 1,526 GPH to properly filter the pond.

Installing the pond and plants is only the first step in water gardening. It takes patience, experimentation, and usually some consultation with experienced water gardeners to achieve a balance between plants, fish, and waterborne oxygen, nutrients, and waste that will sustain all happily while keeping algae, diseases, insects, and predators at acceptable levels.

Growing pond plants

One water lily, a few upright-growing plants, and a bundle of submerged plants (which help keep the water clean) are enough for a medium-size pond. An increasing number of nurseries and garden centers stock water lilies and other water plants. For a larger selection, your nursery or garden center may be able to recommend a specialist supplier.

These plants are grown in containers filled with heavy garden soil (not potting soil, which contains ingredients that float). You can buy special containers designed for aquatic plants, or simply use plastic pails or dishpans. Line basketlike containers with burlap to keep the soil from leaking out the holes. A water lily needs at least 2 to 3 gal. of soil; the more, the better. Most other water plants, such as dwarf papyrus, need 1 to 2 gal. of soil.

After planting, add a layer of gravel on the surface to keep soil from clouding the water and to protect roots from marauding fish. Soak the plant and soil thoroughly. Then set the container in the pond, positioning it so the water over the soil is 6 to 18 in. deep for water lilies, 0 to 6 in. for most other plants.

For maximum bloom, push a tablet of special water-lily fertilizer into the pots once or twice a month throughout the summer. Most water plants are easy to grow and carefree, although many are tropicals that die after hard frost, so you'll have to replace them each spring.

PLANTING WATER PLANTS

Set water plants in a container of heavy garden soil. Then cover soil surface with gravel to keep soil from floating away.

Gravel

1- to 3-gal. dishpan or special container

Heavy garden soil

Building a Retaining Wall

Contours and sloping terrain can add considerable interest to a home landscape. But you can have too much of a good thing. Two designs in this book employ retaining walls to alter problem slopes. The wall shown on p. 62 eliminates a small but abrupt grade change, producing two almost level surfaces and the opportunity to install attractive plantings on them. On p. 70 two low retaining walls help turn a steep slope into a showpiece.

Retaining walls can be handsome landscape features in their own right. Made of cut stone, fieldstone, brick, landscape timbers, or concrete, they can complement the materials and style of your house or nearby structures. However, making a stable, long-lasting retaining wall of these materials can require tools and skills many homeowners do not possess.

For these reasons we've instead chosen retaining-wall systems made of precast concrete for designs in this book.

Readily available in a range of sizes, surface finishes, and colors, these systems require few tools and no special skills to install. They have been engineered to resist the forces that soil, water, freezing, and thawing bring to bear on a retaining wall. Install these walls according to the manufacturer's specifications, and you can be confident that they will do their job for many years.

A number of systems are available in the region through nurseries, garden centers, and local contracting suppliers (search online for "wall block suppliers near me"). But they all share basic design principles. Like traditional dry-stone walls, these systems rely largely on weight and friction to contain the weight of the soil. In many systems, interlocking blocks or pegs help align the courses and increase the wall's strength. In all systems, blocks must rest on a solid, level base. A freely draining backfill of crushed stone is essential to avoid buildup of water pressure (both liquid and frozen) in the retained soil, which can buckle even a heavy wall.

The construction steps shown here are typical of those recommended by most system manufacturers for retaining walls up to 3 to 4 ft. tall; be sure to follow the manufacturer's instructions for the system you choose. (Some installation guides are excellent; others are less helpful. Weigh the quality of instructions in your decision of which system to buy.) For higher walls, walls on loose soil or heavy clay soils, and walls retaining very steep slopes, it is prudent to consult with a landscape architect or contractor.

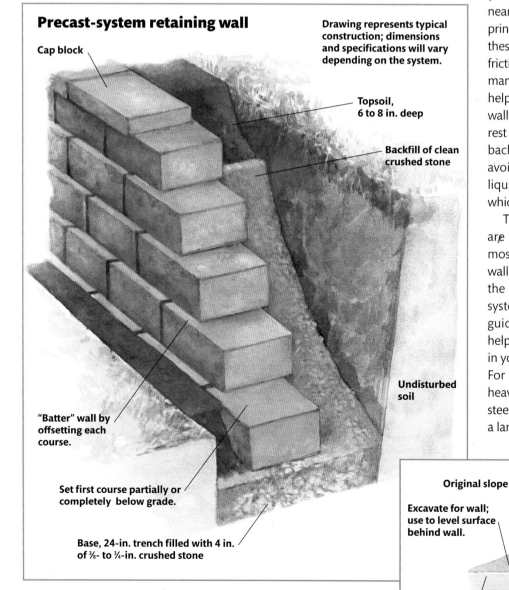

Precast-system retaining wall

Drawing represents typical construction; dimensions and specifications will vary depending on the system.

Cap block

Topsoil, 6 to 8 in. deep

Backfill of clean crushed stone

"Batter" wall by offsetting each course.

Set first course partially or completely below grade.

Base, 24-in. trench filled with 4 in. of ⅜- to ¾-in. crushed stone

Undisturbed soil

Original slope

Excavate for wall; use to level surface behind wall.

New grade level

30–45° from plumb

New grade

Building a wall

Installing a wall system is just about as simple as stacking up children's building blocks. The most important part of the job is establishing a firm, level base. Start by laying out the wall with string and hose (for curves) and excavating a base trench.

As the boxed drawing shows, the position of the wall in relation to the base of the slope determines the height of the wall, how much soil you move, and the leveling effect on the slope. Unless the wall is very long, it is a good idea to excavate along the entire length and fine-tune the line of the wall before beginning

the base trench. Remember to excavate back far enough to accommodate the stone backfill. Systems vary, but a foot of crushed-stone backfill behind the blocks is typical. (For the two-wall design, build the bottom wall first, then the top.)

Systems vary in the width and depth of trench and type of base material, but in all of them, the trench must be level across its width and along its length. We've shown a 4-in. layer of ⅜- to ¾-in. crushed stone (blocks can slip sideways on rounded aggregate or pea gravel, which also don't compact as well). Depending on the system and the circumstances, a portion or all of the first course lies below grade, so the soil helps hold the blocks in place.

Add crushed stone to the trench, level it with a rake, and compact it with a hand tamper or mechanical compactor. Lay the first course of blocks carefully ❶. Check frequently to make sure the blocks are level across their width and along their length. Stagger vertical joints

as you stack subsequent courses. Offset the faces of the blocks so the wall leans back into the retained soil. Some systems design this "batter" into their blocks; others allow you to choose from several possible setbacks.

As the wall rises, shovel backfill behind the blocks ❷. Clean crushed rock drains well; some systems suggest placing a barrier of landscaping fabric between the rock and the retained soil to keep soil from migrating into the fill and impeding drainage.

Thinner cap blocks finish the top of the wall ❸. Some wall systems recommend cementing these blocks in place with a weatherproof adhesive. The last 6 to 8 in. of the backfill should be topsoil, firmed into place and ready for planting.

BUILDING A WALL

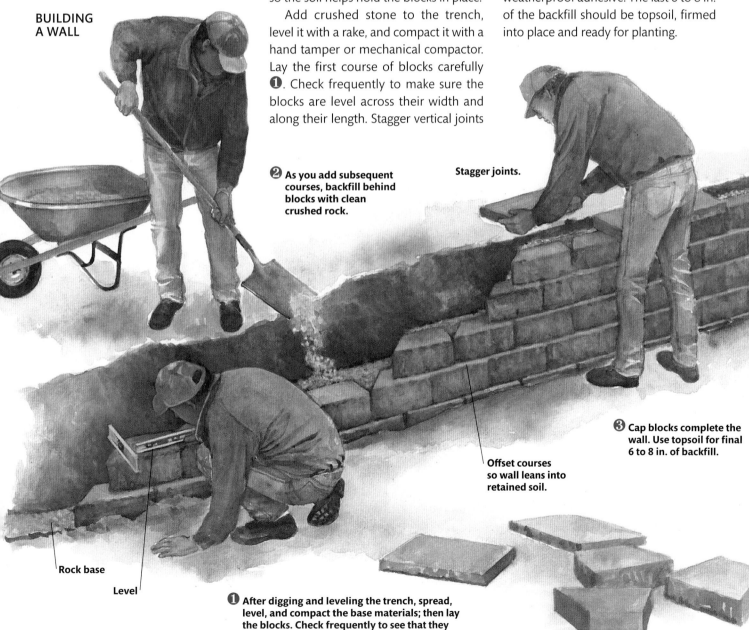

❷ As you add subsequent courses, backfill behind blocks with clean crushed rock.

Stagger joints.

❸ Cap blocks complete the wall. Use topsoil for final 6 to 8 in. of backfill.

Offset courses so wall leans into retained soil.

Rock base

Level

❶ After digging and leveling the trench, spread, level, and compact the base materials; then lay the blocks. Check frequently to see that they are level across their width and length.

Wall parallel with a slope: Stepped base

Construct walls running parallel with a slope in "steps," each with a level base.

Backfill so grade behind finishes level with top of wall.

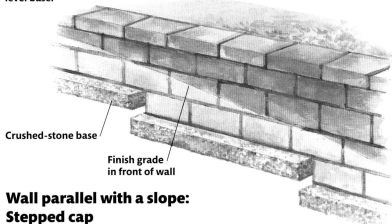

Crushed-stone base

Finish grade in front of wall

Wall parallel with a slope: Stepped cap

Sometimes the top of a wall needs to step up or down to accommodate grade changes in the slope behind.

Cap block

A "return" corner

Where you want the slope to extend beyond the end of the wall, make a corner that cuts into the slope.

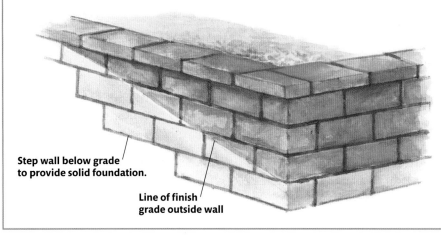

Step wall below grade to provide solid foundation.

Line of finish grade outside wall

Sloped sites

If your site slopes along the wall's length, you'll need to "step" the bottom of the wall, as shown at top left. Create a length of level trench along the lowest portion of the site; then work up the slope, creating steps as necessary.

The top of the wall can also step if the slope dissipates at one end. (See middle left.) Such slopes are common on sites such as the one shown on p. 70, which slopes away from the house and toward the driveway. Here the base of the wall will rest on level ground, but the slope behind the wall decreases along the wall's length. The design on p. 70 shows one solution to this dilemma—a wall of uniform height with a "return" corner at the street end (see bottom left), backfilled to raise the grade behind to the top of the wall. Another solution, shown at center left, is to step the wall down as the slope decreases, which saves material, produces a different look, but still works with the planting design.

Curves and corners

Wall-system blocks are designed so that curves are no more difficult to lay than straight sections. Corners may require that you cut a few blocks or use specially designed blocks, but they are otherwise uncomplicated. If your wall must fit a prescribed length between corners, consider working from the corners toward the middle (after laying a base course). Masons use this technique, which also avoids exposing cut blocks at the corners.

You can cut blocks with a mason's chisel and mallet or rent a mason's saw. Chiseling works well where the faces of the blocks are rough textured, so the cut faces blend right in. A saw is best for smooth-faced blocks and projects requiring lots of cutting.

Where the wall doesn't run the full length of the slope, the best-looking and most structurally sound termination is a corner constructed to cut back into the slope, as shown at bottom left.

Steps

Steps in a low retaining wall are not difficult to build, but they require forethought and careful layout. Systems differ on construction details. The drawing below shows a typical design where the blocks and stone base rest on "steps" cut into firm subsoil. If your soil is less stable or is recent fill, you should excavate the entire area beneath the steps to the same depth as the wall base and build a foundation of blocks, as shown in the boxed drawing.

These steps are independent of the adjacent "return" walls, which are vertical, not battered (stepped back). In some systems, steps and return walls are interlocked. To match a path, you can face the treads with the same stone, brick, or pavers, or you can use the system's cap blocks or special treads.

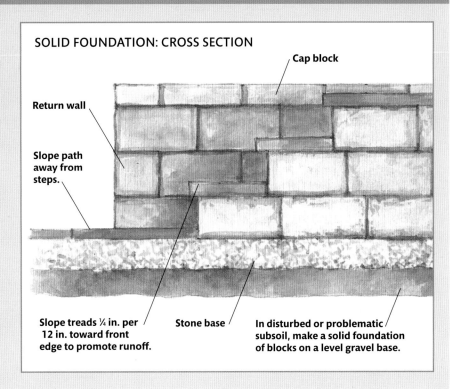

SOLID FOUNDATION: CROSS SECTION

Cap block

Return wall

Slope path away from steps.

Slope treads ¼ in. per 12 in. toward front edge to promote runoff.

Stone base

In disturbed or problematic subsoil, make a solid foundation of blocks on a level gravel base.

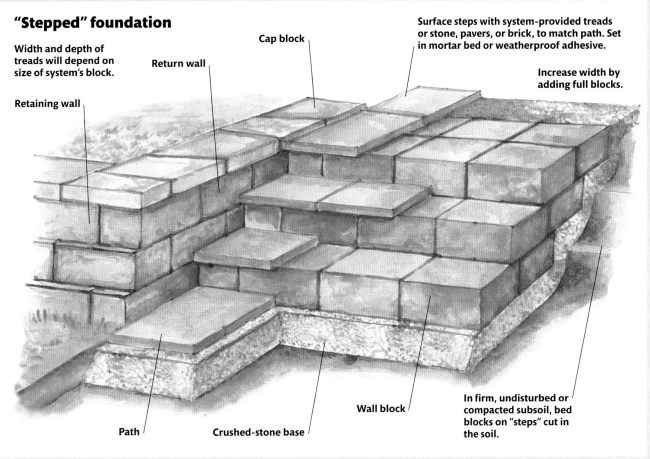

"Stepped" foundation

Width and depth of treads will depend on size of system's block.

Return wall

Cap block

Surface steps with system-provided treads or stone, pavers, or brick, to match path. Set in mortar bed or weatherproof adhesive.

Increase width by adding full blocks.

Retaining wall

Path

Crushed-stone base

Wall block

In firm, undisturbed or compacted subsoil, bed blocks on "steps" cut in the soil.

Fences, Arbors, and Trellises

Novices who have no trouble tackling a simple flagstone path often get nervous when it comes time to erect a fence, an arbor, or even a trellis. While such projects can require more skill and resources than others in the landscape, the ones in this book have been designed with less-than-confident do-it-yourself builders in mind. The designs are simple, the materials are readily available, and the tools and skills will be familiar to anyone accustomed to ordinary home maintenance.

First we'll introduce you to the materials and tools needed for the projects. Then we'll present the small number of basic operations you'll employ when building them. Finally, we'll provide drawings and comments on each of the projects.

Tools and materials

Even the least-handy homeowner is likely to have most of the tools needed for these projects: claw hammer, crosscut handsaw, brace-and-bit or electric drill, adjustable wrench, combination square, tape measure, carpenter's level, and sawhorses. You may even have Grandpa's old posthole digger. Many will have a handheld power circular saw, which makes faster (though noisier) work of cutting parts to length. A cordless drill/screwdriver is invaluable if you're substituting screws for nails. If you have more than a few holes to dig, consider renting a gas-powered posthole digger. A 12-in.-diameter hole will serve for 4x4 posts; if possible, get a larger-diameter digger for 6x6 posts.

Materials

Of the materials offering strength, durability, and attractiveness in outdoor settings, wood is the easiest to work and affords the quickest results. While almost all commercially available lumber is strong enough for landscape structures, most decay quickly when in prolonged contact with soil and water. Cedar, cypress, and redwood, however, contain natural preservatives and are excellent for landscape use. Alternatively, a range of softwoods (such as pine, fir, and hemlock) are pressure-treated with preservatives and will last for many years. Parts of structures that do not come in contact with soil or are not continually wet can be made of ordinary construction-grade lumber, but unless they're regularly painted, they will not last as long as treated or naturally decay-resistant material.

In addition to dimension lumber, several of the designs incorporate lattice, which is thin wooden strips crisscrossed to form patterns of diamonds or squares. Premade lattice is widely available in sheets 4 ft. by 8 ft. and smaller. Lattice comes in decay-resistant woods as well as in treated and untreated softwoods. Local supplies vary, and you may find lattice made of thicker or narrower material.

Fasteners

For millennia, even basic structures such as these would have been assembled with complicated joints. Today, with simple nailed, bolted, or screwed joints, a few hours' practice swinging a hammer or wielding a cordless electric screwdriver is all the training necessary.

All these structures can be assembled using nails. But screws are stronger and, if you have a cordless screwdriver, make assembly easier. Buy common or box nails that are galvanized to prevent rust. Self-tapping screws ("deck" screws) require no pilot holes. For rust resistance, buy galvanized screws or screws treated with zinc dichromate.

Galvanized metal connectors are available to reinforce the joints used in these projects. For novice builders, connectors are a great help in aligning parts and making assembly easier. (Correctly fastened with nails or screws, the joints are strong enough without connectors.)

Finishes

Cedar, cypress, and redwood are handsome when left unfinished to weather, when treated with clear or colored stains, or when painted. Pressure-treated lumber is best painted or stained.

Outdoor stains are becoming increasingly popular. Clear or lightly tinted stains can preserve or enhance the rich reddish browns of cedar, cypress, and redwood. Stains also come in a range of colors that can be used like paint. Because they penetrate the wood rather than forming a film, stains don't form an opaque surface, but stains won't peel or chip like paint and are therefore easier to touch up and refinish.

When choosing a finish, take account of what plants are growing on or near the structure. It's a lot of work to remove yards of vines from a trellis or squeeze between a large shrub and a fence to repaint; consider an unfinished decay-resistant wood or an initial stain that you allow to weather.

Setting posts

All the projects are anchored by firmly set, vertical posts. In general, the taller the structure, the deeper the post should be set. For the arbors and the tallest fences, posts should be at least 3 ft. deep. Posts for fences up to 4 ft. tall can be set 2 ft. deep. To avoid post movement caused by expansion and contraction of the soil during freeze-thaw cycles, it's a good idea to set all arbor posts below the frost line. This depth is greater in colder climates; check with local building authorities.

The length of the posts you buy depends, of course, on the depth at which they are set and their finished heights. When calculating lengths of arbor posts, remember that the tops of the posts must be level. The easiest method of achieving this is to cut the posts to length after installation. For example, buy 12-ft. posts for an arbor finishing at 8 ft. above grade and set 3 ft. in the ground. The convenience is worth the expense of the foot or so you cut off. The site and personal preference can determine whether you cut fence posts to length after installation or buy them cut to length and add or remove fill from the bottom of the hole to position them at the correct heights.

Arbor posts

Take care when positioning arbor posts. The corners of the structure must be right angles, and the sides must be parallel. Locating the corners with batter boards and string is fussy but accurate. Make the batter boards by nailing 1x2 stakes to scraps of 1x3 or 1x4, and position them about 1 ft. from the approximate location of each post as shown in the boxed drawing, right. Locate the exact post positions with string; adjust the string so the diagonal measurements are equal, which ensures that the corners of the structure will be at right angles.

At the intersections of the strings, locate the postholes by eye or with a plumb bob ❶. Remove the strings and dig the holes; then reattach the strings to position the posts exactly ❷. Plumb and brace the posts carefully. Check positions with the level and by measuring between adjacent posts and across diagonals. Diagonal braces between adjacent posts will stiffen them and help align their faces ❸. Then add concrete ❹ and let it cure for a day.

To establish the height of the posts, measure up from grade on one post, then use a level and straightedge to mark the heights of the other posts from the first one. Where joists will be bolted to the faces of the posts, you can install the joists and use their top edges as a handsaw guide for cutting the posts to length.

SETTING ARBOR POSTS

❶ Position the posts with batter boards, taut string, and a plumb bob.

Batter board

Taut string

Plumb bob

BATTER BOARDS
Set L-shaped batter boards at each corner and stretch string to position the posts exactly.

1x2 stakes and 1x3 boards

Taut string

Taut string

18 to 24 in.

For square or rectangular post layout, diagonal measurements should be equal.

❷ Remove the string to dig the holes; then reattach it and align the outer faces of the posts with the string while you plumb and brace them.

❸ Check distances between posts at top. Add diagonal bracing between posts to fix positions.

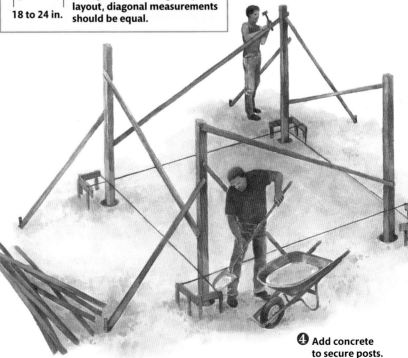

❹ Add concrete to secure posts.

Fence posts

Lay out and set the end or corner posts of a fence first, then add the intermediate posts. Dig the holes by hand or with a power digger ❶. To promote drainage, place several inches of gravel at the bottom of the hole for the post to rest on. Checking with a carpenter's level, plumb the post vertically and brace it with scrap lumber nailed to stakes ❷. Then add a few more inches of gravel around the post's base.

If your native soil compacts well, you can fix posts in place with tamped earth. Add the soil gradually, tamping it continuously with a heavy iron bar or 2x4. Check regularly with a level to see that the post doesn't get knocked out of plumb. This technique suits rustic or informal fences, where misalignments caused by shifting posts aren't noticeable or damaging.

For more formal fences, or where soils are loose or fence panels are buffeted by winds or snow, it's prudent to fix posts in concrete ❸. Mix enough concrete to set the two end posts; as a rule of thumb, figure one 80-lb. bag of premixed concrete per post. As you shovel it in, prod the concrete with a stick to settle it, particularly if you've added rubble to extend the mix. Build

SETTING A FENCE POST

❷ **Plumb the post, checking on adjacent faces with a level. Hold it in position with stakes and braces.**

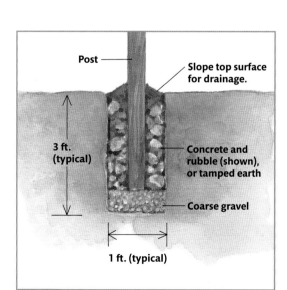

❶ **Position the end or corner posts; then dig holes for them.**

Post

Slope top surface for drainage.

3 ft. (typical)

Concrete and rubble (shown), or tamped earth

Coarse gravel

1 ft. (typical)

❸ **Fill the hole with concrete and rubble.**

the concrete slightly above grade, and slope it away from the post to aid drainage.

Once the end posts are set, stretch a string between the posts. (The concrete should cure for 24 hours before you nail or screw rails and panels in place, but you can safely stretch string while the concrete is still wet.) Measure along the string to position the intermediate posts; drop a plumb bob from the string at each intermediate post position to gauge the center of the hole below ❹. Once all the holes have been dug, again stretch a string between the end posts, near the top. Set the intermediate posts as described previously; align one face with the string and plumb adjacent faces with the carpenter's level ❺. Check positions of intermediate posts a final time with a tape measure before adding concrete.

If the fence is placed along a slope, the top of the slats or panels can step down the slope or mirror it (as shown in the drawings below). Either way, make sure that the posts are plumb, rather than leaning with the slope.

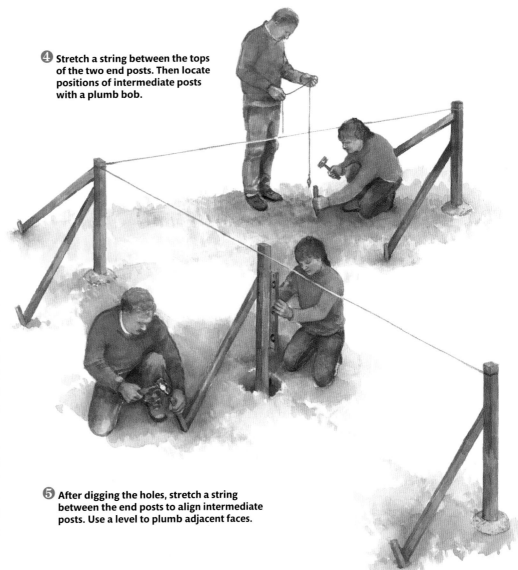

❹ **Stretch a string between the tops of the two end posts. Then locate positions of intermediate posts with a plumb bob.**

❺ **After digging the holes, stretch a string between the end posts to align intermediate posts. Use a level to plumb adjacent faces.**

Fencing a slope

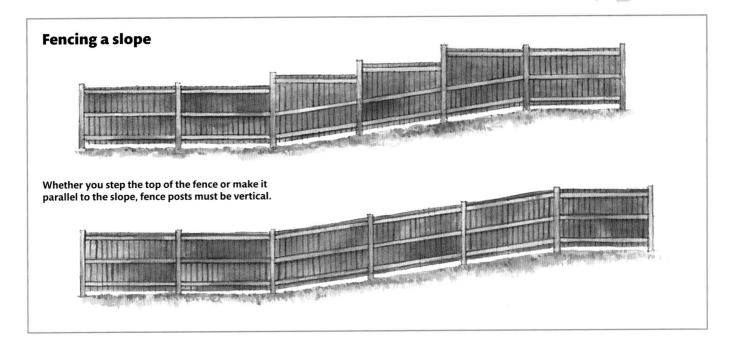

Whether you step the top of the fence or make it parallel to the slope, fence posts must be vertical.

Joints

The components of the fences, arbors, and trellises used in this book are attached to the posts and to each other with the simple joints shown below. Because all the parts are made of dimensioned lumber, the only cuts you'll need to make are to length. For strong joints, cut ends as square as you can, so the mating pieces make contact across their entire surfaces. If you have no confidence in your sawing, many lumberyards will cut pieces to length for a modest fee.

Novices often find it difficult to keep two pieces correctly positioned while trying to drive a nail into them, particularly when the nail must be driven at an angle, called "toenailing". If you have this problem, consider assembling the project with screws, which draw the pieces together, or with metal connectors, which can be nailed or screwed in place on one piece and then attached to the mating piece.

For several designs, you need to attach lattice panels to posts. The panels are made by sandwiching store-bought lattice

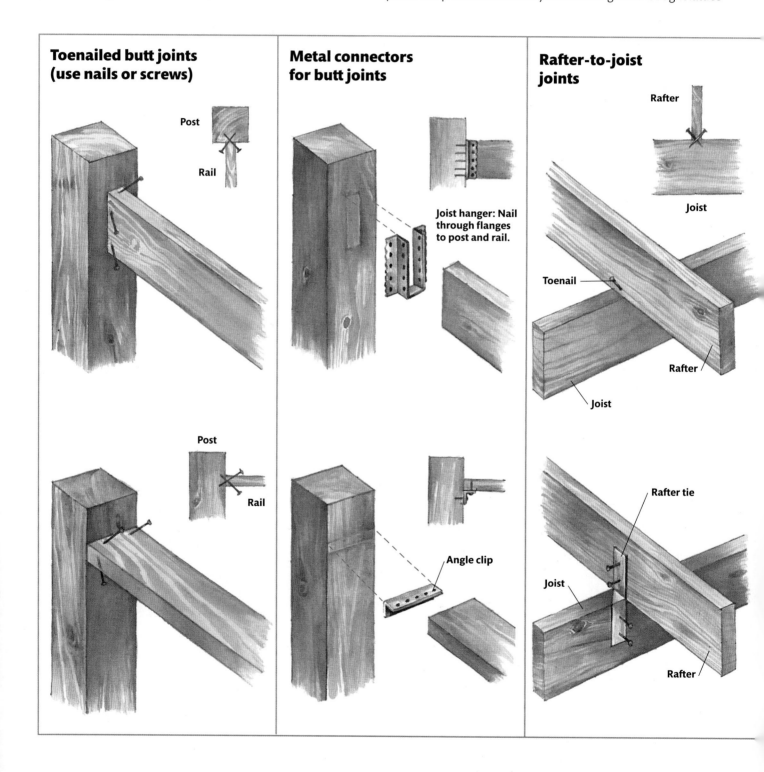

Toenailed butt joints (use nails or screws)

Post

Rail

Post

Rail

Metal connectors for butt joints

Joist hanger: Nail through flanges to post and rail.

Angle clip

Rafter-to-joist joints

Rafter

Joist

Toenail

Rafter

Joist

Rafter tie

Joist

Rafter

between frames of dimension lumber (construction details are given on the following pages). While the assembled panels can be toenailed to the posts, novices may find that the job goes easier using one or more types of metal connector, as shown in the drawing at below right. Attach the angle clips or angle brackets to the post; then position the lattice panel and fix it to the connectors. For greatest strength and ease of assembly, attach connectors with self-tapping screws driven by an electric or cordless screwdriver or drill-driver.

In the following pages, we'll show construction details of the fences, arbors, and trellises presented in the Portfolio of Designs. (The page number indicates the design.) Where the basic joints discussed here can be used, we have shown the parts but left choice of fasteners to you. Typical fastenings are indicated for other joints. We have kept the constructions shown here simple and straightforward. They are not the only possibilities, and we encourage experienced builders to adapt and alter constructions as well as designs to suit differing situations and personal preferences.

Frame corner with metal connector

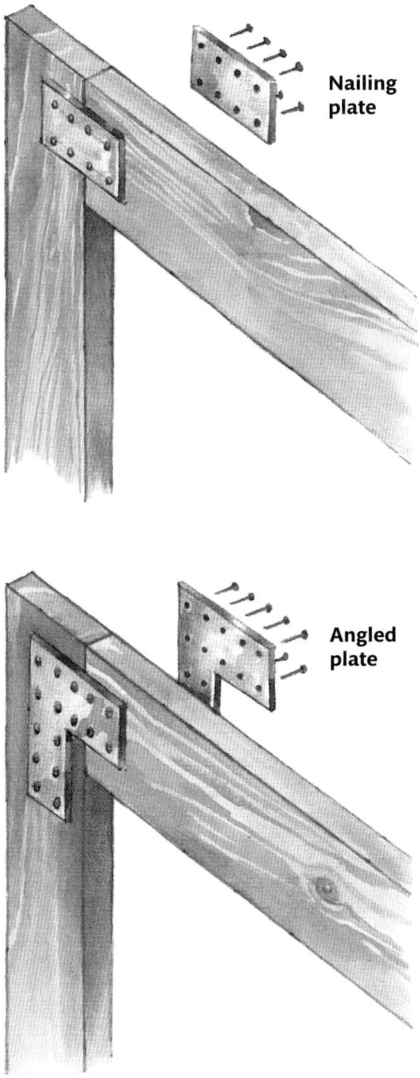

Nailing plate

Angled plate

Attaching framed lattice panels to posts

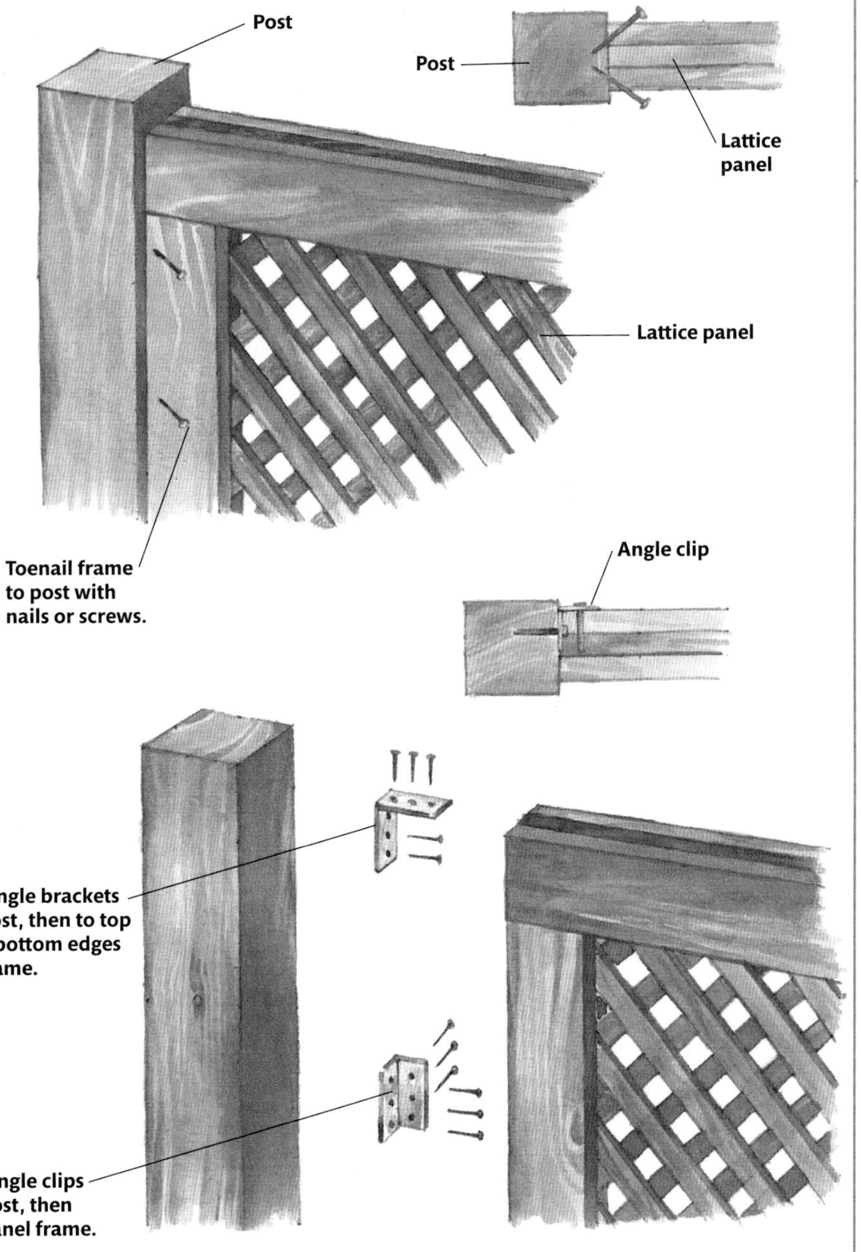

Post

Post

Lattice panel

Lattice panel

Toenail frame to post with nails or screws.

Angle clip

Fix angle brackets to post, then to top and bottom edges of frame.

Fix angle clips to post, then to panel frame.

Lattice-panel fence
(p. 57)

Separating the driveway from the backyard, this low fence is a barrier to balls and animals. The lattice is sandwiched in a frame of 1x3s and 1x2s. Note how the 1x2s are positioned to form an interlocking joint. (Alternatively, you could use the lattice-panel construction shown on p. 194.)

Panels wider than 6 ft. are awkward to construct and to install. It is easiest to construct the panels on a large flat surface (a garage or basement floor) ❶. Lay out the 1x3s that form one face of the panel; then nail the 1x2s to them ❷. Add the lattice, then the other layer of 1x3s ❸. As you work, regularly check that the panel is square, its corners at right angles. (Use a framing square or measure across the diagonals to check that they are equal.) If the lattice rattles in its groove, you can add ¾-in. quarter round as shown in the lower box to tighten the fit.

Depending on whether you have more confidence as a post setter or a panel builder, you can build the panels first, then use them to space the posts, or set the posts first and build the panels to fit. Either way, attach the panels to the posts by toenailing (with nails or screws)

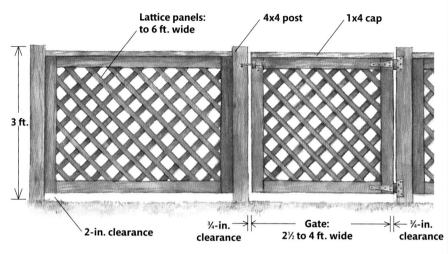

Lattice panels: to 6 ft. wide
4x4 post
1x4 cap
3 ft.
2-in. clearance
¾-in. clearance
Gate: 2½ to 4 ft. wide
¾-in. clearance

PANEL CONSTRUCTION

1x3
Framing square

❶ Lay out one face of the panel on a flat surface, checking the corners with a framing square.

CORNER DETAIL

1x2
1x3

❷ Nail the inner 1x2s in place, overlapping the face joints at the corners, as shown in the box above.

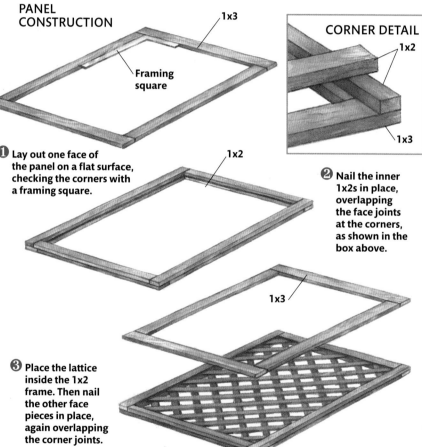

1x2

1x3

❸ Place the lattice inside the 1x2 frame. Then nail the other face pieces in place, again overlapping the corner joints.

FENCE CONSTRUCTION DETAIL

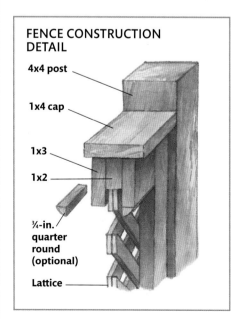

4x4 post
1x4 cap
1x3
1x2
¾-in. quarter round (optional)
Lattice

or with metal connectors along the lengths of the upright members. Add the 1x4 cap last.

The gate is just a lattice panel attached with sturdy strap hinges to one gate post and latched to the other. Allow ¾-in. clearance between each post and the gate. To counter the tendency to sag, you can add a diagonal brace on one or both sides, running from the top of the latch edge to the bottom of the hinge edge. If your path is wider than 4 ft., make a double gate, hinged on both sides; a single wide gate is clumsy and prone to sagging.

Lattice trellis
(pp. 66–69)

The trellises in this design support flowering vines in summer and dress up the garage wall in winter. Sheets of lattice 4 ft. wide are supported by 4x4 posts tucked behind the fascia board of the garage roof. Adding small triangles to the lattices creates arched alcoves to frame the plantings between trellises.

To position the postholes, drop a plumb bob from the fascia. The outer faces of the posts are 4 ft. apart, the width of the largest lattice sheets. To steady the tops of the posts, fix them to the soffit (preferably through the soffit into one of the 2x4 soffit nailers) with metal angle brackets. Toenail the angled 2x4 support to the post and soffit; then piece-in a triangle of lattice. You'll need to add a nailer to the post to provide a place to fix the lattice. The optional trim piece nailed to the outer faces of the posts and 2x4 support hides the ends of the lattice.

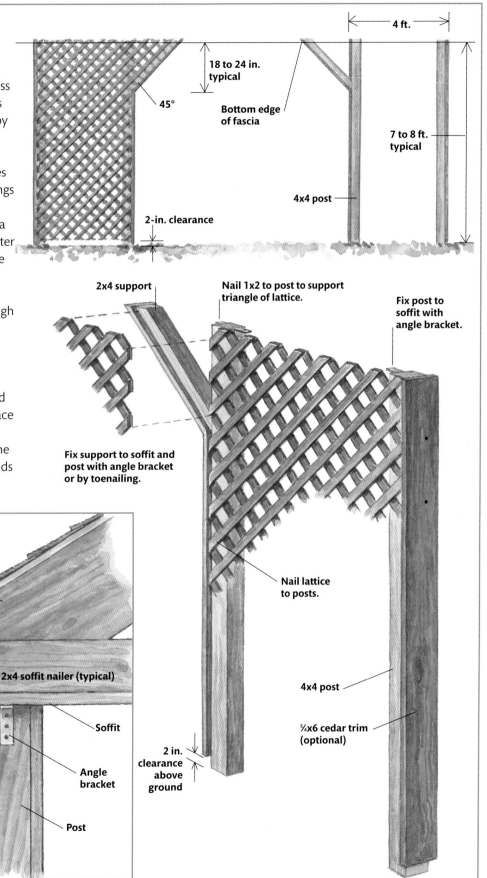

4 ft.

18 to 24 in. typical

45°

Bottom edge of fascia

7 to 8 ft. typical

4x4 post

2-in. clearance

2x4 support

Nail 1x2 to post to support triangle of lattice.

Fix post to soffit with angle bracket.

Fix support to soffit and post with angle bracket or by toenailing.

Nail lattice to posts.

4x4 post

¾x6 cedar trim (optional)

2 in. clearance above ground

POSITION AND ATTACHMENT OF POST

Roof rafter

Gutter

Fascia

2x4 soffit nailer (typical)

Soffit

Position post, lattice, and trim piece behind fascia.

Angle bracket

Lattice

Post

Trim piece extends beyond post 1 in.

Hideaway arbor
(pp. 94–97)

This cozy enclosure shelters a bench and supports vines to shade and soothe the occupants. Once the posts are set in place, this project can be finished in a few hours.

Although nails or screws will hold the double 2x6 joists in place, carriage bolts are far superior. Tack the joists in place with nails. Then bore holes through post and both joists with a long electrician's auger bit. Toenailing or metal rafter ties will hold the rafters in place. You can angle the ends of the joists and rafters with a handsaw; use a handheld electric jigsaw to cut the ogee pattern.

Lattice nailed or screwed to each post provides climbing support for the vines. Sandwich the lattice between 1x2 trim along the edges to support and dress it up. If the lattice is stiff enough, you can omit the trim.

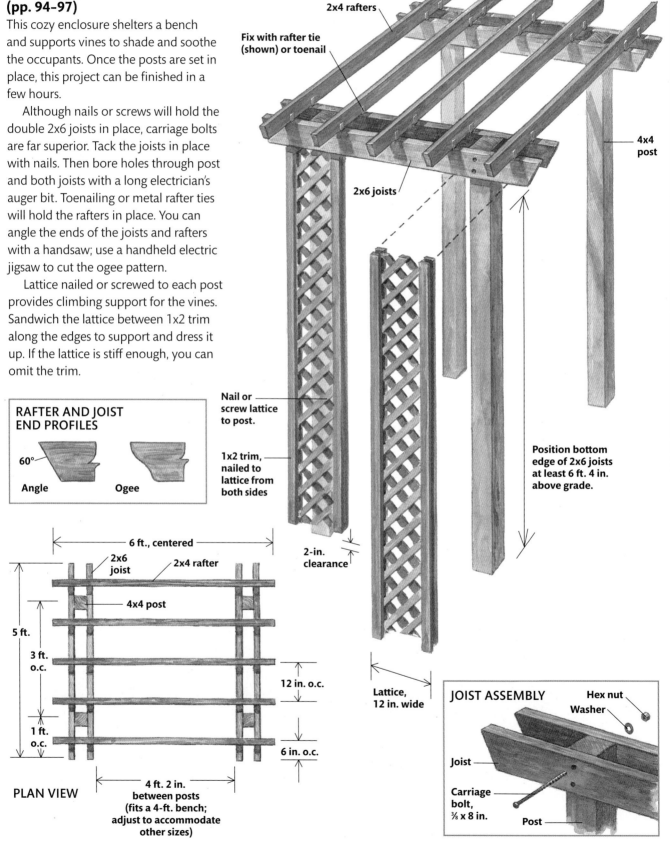

RAFTER AND JOIST END PROFILES

60° — **Angle**

Ogee

2x4 rafters

Fix with rafter tie (shown) or toenail

4x4 post

2x6 joists

Position bottom edge of 2x6 joists at least 6 ft. 4 in. above grade.

Nail or screw lattice to post.

1x2 trim, nailed to lattice from both sides

2-in. clearance

Lattice, 12 in. wide

PLAN VIEW

6 ft., centered

2x6 joist

2x4 rafter

4x4 post

5 ft.

3 ft. o.c.

1 ft. o.c.

12 in. o.c.

6 in. o.c.

4 ft. 2 in. between posts (fits a 4-ft. bench; adjust to accommodate other sizes)

JOIST ASSEMBLY

Hex nut

Washer

Joist

Carriage bolt, ⅜ x 8 in.

Post

Louvered fence
(pp. 88–89)

Made of vertical slats set at an angle, this 6-ft.-tall fence allows air circulation to plants and people near the patio while providing a privacy screen. Be sure to check local codes about height and setback from property lines.

The slats are supported top and bottom by 2x4 rails; a 2x6 beneath the bottom rail stiffens the entire structure, keeps the slat assembly from sagging, and adds visual weight to the design. Set the posts, then cut the rails to fit between them. Toenailed nails or screws or metal connectors are strong enough, but you can add a 2x4 nailer between the rails (as shown in the drawing at bottom right) to make positioning and assembly easier.

Position the 1x6 slats with a spacer block 1½ in. wide and angled 45° at its ends. Nailing or screwing down through the top rail is easy. Nailing up through the bottom rail is more difficult; instead, you could toenail through the edges or faces of the slats into the bottom rail.

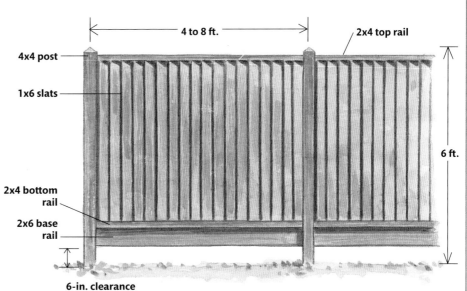

4 to 8 ft.

2x4 top rail

4x4 post

1x6 slats

2x4 bottom rail

2x6 base rail

6 ft.

6-in. clearance

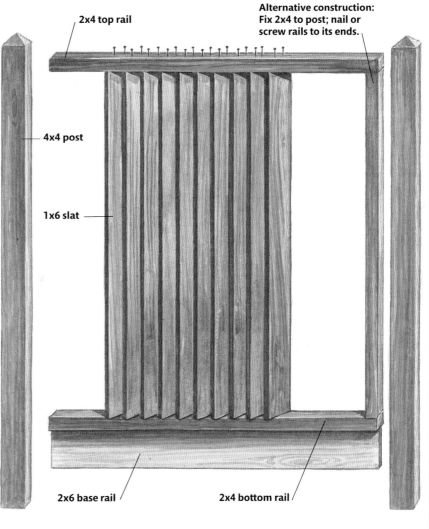

2x4 top rail

Alternative construction: Fix 2x4 to post; nail or screw rails to its ends.

4x4 post

1x6 slat

2x6 base rail

2x4 bottom rail

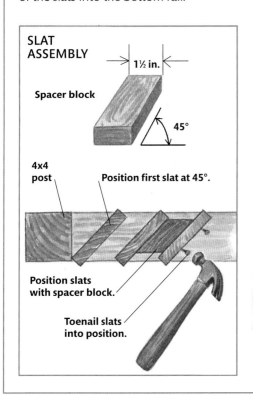

SLAT ASSEMBLY

1½ in.

Spacer block

45°

4x4 post

Position first slat at 45°.

Position slats with spacer block.

Toenail slats into position.

Good-neighbor fence
(pp. 74–76)

A variation on the traditional picket fence, this design provides privacy and good looks to neighbors on both sides, in addition to serving as a backdrop for a perennial border.

This is a simple fence to construct. Just set the posts, cut top and bottom rails to fit between them, and attach the slats. Note that the slats overlap roughly ½ in.; a 4½-in.-wide spacer block (1 in. narrower than the actual 5½-in. width of the 1x6s) makes positioning them a snap. Use two screws or nails positioned diagonally for each slat-to-rail connection.

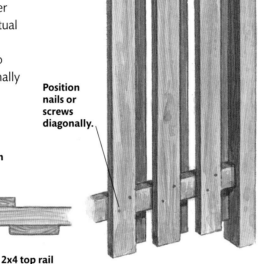

1x6 slats
4x4 post
2x4 top rail
Position nails or screws diagonally.

PLAN VIEW Slats overlap on each side ½ in.

4x4 post
2x4 top rail

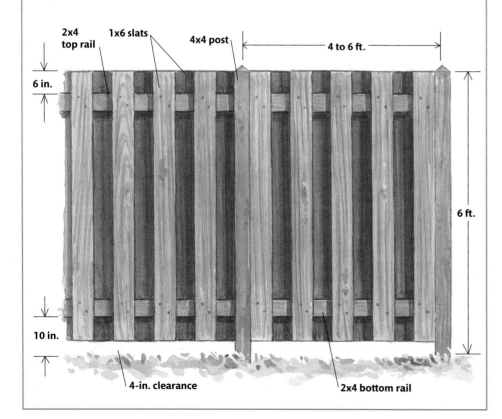

2x4 top rail
1x6 slats
4x4 post
4 to 6 ft.
6 in.
6 ft.
10 in.
4-in. clearance
2x4 bottom rail

Lattice skirting for a deck
(pp. 78–80)

The lattice in this project provides support for vines, while giving the base of the deck some airy visual weight. Of all the projects, this is the most dependent upon the configuration of your deck. In our example, we show a 2x4 framework fitted to a deck whose posts are 8 ft. on center. The frame supports the edges and center of 4x8 sheets of lattice applied vertically. If the lattice is stiff enough, the central horizontal supports could be omitted. Taller decks or different post spacings will require slightly different positioning of the lattice sheets to fill the area and a different framing pattern to support the lattice edges.

Nail or screw the top 2x4 frame rail to the deck joists. Then nail the 2x6 base rail and 2x4 bottom rail between existing posts. Fix 2x4 side rails to the posts, and cut and toenail the central vertical support in place; then add the central horizontal supports. Position the frame back from the front edge of the posts by the thickness of the lattice and 1x2 trim, as shown here. (The trim is optional; alter the frame position if you omit it.) Note that the central supports are oriented with their wide faces out, to facilitate nailing two lattice sheets edge to edge.

To accommodate the 4-ft.-wide lattice panels on the side of the deck, we've added a new post, sunk in the ground and fixed at top to the deck. A similar 2x4 frame supports the lattice.

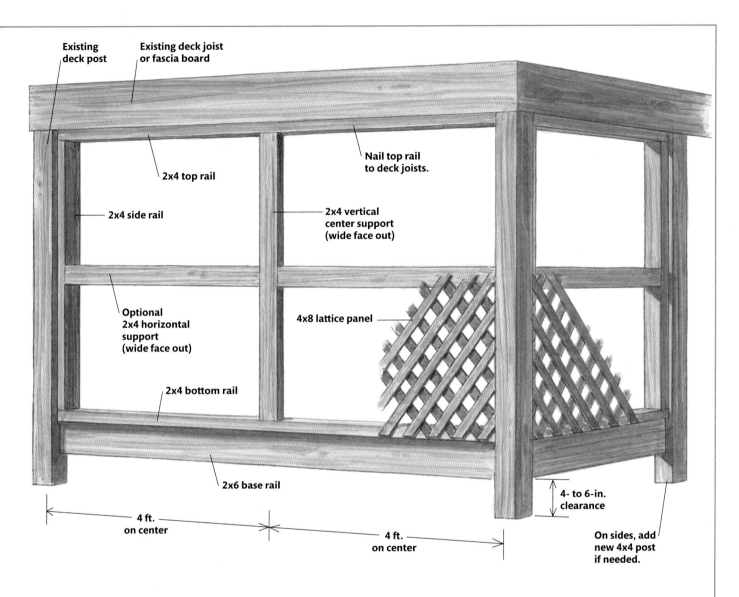

Existing deck post

Existing deck joist or fascia board

2x4 top rail

Nail top rail to deck joists.

2x4 side rail

2x4 vertical center support (wide face out)

Optional 2x4 horizontal support (wide face out)

4x8 lattice panel

2x4 bottom rail

2x6 base rail

4- to 6-in. clearance

4 ft. on center

4 ft. on center

On sides, add new 4x4 post if needed.

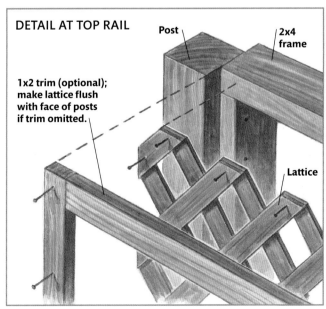

DETAIL AT TOP RAIL

Post

2x4 frame

1x2 trim (optional); make lattice flush with face of posts if trim omitted.

Lattice

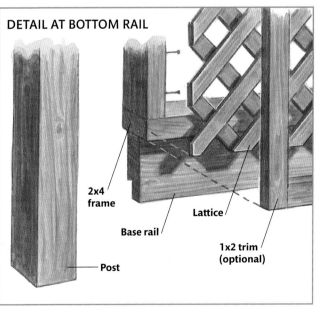

DETAIL AT BOTTOM RAIL

2x4 frame

Base rail

Lattice

1x2 trim (optional)

Post

Entry arbor and fence
(pp. 44–47)

This arbor makes an event of the passage from sidewalk to front door or from one part of your property to another. Two versions are shown in the Portfolio. One features the arbor alone; the other adds a picket fence.

Hefty 6x6 posts provide real presence here; the 12-footers you'll need are heavy, so engage a couple of helpers to save your back. As with the previous arbor, once the posts are set, the job is easy. You can toenail the 3x6 beams to the tops of the posts and the 2x4 rafters to the beams. (Or you can fix them with long spikes or lag screws, 10 in. and 8 in. long, respectively. This job is easier if you drill pilot holes, with bits slightly thinner than the spikes.) Attach the 2x2 cross rafters with screws or nails. If you can't buy 3x6s, you can nail two 2x6s together face to face.

Sandwich lattice between 1x3s to make the side panels and fix them between posts with nails, screws, or metal connectors. Alternating the corner overlap, as shown on the drawing, makes a stronger frame.

The fence forms small enclosures on either side of the arbor before heading off across the property. To match the arbor, use 6x6 posts for the enclosures; then switch to 4x4s if you wish, spacing them no farther apart than 8 ft.

You can purchase ready-made lengths of picket fence, but it is easy enough to make yourself. Set the posts; then cut and fit 2x4 rails on edge between them. Space 1x3 picket slats 1½ in. apart. The drawing on the facing page shows large round wooden finials atop the fence posts; you can buy various types of ready-made finials, or you could work a heavy bevel around the top end of the posts themselves.

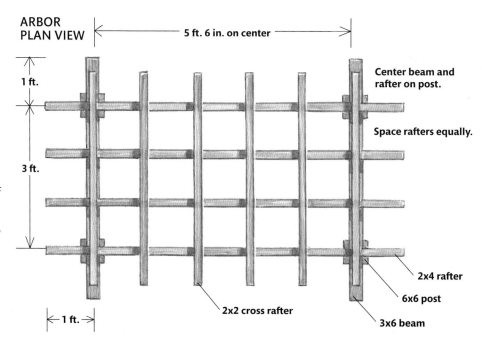

ARBOR PLAN VIEW

5 ft. 6 in. on center

1 ft.

3 ft.

1 ft.

Center beam and rafter on post.

Space rafters equally.

2x4 rafter

6x6 post

3x6 beam

2x2 cross rafter

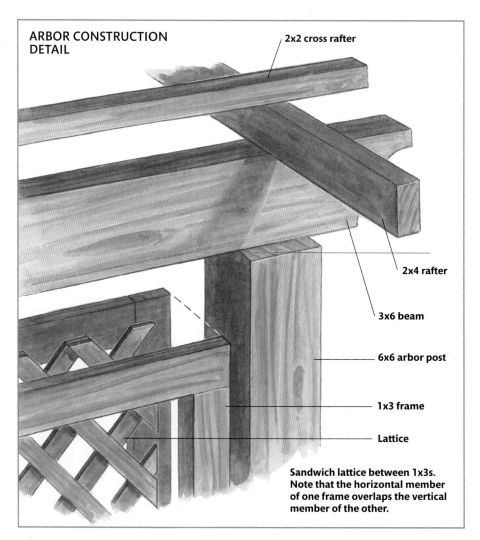

ARBOR CONSTRUCTION DETAIL

2x2 cross rafter

2x4 rafter

3x6 beam

6x6 arbor post

1x3 frame

Lattice

Sandwich lattice between 1x3s. Note that the horizontal member of one frame overlaps the vertical member of the other.

ARBOR SIDE ELEVATION DETAIL

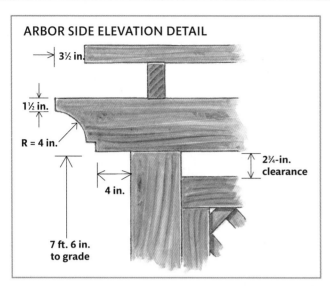

3½ in.

1½ in.

R = 4 in.

4 in.

2¾-in. clearance

7 ft. 6 in. to grade

FENCE PLAN VIEW

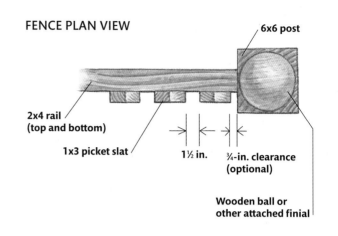

6x6 post

2x4 rail (top and bottom)

1x3 picket slat

1½ in.

¾-in. clearance (optional)

Wooden ball or other attached finial

Entry arbor and fence

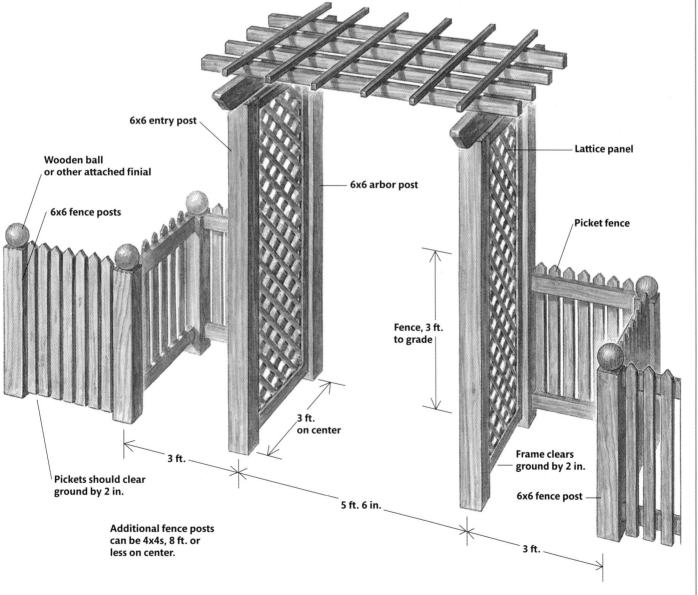

6x6 entry post

Wooden ball or other attached finial

6x6 fence posts

6x6 arbor post

Lattice panel

Picket fence

Fence, 3 ft. to grade

3 ft. on center

3 ft.

Pickets should clear ground by 2 in.

Additional fence posts can be 4x4s, 8 ft. or less on center.

5 ft. 6 in.

Frame clears ground by 2 in.

6x6 fence post

3 ft.

Preparing the Soil for Planting

The better the soil, the better the plants. Soil quality affects how fast plants grow, how big they get, how good they look, and how long they live. But on many residential lots, the soil is shallow and infertile. Unless you're lucky enough to have a better-than-average site where the soil has been cared for and amended over the years, perhaps for use as a vegetable garden or flower bed, you should plan to improve your soil before planting in it.

If you were planting just a few trees or shrubs, you could prepare individual planting holes for them and leave the surrounding soil undisturbed. However, for nearly all the plantings in this book, digging individual holes is impractical,

and it's much better for the plants if you prepare the soil throughout the entire area that will be planted. (The major exception is when you're planting under a tree, which we'll discuss on p. 198.)

For most of the situations shown in this book, you could prepare the soil with hand tools—a spade, digging fork, and rake. The job goes faster, though, if you use a rototiller, and a rototiller is better than hand tools for mixing amendments into the soil. Unless you grow vegetables, you probably won't use a rototiller often enough to justify buying one yourself, but you can easily borrow or rent a rototiller or hire someone with a tiller to come and prepare your site.

Common fertilizers and soil amendments

The following materials serve different purposes. Follow soil-test recommendations or the advice of an experienced gardener in choosing which amendments would be best for your soil. If so recommended, you can apply two or three of these amendments at the same time, using the stated rate for each one.

Material	Description	Amount for 100 sq. ft.
Bagged steer manure	A weak all-purpose fertilizer.	6–8 lb.
Dried poultry manure	A high-nitrogen fertilizer.	2 lb.
5-5-5 all-purpose fertilizer	An inexpensive and popular synthetic fertilizer.	2 lb.
Superphosphate or rock phosphate	Supplies phosphorus. Work into the soil as deep as possible.	2–4 lb.
Greensand	Supplies potassium and many trace elements.	2–4 lb.
Regular or dolomitic limestone	Used primarily to sweeten acid soil.	5 lb.
Gypsum	Helps loosen clay soil. Also helps reduce salt buildup in roadside soil.	2 lb.
Wood ashes	Supply potassium, phosphorus, and lime.	2–4 lb.

Loosen the soil

After you've removed any sod or other vegetation from the designated area (see pp. 164–165), the first step is digging or tilling to loosen the soil ❶. Do this on a day when the soil is moist—not so wet that it sticks to your tools or so dry that it makes dust. Start at one end of the bed and work back and forth until you reach the other end. Try to dig down at least 8 in., or deeper if possible. If the ground is very compacted, you'll have to make repeated passes with a tiller to reach 8 in. deep. Toss aside any large rocks, roots, or debris that you encounter. When you're working near a house or other buildings, watch out for buried wires, cables, and pipes. Most town and city governments have a number you can call to request that someone help you locate buried utilities.

After this initial digging, the ground will probably be very rough and lumpy. Farmers used to plow in the fall and let frost break the clods apart over the winter. That's still a good system; if you plan ahead and do the initial digging in fall, it's easy to finish preparing the soil in spring. But you can do the whole job in one day, too, if you want to. Whump the clods with the back of a digging fork or make another pass with the tiller. Continue until you've reduced all the clumps to the size of apples.

Loosening the existing soil comes first, because that's when you can dig as deep as possible. Then add some topsoil and rake it around if you want to fill in some low spots, refine the grade, or raise the planting area above the surrounding grade for improved visibility and better drainage. Unless you need just a few bags of it, order screened topsoil by the cubic yard from a landscape contractor.

Add organic matter

Common dirt (and purchased topsoil, too) consists mainly of rock and mineral fragments of various sizes—which are mostly coarse and gritty in sandy soil, and dust-fine in clay soil. One of the best things you can do to improve any kind of soil for garden plants is to add some organic matter. Sold in bags or in bulk at nurseries and garden centers, organic materials include all kinds of composted plant parts and animal manures.

How much organic matter should you use? Spread a layer 2 to 3 in. thick across the entire area you're working on ❷. At this thickness, a cubic yard (about one heaping pickup-truck load) of bulk material, or six bales of peat moss, will cover 100 to 150 sq. ft. If you're working on a large area and need several cubic yards of organic matter, have it delivered. Ask the driver to dump the pile as close to your project area as possible; it's worth allowing the truck to drive across your lawn to get there. You can spread a big truckload of material in just a few hours if you don't have to cart it very far.

Add fertilizers and mineral amendments

Organic matter improves the soil's texture and helps it retain water and nutrients, but it doesn't actually supply many nutrients. To provide the nutrients that plants need, you need to use organic or synthetic fertilizers and powdered minerals. It's most helpful if you mix these materials into the soil before you do any planting, putting them down into the root zone as shown in the drawing ❸, but you can also sprinkle them on top of the soil in subsequent years to maintain a planting.

Getting a sample of soil tested (a service that's usually available free or at low cost through your County Extension Service) is the most accurate way to determine how much of which nutrients is needed. Less precise, but often adequate, is asking the advice of an experienced gardener in your neighborhood. Test results or a gardener's advice will point out any significant deficiencies in your soil, but these are uncommon. Most soil just needs a moderate, balanced dose of nutrients.

Most important is to avoid using too much of any fertilizer or mineral. Don't guess at this; measure and weigh carefully. Calculate your plot's area. Follow your soil-test results, instructions on a commercial product's package, or the general guidelines given in the chart above, and weigh out the appropriate amount, using a kitchen or bathroom scale. Apply the material evenly across the plot with a spreader or by hand.

PREPARING THE SOIL FOR PLANTING

❶ Use a spade, digging fork, or tiller to dig at least 8 in. deep and break the soil into rough clods. Discard rocks, roots, and debris. Watch out for underground utilities.

❷ Spread a 2- to 3-in. layer of organic matter on top of the soil.

❸ Sprinkle measured amounts of fertilizer and mineral amendments evenly across the entire area, and mix thoroughly into the soil.

Mix and smooth the soil

Finally, use a digging fork or tiller and go back and forth across the bed again until the added materials are mixed thoroughly into the soil and everything is broken into nut-size or smaller lumps ❹. Then use a rake to smooth the surface ❺.

At this point, the soil level may look too high compared with adjacent pavement or lawn, but don't worry. It will settle a few inches over the next several weeks and end up close to its original level.

Working near trees

Plantings under the shade of lovely old trees can be cool lovely oases, like the ones shown on pp. 106–109. But to establish the plants, you'll need to contend with the tree's roots. Contrary to popular belief, most tree roots are in the top few inches of the soil, and they extend at least as far away from the trunk as the limbs do. If you dig anyplace in that area, you'll probably cut or bruise some of the tree's roots. When preparing for planting beneath a tree, therefore, it is important to disturb as few roots as possible.

It is natural for a tree's trunk to flare out at the bottom and for the roots near the trunk to be partly above ground. Don't bury them. However, if the soil has eroded away from roots farther out from the trunk, it's okay to add a layer of soil up to several inches deep and top the new soil with a thinner layer of mulch. Adding some soil like this makes it easier to start ground covers or other plants underneath a tree. (See p. 205 for planting instructions.) Just don't overdo it—covering roots with too much soil can starve them of oxygen, damaging or killing them, and piling soil close to the trunk can rot the bark.

❹ Use a tiller or digging fork to mix everything together, again working as deep as possible.

❺ Finish by smoothing the surface with a rake.

Making neat edges

All but the most informal landscapes look best if you define and maintain neat edges between the lawn and any adjacent plantings. There are several ways to do this, varying in appearance, effectiveness, cost, and convenience. For the Mid-Atlantic region, the best methods are cut brick or stone and plastic strip edges. Several other prefab edging systems that you may see in catalogs work well only in warmer climates; they tend to frost-heave in cold winters. In any case, the time to install an edging is after you prepare the soil but before you plant the bed.

Cut edge

Lay a hose or rope on the ground to mark the line where you want to cut. Then cut along the line with a sharp spade or edging tool. Lift away any grass that was growing into the bed (or any plants that were running out into the lawn). Use a rake or hoe to smooth out a shallow trench on the bed side of the cut. Keep the trench empty; don't let it fill up with mulch.

Pros and cons: Free. Good for straight or curved edges, level or sloped sites. You have to recut the edge at least twice a year, in spring and late summer, but you can cut 50 to 100 ft. in an hour or so. Don't cut the trench too deep; if a mower wheel slips down into it, you scalp the lawn. Crabgrass and other weeds may sprout in the exposed soil.

Brick mowing strip

Dig a trench about 8 in. wide and 4 in. deep around the edge of the bed. Fill it halfway with sand; then lay bricks on top, setting them level with the soil on the lawn side. You'll need three bricks per foot of edging. Sweep extra sand into any cracks between the bricks. You'll probably have to reset a few frost-heaved bricks each spring. You can substitute cut stone blocks or concrete pavers for bricks.

Pros and cons: Good for straight or curved edges on level or gently sloped sites. Looks good in combination with brick walkways, or brick house. Fairly easy to install and maintain. Some kinds of grass and plants will grow under, between, or over the bricks.

Plastic strip edging

Garden centers and home-improvement stores sell heavy-duty plastic edging in strips 5 or 6 in. wide and 20 or 50 ft. long. To install it, use a sharp tool to cut straight down through the sod around the edge of the bed. Hold the edging so the round lip sits right at soil level, and drive the stakes through the bottom of the edging and into the undisturbed soil under the lawn. Stakes, which are supplied with the edging, should be at least 8 in. long and set about 3 ft. apart.

Pros and cons: Good for straight or curved edges, but only on relatively level sites. Neat and carefree when well installed, but installation is a two- or three-person job. If the lip isn't set right on the ground, you're likely to hit it with the mower blade. Liable to frost-heave unless it's very securely staked. Hard to drive stakes in rocky soil. Some kinds of grass and ground covers can grow across the top of the edging.

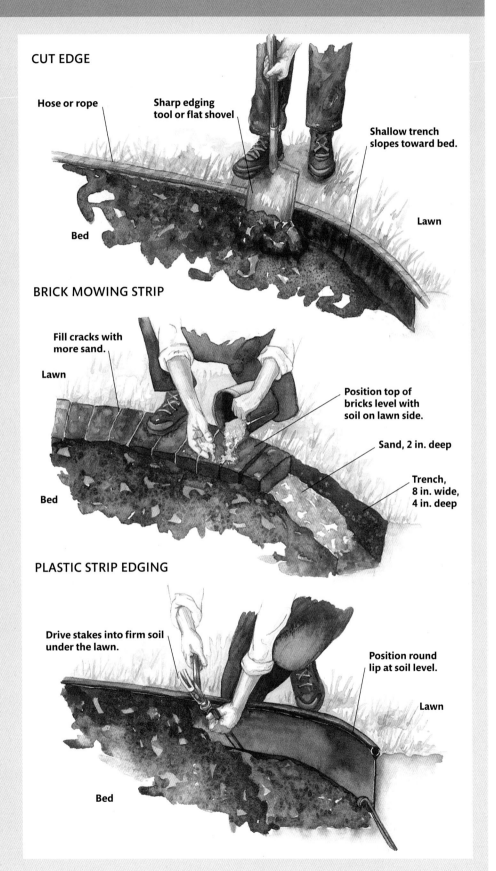

CUT EDGE

Hose or rope

Sharp edging tool or flat shovel

Shallow trench slopes toward bed.

Lawn

Bed

BRICK MOWING STRIP

Fill cracks with more sand.

Lawn

Position top of bricks level with soil on lawn side.

Sand, 2 in. deep

Trench, 8 in. wide, 4 in. deep

Bed

PLASTIC STRIP EDGING

Drive stakes into firm soil under the lawn.

Position round lip at soil level.

Lawn

Bed

Buying Plants

Once you have chosen and planned a landscape project, make a list of the plants you want and start thinking about where to get them. You'll need to locate the kinds of plants you're looking for, choose good-quality plants, and get enough of the plants to fill your design area.

Where and how to shop

You may already have a favorite place to shop for plants. If not, search the internet for Nursery Stock, Nurserymen, Garden Centers, and Landscape Contractors, and choose a few places to visit. Take your shopping list, find a salesperson, and ask for help. The plants in this book are commonly available in the Mid-Atlantic region, but you may not find everything you want at one place. The salesperson may refer you to another nursery, offer to special-order plants, or recommend similar plants as substitutes.

If you're buying too many plants to carry in your car or truck, ask about delivery—it's usually available and sometimes free. Some nurseries offer to replace plants that fail within a limited guarantee period, so ask about that, too.

The staff at a good nursery or garden center will usually be able to answer most of the questions you have about which plants to buy and how to care for them. If you can, go shopping on a rainy weekday when business is slow so staff will have time to answer your questions.

Don't be lured by the low prices of plants for sale at supermarkets or discount stores unless you're sure you know exactly what you're looking for and what you're looking at. The salespeople at these stores rarely have the time or knowledge to offer you much help, and the plants are often disorganized, unlabeled, and stressed by poor care.

If you can't find a plant locally or have a retailer order it for you, you can always order it yourself from an online plant retailer nursery. Most mail-order nurseries produce good plants and pack them well, but if you haven't dealt with a business before, be smart and place a minimum order first. Judge the quality of the plants that arrive; then decide whether or not to order larger quantities from that firm.

Timing

It's a good idea to plan ahead and start shopping for plants before you're ready to put them in the ground. That way, if you can't find everything on your list, you'll have time to keep shopping around, place special orders, or choose substitutes. Most nurseries will let you "flag" an order for later pickup or delivery, and they'll take care of the plants in the meantime. Or you can bring the plants home; just remember to check the soil in the containers every day and water if needed.

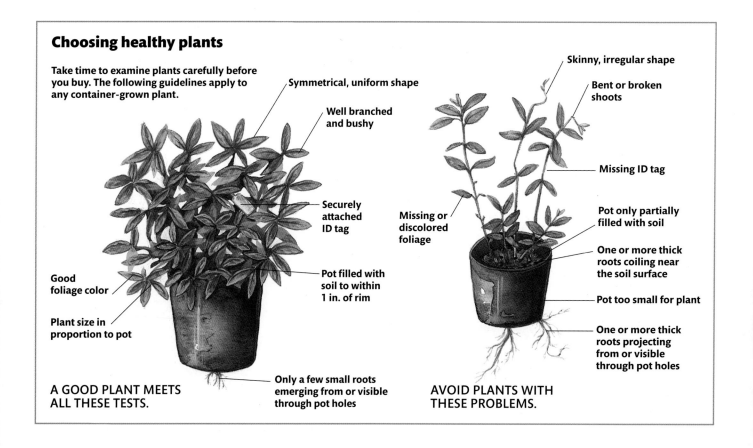

Choosing healthy plants

Take time to examine plants carefully before you buy. The following guidelines apply to any container-grown plant.

Symmetrical, uniform shape

Well branched and bushy

Securely attached ID tag

Good foliage color

Plant size in proportion to pot

Pot filled with soil to within 1 in. of rim

Only a few small roots emerging from or visible through pot holes

A GOOD PLANT MEETS ALL THESE TESTS.

Skinny, irregular shape

Bent or broken shoots

Missing ID tag

Missing or discolored foliage

Pot only partially filled with soil

One or more thick roots coiling near the soil surface

Pot too small for plant

One or more thick roots projecting from or visible through pot holes

AVOID PLANTS WITH THESE PROBLEMS.

Choosing particular plants

If you need, for example, five mugo pines and the nursery or garden center has a whole block of them, how do you choose which five to buy? The sales staff may be too busy to help you decide; you often have to choose by yourself.

Most plants nowadays are grown in containers, so it's possible to lift them one at a time and examine them from all sides. Following the guidelines shown in the drawings opposite, evaluate each plant's shape, size, health and vigor, and root system.

Trees and shrubs are frequently sold "balled-and-burlapped," that is, with a ball of soil and roots wrapped tightly in burlap. For these plants, look for strong limbs with no broken shoots, an attractive profile, and healthy foliage. Then press your hands against the burlap-covered root ball to make sure that it feels firm, solid, and damp, not loose or dry. (If the ball is buried within a bed of wood chips, carefully pull the chips aside; then push them back after inspecting the plant.)

To make the final cut when you're choosing a group of plants, line them up side by side and select the ones that are most closely matched in height, bushiness, and foliage color. If your design includes a hedge or mass planting where uniformity is very important, it's a good idea to buy a few extra plants as potential replacements in case of damage or loss. It's easier to plan ahead than to find a match later. Plant the extras in a spare corner and you'll have them if you need them.

Sometimes a plant will be available in two or more sizes. Which is better? That depends on how patient you are. The main reason for buying bigger plants is to make a landscape look impressive right away. If you buy smaller plants and set them out at the same spacing, the planting will look sparse at first, but it will soon catch up. A year after planting, you can't tell if a perennial came from a quart- or gallon-size pot: they look the same. For shrubs, the difference between one size pot and the next usually represents one year's growth.

The Planting Process

Throughout the Mid-Atlantic region, spring is the best season for planting. You can start planting as soon as the soil thaws and the nurseries open, and continue through May with good results. Planting in spring gives the plants a whole growing season to send out roots and get established before facing the rigors of winter. The second-best time for planting is from mid-September to early November, after the heat of summer but before hard frosts. If you want to plant during the summer, do it on a cloudy day when rain is forecast for the next day or so.

Compared with preparing the soil, putting plants in the ground goes quite quickly. If you're well prepared, you can plant a whole bed in just an hour or two.

Try to stay off the soil

Throughout the planting process, do all you can by reaching in from outside the bed—don't step on the newly prepared soil if you can help it. Stepping or walking in the bed compacts the soil and makes it harder to dig planting holes. Use short boards or scraps of plywood as temporary steppingstones if you do need to walk around on the soil. As soon as you can decide where to put them, you might want to lay permanent steppingstones for access to plants that need regular maintenance.

Check placement and spacing

The first step in planting is to mark the position of each plant. The simplest way to do this is to arrange the plants themselves on the bed. Use an empty pot or a stake to represent any plant that's too heavy to move easily. Use a yardstick to check the spacing, and set the plants in place.

Then step back and take a look. Walk around and look from all sides. Go into the house and look out the window. What do you think? Should any of the plants be adjusted a little? Don't worry if the planting looks a little sparse now—it should. Plants almost always grow faster and get bigger than you can imagine when you're first setting them out, and it's almost always better to allow space and wait a few years for them to fill in than to crowd them too close together at first and have to keep pruning and thinning them later.

PLANTING POINTERS

When working on top of prepared soil, kneel on a piece of plywood to distribute your weight.

Use empty pots or stakes to mark positions of plants not yet purchased or too heavy to move frequently.

Moving through the job

When you're satisfied with the arrangement, mark the position of each plant with a stake or stone, and set the plants aside out of the way, so you won't knock them over or step on them as you proceed. Start planting in order of size. Do the biggest plants first, then move on to the medium-size and smaller plants. If all the plants are about the same size, start at the back of the bed and work toward the front, or start in the center and work to the edges.

Position trees and shrubs to show their best side

Most trees and shrubs are slightly asymmetric. There's usually enough irregularity in their branching or shape that one side looks a little fuller or more attractive than the other sides do. After you've set a tree or shrub into its hole, step back and take a look. Then turn it partway, or try tilting or tipping it a little to one side or the other. Once you've decided which side and position looks best, start filling in the hole with soil. Stop and check again before you firm the soil into place.

The fine points of spacing

When you're planting a group of the same kind of plants, such as perennials or ferns, it normally looks best if you space them informally, in slightly curved or zigzag rows, with the plants in one row offset from those of the next row. Don't arrange plants in a straight row unless you want to emphasize a line, such as the edge of a bed. After planting, step back and evaluate the effect. If you want to adjust the placement or position of any plant, now is the time to do so.

Rake, water, and mulch

Use a garden rake to level out any high and low spots that remain after planting. Water enough to settle the soil into place around the roots. Mulch the entire planting area with 1 to 3 in. of composted bark, wood chips, or other organic matter. Mulch is indispensable for controlling weeds and regulating the moisture and temperature of the soil. If you're running out of time, you don't have to spread the mulch right away, but try to get it done within the next week or so.

Using annuals as fillers

The plants in our designs have been spaced so they will not be crowded at maturity. Buying more plants and spacing them closer may fill things out faster, but in several years (for perennials; longer for shrubs) you'll need to remove plants or prune them frequently.

If you want something to fill the gaps between newly planted perennials, shrubs, or ground covers for that first year or two, use some annuals. The best annual fillers are compact plants that grow only 6 to 10 in. tall. These will hide the soil or mulch and make a colorful carpet. Avoid taller annuals, because they can shade or smother your permanent plantings.

The following annuals are all compact, easy to grow, readily available, and inexpensive. Seeds of those marked with a symbol (✿) can be sown directly in the garden about the time of last frost. For the others, buy six-packs or flats of plants. Thin seedlings or space plants 8 to 12 in. apart.

Annual phlox ✿: Red, pink, or white flowers. Good for hot dry sites.
China pink ✿: Red, pink, white, or bicolor flowers. Blooms all summer.
Dusty miller: Silvery foliage, often lacy-textured. No flowers.
Edging lobelia: Dark blue, magenta, or white flowers. Likes afternoon shade.

Flossflower: Fluffy blue, lavender, or white flowers. Choose dwarf types.
Garden verbena: Bright red, pink, purple, or white flowers. Good for hot dry sites.
Globe candytuft ✿: Pink or white flowers. Grows and blooms fast, then goes to seed.
Moss rose: Bright flowers in many colors. Ideal for hot dry sites.
Pansy and viola: Multicolored flowers. Grow best in cool weather.
Sweet alyssum ✿: Fragrant white or lilac flowers. Blooms for months. Very easy.
Wax begonia: Rose, pink, or white flowers. Good for shady sites but also takes sun.

Planting Basics

Most of the plants that you buy for a landscaping project today are grown and sold in individual plastic containers, but large shrubs and trees may be balled-and-burlapped. Mail-order plants may come bare-root. And ground covers are sometimes sold in flats. In any case, the basic concern is the same: Be careful what you do to a plant's roots. Spread them out; don't fold or coil them or cram them into a tight hole. Keep them covered; don't let the sun or air dry them out. And don't bury them too deep; set the top of the root ball level with the surrounding soil.

Planting container-grown plants

The steps are the same for any plant, no matter what size container it's growing in. Dig a hole that's a little wider than the container but not quite as deep ❶. Check by setting the container into the hole—the top of the soil in the container should be slightly higher than the surrounding soil. Dig several holes at a time, at the positions that you've already marked out.

Remove the container ❷. With one hand, grip the plant at the base of its stems or leaves, like pulling a ponytail, while you tug on the pot with the other hand. If the pot doesn't slide off easily,

don't pull harder on the stems. Try whacking the pot against a hard surface; if it still doesn't slide off, use a strong knife to cut or pry it off.

Examine the plant's roots ❸. If there are any thick, coiled roots, unwind them and cut them off close to the root ball, leaving short stubs. If the root ball is a mass of fine, hairlike roots, use the knife to cut three or four slits from top to bottom, about 1 in. deep. Pry the slits apart and tease the cut roots to loosen them. This cutting or slitting may seem drastic, but it's actually good for the plant because it forces new roots to grow out into the surrounding soil. Work quickly. Once you've taken a plant out of its container, get it in the ground as soon as possible. If you want to prepare several plants at a time, cover them with an old sheet or tarp to keep the roots from drying out.

Set the root ball into the hole ❹. Make sure that the plant is positioned right, with its best side facing out, and that the top of the root ball is level with or slightly higher than the surface of the bed. Then add enough soil to fill in the hole, and pat it down firmly.

PLANTING CONTAINER-GROWN PLANTS

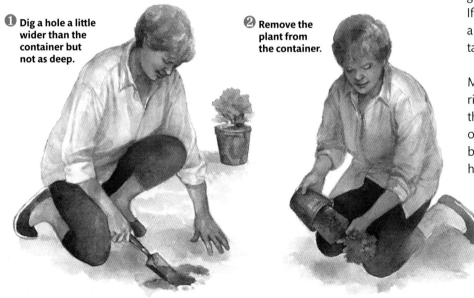

❶ Dig a hole a little wider than the container but not as deep.

❷ Remove the plant from the container.

❸ Unwind any large, coiled roots and cut them off short. Cut vertical slits through masses of fine roots.

❹ Position the plant in the hole, and fill in around it with soil.

Planting a balled-and-burlapped shrub or tree

Nurseries often grow shrubs and trees in fields, then dig them with a ball of root-filled soil and wrap a layer of burlap snugly around the ball to keep it intact. The problem is that even a small ball of soil is very heavy. A root ball that is a foot wide is a two-person job. For larger root balls, ask the nursery to deliver and plant it. Here's how to proceed with plants that are small enough that you can handle them.

Dig a hole several inches wider than the root ball but not quite as deep as the root ball is high. Firm the soil so the plant won't sink. Set the plant into the hole, and lay a stick across the top of the root ball to make sure it's at or a little higher than grade level. Be sure to cut or untie any twine that wraps around the trunk. If the root ball is enclosed in a wire basket, remove it before placing the plant in the hole. Fold the burlap down around the sides of the ball. Don't try to pull the burlap out altogether—roots can grow out through it, and it will eventually decompose. Fill soil all around the sides of the ball and pat it down firmly. Spread only an inch of soil over the top of the ball.

The top of the ball should be level with the surrounding soil. Cut twine that wraps around the trunk. Fold down the burlap, but don't remove it.

Planting bare-root plants

Mail-order nurseries sometimes dig perennials, roses, and other plants when the plants are dormant, cut back the tops, and wash all the soil off the roots, to save space and weight when storing and shipping them. If you receive a plant in bare-root condition, unwrap it, trim away any roots that are broken or damaged, and soak the roots in a pail of water for several hours.

To plant, dig a hole large enough that you can spread the roots across the bottom without folding them. Start covering the roots with soil, then lay a stick across the top of the hole and hold the plant against it to check the planting depth, as shown in the drawing. Raise or lower the plant if needed in order to bury just the roots, not the buds. Add more soil, firming it down around the roots, and continue until the hole is full.

Dig a hole wide enough that you can spread out the roots. A stick helps position the plant at the correct depth as you fill the hole with soil.

Planting ground covers from flats

Sometimes ground covers are sold in flats of 25 or more rooted cuttings. Start at one corner, reach underneath the soil, and lift out a portion of the flat's contents. Working quickly, because the roots are exposed, tease the cuttings apart, trying not to break off any roots, and plant them individually. Then lift out the next portion and continue planting.

Remove a clump of little plants; tease their roots apart; and plant them quickly.

Planting bulbs

Plant spring-blooming bulbs in October and November. If the soil in the bed was well prepared, you can use a trowel to dig holes for planting individual bulbs; where you have room, you can dig a wider hole or trench for planting a group of bulbs all at once. The perennials, ground covers, shrubs, and trees you planted earlier in the fall or in the spring will still be small enough that you won't disturb their roots. As a rule of thumb, plant small (grape- or cherry-size) bulbs about 2 in. deep and 3 to 5 in. apart, and large (walnut- or egg-size) bulbs 4 to 6 in. deep and 6 to 10 in. apart.

Plant bulbs with the pointed end up, at a depth and spacing determined by the size of the bulb.

Basic Landscape Care

Planting under a tree

When planting beneath a mature tree, as for the design on pp. 106–109, remember that most tree roots are in the top few inches of the soil, and they extend at least as far away from the trunk as the limbs do. For areas of ground cover and most container-grown perennials, you can add topsoil and organic amendments up to about 6 in. deep over the entire area; then set the plants out in the new soil. Larger plants need deeper holes. Whether you dig their planting holes in existing soil or through a layer of added topsoil, dig carefully, disturbing as few tree roots as possible. If you find a large root, move the planting hole rather than sever the root.

Confining perennials

Yarrow, bee balm, artemisia, and various other perennials, grasses, and ferns easily take over landscape beds with their underground runners. To confine these plants to a limited area, install a barrier when you plant them. Cut the bottom off a 5-gal. or larger plastic pot, bury the pot so its rim is above the soil, and plant the perennial inside. You'll need to lift, divide, and replant part of the perennial every second or third year.

Position rim above soil surface.

Remove bottom of pot.

The landscape plantings in this book will grow increasingly carefree from year to year as the plants mature, but of course you'll always need to do some regular maintenance. Depending on the design you choose, this ongoing care may require as much as a few hours a week during the season or as little as a few hours a year. No matter what you plant, you'll have to control weeds, use mulch, water as needed, and do spring and fall cleanups. Trees, shrubs, and vines may need staking or training at first and occasional pruning or shearing afterward. Perennials, ground covers, and grasses may need to be cut back, staked, deadheaded, or divided. Performing these tasks, which are explained on the following pages, is sometimes hard work, but for many gardeners it is enjoyable labor, a chance to get outside in the fresh air. Also, spending time each week with your plants helps you identify and address problems before they become serious.

Mulches and fertilizers

Covering the soil in all planted areas with a layer of organic mulch does several jobs at once: it improves the appearance of your garden while you're waiting for the plants to grow, reduces the number of weeds that emerge, reduces water loss from the soil during dry spells, moderates soil temperatures, and adds nutrients to the soil as it decomposes. Inorganic mulches such as clear or black plastic, landscape fabric, and gravel also provide some of these benefits, but their conspicuous appearance and the difficulty of removing them if you ever want to change the landscape are serious drawbacks.

Many materials are used as mulches; the box on p. 206 presents the most common, with comments on their advantages and disadvantages. Consider appearance, availability, cost, and convenience when you're comparing different products. Most garden centers have a few kinds of bagged mulch materials, but for mulching large areas, it's easier and cheaper to have a landscape contractor or other supplier deliver a truckload of bulk mulch. A landscape looks best if you see the same mulch throughout the entire planting area, rather than a patchwork of different mulches. You can achieve a uniform look by spreading a base layer of homemade compost, rotten hay, or other inexpensive material and topping that with a neater-looking material such as bark chips, shredded bark, or cocoa hulls.

It takes at least a 1-in. layer of mulch to suppress weeds, but there's no need to spread it more than 3 in. deep. As you're spreading it, don't put any mulch against the stems of any plants, because that can lead to disease or insect problems. Put most of the mulch between plants, not right around them. Check the mulch each spring when you do an annual garden inspection and cleanup. Be sure it's pulled back away from the plant stems. Rake the surface of the mulch lightly to loosen it, and top it up with a fresh layer if the old material has decomposed.

Fertilizer

Decomposing mulch frequently supplies enough nutrients to grow healthy plants, but using fertilizer helps if you want to boost the plants—to make them grow faster, get larger, or produce more flowers. There are dozens of fertilizer products on the market—liquid and granular, fast-acting and slow-release, organic and synthetic. Choose whichever you prefer; they all give good results if applied as directed. And observe the following precautions: Don't overfertilize, don't fertilize when the soil is dry, and don't fertilize after midsummer, because plants need to slow down and finish the season's growth before cold weather comes.

Mulch materials

Bark products
Bark nuggets, chipped bark, shredded bark, and composted bark, usually from conifers, are available in bags or in bulk. All are attractive, long-lasting, medium-price mulches.

Chipped tree trimmings
The chips from utility companies and tree services are a mixture of wood, bark, twigs, and leaves. These chips cost less than pure bark products (you may be able to get a load for free), but they don't look as good and you have to replace them more often, because they decompose fast.

Sawdust and shavings
These are cheap or free at sawmills and woodshops. They make good path coverings, but they aren't ideal mulches, because they tend to pack down into a dense, water-resistant surface.

Hulls and shells
Cocoa hulls, buckwheat hulls, peanut shells, and nut shells are available for pickup at food-processing plants and are sometimes sold in bags or bulk at garden centers. They're all attractive, long-lasting mulches. Price varies from free to quite expensive, depending on where you get them.

Tree leaves
A few big trees may supply all the mulch you need, year after year. You can just rake the leaves onto the bed in fall, but they'll probably blow off it again. It's better to chop them up with the lawn mower, pile them in compost bins for the winter, and spread them on the beds in late spring. If you have the space for two sets of compost bins, give leaves an extra year to decompose before spreading them. Pine needles make good mulch, too, especially for rhododendrons, mountain laurels, and other acid-loving shrubs. You can spread pine needles in fall, because they cling together and don't blow around.

Grass clippings
A 1- to 2-in. layer of dried grass clippings makes an acceptable mulch that decomposes within a single growing season. Don't pile clippings too thick, though. If you do, the top surface dries and packs into a water-resistant crust, and the bottom layer turns into nasty slime.

Hay and straw
Farmers sell hay that's moldy, old, or otherwise unsuitable for fodder as "mulch" hay. This hay is cheap, but it's likely to include weed seeds, particularly seeds of weedy grasses such as barnyard grass. Straw—the stems of grain crops such as wheat—is usually seed-free but more expensive. Both hay and straw are more suitable for mulching vegetable gardens than landscape plantings because they have to be renewed each year. They are bulky at first but decompose quickly. They also tend to attract rodents.

Gravel
A mulch of pea gravel or crushed rock, spread 1 to 2 in. thick, helps keep the soil cool and moist, and many plants grow very well with a gravel mulch. However, compared with organic materials such as bark or leaves, it's much more tiring to apply a gravel mulch in the first place; it's harder to remove leaves and litter that accumulate on the gravel or weeds that sprout up through it; it's annoying to dig through the gravel if you want to replace or add plants later; and it's extremely tedious to remove the gravel itself, should you ever change your mind about having it there.

Landscape fabrics
Various types of synthetic fabrics, usually sold in rolls 3 to 4 ft. wide and 20, 50, or 100 ft. long, can be spread over the ground as a weed barrier and topped with a layer of gravel, bark chips, or other mulch. Unlike plastic, these fabrics allow water and air to penetrate into the soil. It's useful to lay fabric under paths, but not in planted areas. In a bed, it's a two-person job to install the fabric in the first place, it's inconvenient trying to install plants through holes cut in the fabric, and it's hard to secure the fabric neatly and invisibly at the edges of the bed. The fabric lasts indefinitely, and removing it—if you change your mind—is a messy job.

Clear or black plastic
Don't even think about using any kind of plastic sheeting as a landscape mulch. The soil underneath a sheet of plastic gets bone-dry, while water accumulates on top. Any loose mulch you spread on plastic slips or floats around and won't stay in an even layer. No matter how you try to secure them, the edges of plastic sheeting always pull loose, appear at the surface, degrade in the sun, and shred into tatters.

Watering

Watering is less of a concern for gardeners in the Mid-Atlantic region than in other parts of the country, but even here there are dry spells and droughts when plants could use some extra water. New plantings, in particular, almost always need water more often than rain provides it.

Deciding whether water is needed

Usually only experienced gardeners can judge whether plants need water simply by looking at their leaves. Their appearance can be misleading. Moreover, you can't go by your own feelings about the weather. One of the ironies of the Mid-Atlantic climate is that the air can be very humid, making us humans feel all wet, even though at the same time the soil is so dry that the plants around us are suffering from drought.

Fortunately, there are two very reliable ways of deciding whether you should water. One is to check the soil. Get a paint stirrer or similar piece of unfinished, light-colored wood and use it like a dipstick. Push it down through the mulch and a few inches into the soil, leave it there for an hour or so, and pull it out to see whether moisture has discolored the wood. If so, the soil is moist enough for plants. If not, it's time to water. You have to let the stick dry out before you can use it again; it's handy to have several of these sticks around the garden shed.

The other method is to make a habit of monitoring rainfall by having your own rain gauge or listening to the weather reports, and marking a calendar to keep track of rainfall amounts. In the Mid-Atlantic region, most landscape plants thrive if they get 3 to 4 in. of rain a month. You should make every effort to water new plantings if there's been less than 1 in. of rain in two weeks. In subsequent years, after the plants have had time to put down roots, they can endure three or more weeks with no rain at all; even so, you should water them if you can. In this region, established plants rarely die from drought, but they do show many signs of stress—wilting leaves, premature leaf drop, failure to bloom or to set fruit, and increased susceptibility to insect and disease attacks.

Pay attention to soil moisture or rainfall amounts from March through December, because plants can suffer from dryness throughout that entire period, not just in the heat of summer, and water whenever the soil is dry. As for time of day, you can water whenever the plants need it and you get the chance. Gardening books sometimes warn against watering plants late in the day, saying that plants are more vulnerable to fungal infections if the leaves stay wet at night. That's true, but plants get wet with dew most nights anyway.

How much to water

It's easy to overwater a houseplant but hard to overwater a plant in the ground. Outdoors, you're much more likely to water too little than too much. You could spend an hour with hose in hand, watering the plants in a flower bed, and supply the equivalent of ¼ in. of rain or less. Holding a hose or carrying a bucket is practical for watering new plantings only where the plants are few, small, or relatively widely spaced. To thoroughly water an area that's filled with plants, you need a system that allows you to turn on the water, walk away, and come back later. An oscillating sprinkler on the end of a hose works fine, or you can weave a soaker hose through the bed.

No matter how you water, you should monitor how much water you have applied and how evenly it was distributed. If you're hand-watering or using a soaker hose, the watering pattern may be quite uneven. Put several wooden "dipsticks" in different parts of the bed to make sure that all areas have received enough water to moisten the sticks. Monitor the output of a sprinkler by setting tuna-fish cans around the bed and checking to see how much water they catch, like measuring rainfall. Let the sprinkler run until there's about an inch of water in each can.

CHECKING SOIL MOISTURE

Stick a paint stirrer or similar piece of light-colored, unfinished wood down through the mulch and into the soil. Pull it up after an hour. If the bottom of the stick looks and feels damp, the soil is moist enough for plants.

MONITORING A SPRINKLER

Set several tuna-fish cans throughout the area, and let the sprinkler run until about 1 in. of water has collected in each can.

Controlling weeds

Weeds are not much of a problem in established landscapes. Once the "good" plants have grown big enough to merge together, they tend to crowd or shade out all but the most persistent weeds. But weeds can be troublesome in a new landscape unless you take steps to prevent and control them.

There are two main types of weeds: those that mostly sprout up as seedlings and those that keep coming back from perennial roots or runners. Try to identify and eliminate any perennial weeds before you start a landscaping project. Then you'll only have to deal with new seedlings later.

Annual and perennial weeds that commonly grow from seeds include crabgrass, chickweed, dandelions, plantain, purslane, ragweed, and violets. Trees and shrubs such as silver maple, wild cherry, cottonwood, willow, black locust, buckthorn, and honeysuckle produce weedy seedlings, too. For any of these weeds that grow from seeds, the strategy is twofold: try to keep the weed seeds from sprouting, and eliminate any seedlings that do sprout as soon as you see them, while they are still small.

Almost any patch of soil includes weed seeds that are ready to sprout whenever that soil is disturbed. You have to disturb the soil to prepare it before planting, and that will probably cause an initial flush of weeds, but you'll never see that many weeds again if you leave the soil undisturbed in subsequent years. You don't have to hoe, rake, or cultivate around perennial plantings. Leave the soil alone, and fewer weeds will appear. Using mulch helps even more; by shading the soil, it prevents weed seeds from sprouting. And if weed seeds blow in and land on top of the mulch, they'll be less likely to germinate there than they would on bare soil.

Pull or cut off any weeds that appear while they're young and small. Don't let them mature and go to seed. Most weed seedlings emerge in late spring and early summer.

Using herbicides

Two kinds of herbicides can be very useful and effective in maintaining home landscapes, but only if used correctly. You have to choose the right product for the job and follow the directions on the label regarding dosage and timing of application exactly.

Preemergent herbicides. Usually sold in granular form, these herbicides are designed to prevent weed seeds, particularly crabgrass and other annual weeds, from sprouting. One application is typically enough to last through the growing season, but you need to apply the product quite early in spring, at the time forsythias start blooming. If you wait until later, many weeds will already have sprouted, and a preemergent herbicide will not stop them then.

WEEDS THAT SPROUT FROM SEEDS

Simple root systems can be easily pulled while still small.

Plantain   Maple seedling   Dandelion

WEEDS THAT SPROUT BACK FROM PERENNIAL ROOTS OR RUNNERS

Connected by underground runners, the shoots of these weeds need to be pulled repeatedly, smothered with a thick mulch, or killed with an herbicide.

Mother plant

Ground ivy

Runner

Use a disposable, sponge-type paintbrush to apply the herbicide selectively, painting only the weeds. Prepare the solution as directed for spray application. Use only enough to wet the leaves, so none drips off.

USING HERBICIDES ON PERENNIAL WEEDS

Ready-to-use spot-weeder sprays are convenient, but you must aim carefully. Try using a sheet of cardboard as a backdrop to protect desirable plants from herbicide drift.

Caring for Woody Plants

Read the label carefully, and make sure the herbicide you buy is registered for use around the kinds of ground covers, perennials, shrubs, or other plants you have. Measure the area of your bed, weigh out the appropriate amount of granules, and sprinkle them as evenly as possible across the soil. Wear heavy rubber gloves that are rated for use with farm chemicals, not common household rubber gloves, and follow the safety precautions on the product label.

Postemergent herbicides. These chemicals are used to kill plants. Some kinds kill only the aboveground parts of a plant; other kinds are absorbed into the plant and kill it, roots and all. Postemergent herbicides are typically applied as sprays, which you can buy ready-to-use or prepare by mixing a concentrate with water. Look for those that break down quickly, and read the label carefully for registered applications, specific directions, and safety instructions.

Postemergent herbicides work best if applied when the weeds are growing vigorously. You usually have to apply enough to thoroughly wet the plant's leaves, and do it during a spell of dry weather. Applying an herbicide is an effective way to get rid of a perennial weed that you can't dig or pull up, but it's really better to do this before you plant a bed, as it's hard to spray herbicides in an established planting without getting some on your good plants. Aim carefully, and don't spray on windy days. Brushing or sponging the herbicide on the leaves avoids damaging adjacent plants.

Using postemergent herbicides in an established planting is a painstaking job, but it may be the only way to get rid of a persistent perennial weed. For young weed seedlings, it's usually easier and faster to pull them by hand than to spray them.

A well-chosen garden tree, such as the ones recommended in this book, grows naturally into a neat, pleasing shape; won't get too large for its site; is resistant to pests and diseases; and doesn't drop messy pods or other litter. Once established, these trees need very little care from year to year.

Regular watering is the most important concern in getting a tree off to a good start. Don't let it suffer from drought for the first few years. To reduce competition, don't plant ground covers or other plants within 2 ft. of the tree's trunk. Just spread a thin layer of mulch there.

Arborists now dismiss other care ideas that once were common practice. According to current thinking, you don't need to fertilize a tree when you plant it (in fact, most landscape trees never need fertilizing). Keep pruning to a minimum at planting time; remove only dead or damaged twigs, not healthy shoots. Finally, if a tree is small enough that one or two people can carry and plant it, it doesn't need staking and the trunk will grow stronger if unstaked. Larger trees that are planted by a nursery may need staking, especially on windy sites, but the stakes should be removed within a year.

Pruning to direct growth

Pruning shapes plants not only by removing stems, branches, and leaves but also by inducing and directing new growth. All plants have a bud at the base of every leaf. New shoots grow from these buds. Cutting off the end of a stem encourages the lower buds to shoot out and produces a bushier plant. This type of pruning makes a hedge fill out and gives an otherwise lanky perennial or shrub a better rounded shape.

The same response to pruning also allows you to steer the growth of a plant. The bud immediately below the cut will produce a shoot that extends in the direction the bud was pointing. To direct a branch or stem, cut it back to a bud pointing in the direction you want to encourage growth. This technique is useful for shaping young trees and shrubs and for keeping their centers open to light and air.

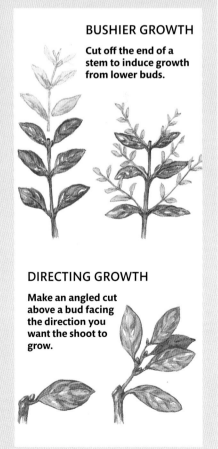

BUSHIER GROWTH

Cut off the end of a stem to induce growth from lower buds.

DIRECTING GROWTH

Make an angled cut above a bud facing the direction you want the shoot to grow.

Training a horizontal espalier

An espaliered tree grown flat against a wall, as on p. 68, or along a fence is a striking addition to the home landscape. Training a Kousa dogwood, Sargent crab apple, or other tree as an espalier isn't difficult, but it does take patience and perseverance.

To support the branches, you'll need to stretch heavy wire between well-anchored 4x4 posts. (In the espalier design mentioned above, the posts could also help support the trellis at each end of the garage.) Wires should be about 20 in. apart and reach as high as you want the espalier to grow.

Start with a tree no more than 4 to 6 ft. tall that has several side shoots. Plant the tree in spring and let it grow unhindered through the summer and fall. Begin shaping the tree the first winter after planting, when it is dormant and leafless. For each wire, choose one shoot to train to the left and another to train to the right. Bring the tip of each shoot to the wire and tie it with soft sisal twine or a strip of cotton cloth. Put a few more ties along the shoot to keep it bent in position, as close to the wire as possible without breaking the shoot. Remove any side shoots that aren't tied to a wire by cutting them off close to the main trunk.

The next summer, add more ties to fasten the limbs' new growth to the wires. In subsequent years, continue tying in the new growth, choose limbs for the upper wires as the tree gets taller, and check the old ties and loosen any that are tight. At the same time, prune away any shoots that point back at the wall, and cut all other side shoots or branches about 4 to 6 in. long. Over time, most of the tree's leaves and flowers will be produced on these short side branches.

Don't cut the top of the main trunk until the tree is as tall as you want it, or the ends of the horizontal limbs until they have spread as wide as you want. This may take several years. After that, prune annually to remove long, ungainly, or weak shoots and to promote compact, shapely growth.

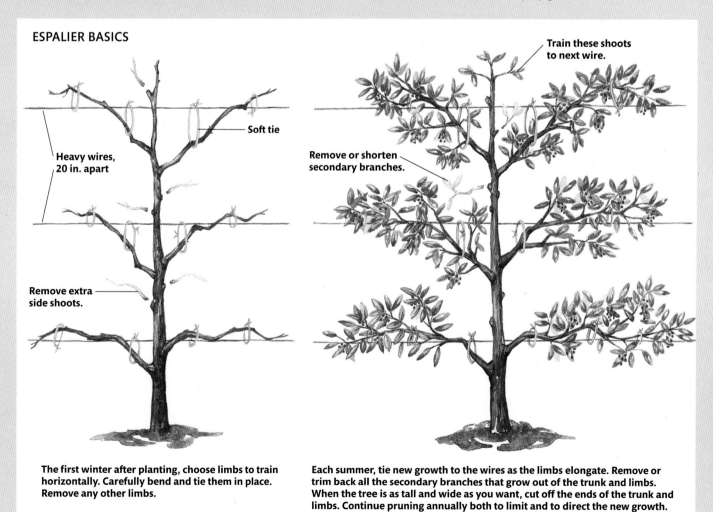

ESPALIER BASICS

Soft tie

Heavy wires, 20 in. apart

Remove extra side shoots.

Train these shoots to next wire.

Remove or shorten secondary branches.

The first winter after planting, choose limbs to train horizontally. Carefully bend and tie them in place. Remove any other limbs.

Each summer, tie new growth to the wires as the limbs elongate. Remove or trim back all the secondary branches that grow out of the trunk and limbs. When the tree is as tall and wide as you want, cut off the ends of the trunk and limbs. Continue pruning annually both to limit and to direct the new growth.

Shaping young trees

Direct a tree's growth by pruning once a year, in winter or summer. (See p. 209.) Don't prune just for the sake of pruning. If you don't have a good reason for making a cut, don't do it. Follow these guidelines:

▎**Use sharp pruning shears, loppers, or saws,** which make clean cuts without tearing the wood or bark.

▎**Cut branches back** to a healthy shoot, leaf, or bud, or cut back to the branch collar at the base of the branch, as shown at right. Don't leave any stubs; they're ugly and prone to decay.

▎**Remove any dead or damaged** branches and any twigs or limbs that are very spindly or weak.

▎**Where two limbs cross over or rub** against each other, save one limb—usually the thicker, stronger one—and prune off the other one.

▎**Prune or widen narrow crotches.** Places where a branch and trunk or two branches form a narrow V are weak spots, liable to split apart as the tree grows. Where the trunk of a young tree exhibits such a crotch or where either of two shoots could continue the growth of a branch, prune off the weaker of the two. Where you wish to keep the branch, insert a piece of wood as a spacer to widen the angle, as shown below. Leave the spacer in place for a year or so.

One trunk or several?

If you want a young tree to have a single trunk, identify the leader or central shoot and let it grow straight up, unpruned. The trunk will grow thicker faster if you leave the lower limbs in place for the first few years, but if they're in the way, you can remove them. At whatever height you choose—usually about 8 ft. off the ground if you want

WHERE TO CUT

When removing the end of a branch, cut back to a healthy leaf, bud, or side shoot. Don't leave a stub. Use sharp pruning shears to make a neat cut that slices the stem rather than tears it.

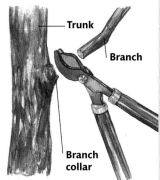

Trunk

Branch

Branch collar

When removing an entire branch, cut just outside the slightly thickened area, called the branch collar, where the branch grows into the trunk.

to walk or see under the tree—select the shoots that will become the main limbs of the tree. Be sure they are evenly spaced around the trunk, pointing outward at wide angles. Remove any lower or weaker shoots. As the tree matures, the only further pruning required will be an annual checkup to remove dead, damaged, or crossing shoots.

Most of the trees in this book, including crape myrtle, fringe tree, Japanese stewartia, Kousa dogwood, redbud, serviceberry, and sweet bay magnolia, are often grown with multiple (usually two to four) trunks, for a graceful, clumplike appearance. When buying a multiple-trunk tree, what's most important is that the trunks should diverge at the base. The more space between them, the better. Prune multiple-trunk trees as previously described for single-trunk trees, and remove some of the branches that are growing toward the center of the clump, so it doesn't get too dense and tangled.

AVOIDING NARROW CROTCHES

A tree's limbs should spread wide, like outstretched arms. If limbs angle too close to the trunk or to each other, there isn't room for them to grow properly and they may split apart after a few years, ruining the tree.

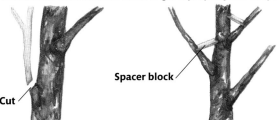

Spacer block

Cut

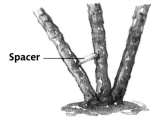

Spacer

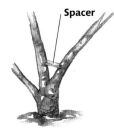

Spacer

SINGLE-TRUNK TREES: Correct narrow crotches on a young tree by removal or by widening the angle with a wooden spacer block. Choose well-spaced shoots to become the main limbs of a shade tree.

MULTIPLE-TRUNK TREES: Whether the stems of a multiple-trunk tree emerge from the ground or from a single trunk near the ground, widen angles if necessary to keep the trunks from touching.

Pruning shrubs

Shrubs are generally carefree plants, but they almost always look better if you do some pruning at least once a year. As a minimum, remove dead twigs from time to time, and if any branches are broken by storms or accidents, remove them as soon as convenient, cutting back to a healthy bud or to the plant's crown. Also, unless the shrub produces attractive seedpods or berries, it's a good idea to trim off the flowers after they fade.

Beyond this routine pruning, some shrubs require more attention. (The entries in Plant Profiles, pp. 114–159, give more information on when and how to prune particular shrubs.) Basically, shrub pruning falls into three categories: selective pruning, severe pruning, and shearing.

Selective pruning means using pruning shears to remove or cut back individual shoots, in order to refine the shape of the bush and maintain its vigor, as well as limit its size. (See the drawing to the right.) This job takes time but produces a very graceful and natural-looking bush. Cut away weak or spindly twigs and any limbs that cross or rub against each other, and cut all the longest shoots back to a healthy, outward-facing bud or to a pair of buds. You can do selective pruning on any shrub, deciduous or evergreen, at any time of year.

Severe pruning means using pruning shears or loppers to cut away most of a shrub's top growth, leaving just short stubs or a gnarly trunk. This kind of cutting back is usually done once a year in late winter or early spring. Although it seems drastic, severe pruning is appropriate in several situations.

It makes certain fast-growing shrubs such as bluebeard and butterfly bush flower more profusely. It keeps others, such as lavender and spirea, compact and bushy, and it stimulates Siberian dogwood to produce canelike stems with bright red bark.

One or two severe prunings done when a shrub is young can make it branch out at the base, producing a bushier specimen or a fuller hedge plant. Nurseries often do this pruning as part of producing a good plant, and if you buy a shrub that's already bushy you don't need to cut it back yourself.

Older shrubs that have gotten tall and straggly sometimes respond to a severe pruning by sprouting out with renewed vigor, sending up lots of new shoots that bear plenty of foliage and flowers. This strategy doesn't work for all shrubs, though—sometimes severe pruning kills a plant. Don't try it unless you know it will work (check with a knowledgeable person at a nursery) or are willing to take a chance.

Shearing means using hedge shears or an electric hedge trimmer to trim the surface of a shrub, hedge, or tree to a neat, uniform profile, producing a solid mass of greenery. Both deciduous and evergreen shrubs and trees can be sheared; those with small, closely spaced leaves and a naturally compact growth habit usually look best. A good time for shearing most shrubs is early summer, after the new shoots have elongated but before the wood has hardened, but you can shear at other times of year, and you may have to shear some plants more than once a year.

If you're planning to shear a plant, start when it is young and establish the shape—cone, pyramid, flat-topped hedge, or whatever. Looking at the profile, always make the shrub wider at the bottom than on top, otherwise the lower limbs will be shaded and won't be as leafy. Shear off as little as needed to maintain the shape as the shrub grows. Once it gets as big as you want it, shear as much as you have to to keep it that size.

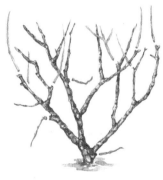

SELECTIVE PRUNING. Remove weak, spindly, bent, or broken shoots (red). Where two branches rub on each other, remove the weakest or the one that's pointing inward (orange). Cut back long shoots to a healthy, outward-facing bud (blue).

SEVERE PRUNING. In late winter or early spring, before new growth starts, cut all the stems back close to the ground.

SHEARING. Trim with hedge clippers to a neat profile.

Making a hedge

To make a hedge that's dense enough that you can't see through it, choose shrubs that have many shoots at the base. If you can only find skinny shrubs, prune them severely the first spring after planting to stimulate bushier growth.

Hedge plants are set in the ground as described on pp. 203–204 but are spaced closer together than they would be if planted as individual specimens. We took that into account in creating the designs and plant lists for this book; just follow the spacings recommended in the designs. If you're impatient for the hedge to fill in, you can space the plants closer together.

A hedge can be sheared, pruned selectively, or left alone, depending on how you want it to look. Slow-growing, small-leaved plants such as boxwood and Japanese holly make rounded but natural-looking hedges with no pruning at all, or you can shear them into any profile you choose and make them perfectly neat and uniform. (Be sure to keep them narrower at the top.) Choose one style and stick with it. Once a hedge is established, you can neither start nor stop shearing it without an awkward transition that may last a few years before the hedge looks good again.

Getting a vine off to a good start

Nurseries often sell clematis, honeysuckle, and other vines as young plants with a single stem fastened to a bamboo stake. To plant them, remove the stake and cut off the stem right above the lowest pair of healthy leaves, usually about 4 to 6 in. above the soil ❶. This forces the vine to send out new shoots low to the ground. As soon as those new shoots have begun to develop (normally within four to six weeks after planting), cut them back to their first pairs of leaves ❷. After this second pruning, the plant will become bushy at the base. Now, as new shoots form, use sticks or strings to direct them toward the base of the support they are to climb ❸.

Once they're started, both clematis and honeysuckle can scramble up a lattice trellis, although it helps if you tuck in any stray ends from time to time. The plants can't climb a smooth surface, however. For them to cover a fence or post, you have to provide something the vine can wrap around. Screw a few eyebolts to the top and bottom of such a support and stretch wire, nylon cord, or polypropylene rope between them. (The wires or cords should be a few inches out from the fence, not flush against it.)

Other vines need different treatments. 'Golden Showers' and other so-called climbing roses don't really climb at all by themselves—you have to fasten them to a support. Twist-ties are handy for this job. Roses grow fast, so you'll have to tie in the new shoots every few weeks from spring to fall. Climbing hydrangea and English ivy are both slow starters, but once under way, they can climb any surface to any height by means of their clinging rootlets and so need no further assistance or care.

After the first year, the vines in this book don't need pruning on a regular basis, but you can cut them back whenever they get too big, and you should remove any dead or straggly stems from time to time.

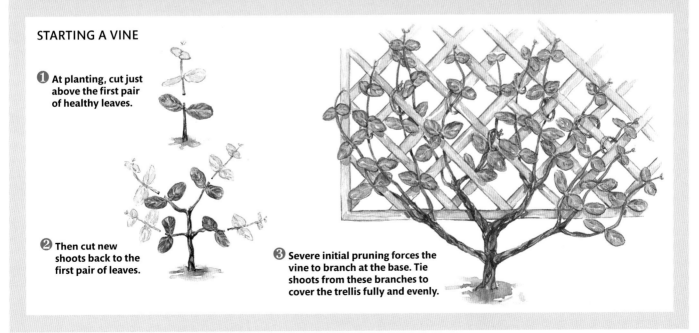

STARTING A VINE

❶ At planting, cut just above the first pair of healthy leaves.

❷ Then cut new shoots back to the first pair of leaves.

❸ Severe initial pruning forces the vine to branch at the base. Tie shoots from these branches to cover the trellis fully and evenly.

Caring for Perennials

Perennials are simply plants that send up new growth year after year. A large group, perennials include flowering plants such as daylilies and astilbes as well as grasses, ferns, and hardy bulbs. Although some perennials need special conditions and care, most of the ones in this book are adaptable and easygoing. Get them off to a good start by planting them in well-prepared soil, adding a layer of mulch, watering as often as needed throughout the first year, and keeping weeds away. After that, keeping perennials attractive and healthy typically requires just a few minutes per plant each year.

Routine annual care

Some of the perennials that are used as ground covers, such as lily-of-the-valley, moneywort, pachysandra, periwinkle, sweet woodruff, and sweet violet, need virtually no care. On a suitable site, they'll thrive for decades even if you pay them no attention at all.

Most garden perennials, though, look and grow better if you clean away the old leaves and stems at least once a year. When to do this depends on the plant. Perennials such as aster, daylily, dwarf fountain grass, hosta, interrupted fern, iris, and peony have leaves and stalks that turn tan or brown after they're frosted in fall. Cut these down to the ground in late fall or early spring; either time is okay.

Perennials such as beach wormwood, bigroot geranium, blue oat grass, Christmas fern, dianthus, Lenten rose, lilyturf, and moss phlox have foliage that is more or less evergreen, depending on the severity of the winter. For those plants, wait until early spring; then cut back any leaves or stems that are discolored or shabby-looking. Don't leave cuttings lying on the soil, because they may contain disease spores. Do not compost diseased stems or leaves.

Right after you've cleared away the dead material is a good time to renew the mulch on the bed. Use a fork, rake, or cultivator to loosen the existing mulch, and add some fresh mulch if needed. Also, if you want to sprinkle some granular fertilizer on the bed, do that now, when it's easy to avoid getting any on the plants' leaves. Fertilizing perennials is optional, but it does make them grow bigger and bloom more than they would otherwise.

Remove faded flowers

Removing flowers as they fade (called "deadheading") makes the garden look neater, prevents unwanted self-sown seedlings, and often stimulates a plant to continue blooming longer than it would if you left it alone, or to bloom a second time later in the season. (This is true for shrubs and annuals as well as for perennials.)

Pick large flowers such as daisies, daylilies, lilies, peonies, and tulips one at a time, snapping them off by hand. Use pruning shears on perennials such as astilbe, bee balm, hosta, lady's mantle, phlox, and yarrow that produce tall stalks crowded with lots of small flowers, cutting the stalks back to the height of the foliage. Use hedge shears on bushy plants that are covered with lots of small flowers on short stalks, such as basket-of-gold, catmint, dianthus, and evergreen candytuft, cutting the stems back by about one-half.

Instead of removing them, you may want to let the flowers remain on coneflower, purple coneflower, false indigo, Siberian iris, 'Autumn Joy' sedum, and the various grasses. These plants all bear conspicuous seedpods or seed heads on stiff stalks that remain standing and look interesting throughout the fall and winter.

Pruning and shearing perennials

Some perennials that bloom in summer or fall respond well to being pruned earlier in the growing season. Bee balm, boltonia, chrysanthemum, garden phlox, gaura, New England aster, Nippon daisy, and 'Autumn Joy' sedum all form tall clumps of stems topped with lots of little flowers. Unfortunately, tall stems are liable to flop over in stormy weather, and even if they don't, too-tall clumps can look leggy or top-heavy. To prevent floppiness, prune these plants when the stems are about 1 ft. tall. Remove the weakest stems from each clump by cutting them off at the ground, then cut all the remaining, strong stems back by about one-third. Pruning in this way keeps these plants shorter, stronger, and bushier, so you don't have to bother with staking them.

Southernwood and 'Valerie Finnis' artemisia are grown more for their foliage than for their flowers. You can use hedge shears to keep them neat, compact, and bushy, shearing off the tops of the stems once or twice in spring and summer.

PRUNING A PERENNIAL

Prune to create neater, bushier clumps of some summer- and fall-blooming perennials such as phlox, chrysanthemums, New England aster, and bee balm. When the stalks are about 1 ft. tall, cut them all back by one-third. Remove the weakest stalks at ground level.

Dividing perennials

Most perennials send up more stems each year, forming denser clumps or wider patches. Dividing is the process of cutting or breaking apart these clumps or patches. This is an easy way to make more plants to expand your garden, to control a plant that might otherwise spread out of bounds, or to renew an old specimen that doesn't look good or bloom well anymore.

Most perennials can be divided as often as every year or two if you're in a hurry to make more plants, or they can go for several years if you don't have any reason to disturb them. You can divide them in early spring, just as new growth is starting, or in late summer and fall, up until a month before hard frost.

There are two main approaches to dividing perennials, as shown in the drawings at right. You can leave the plant in the ground and use a sharp shovel to cut it apart, like slicing a pie, then lift out one chunk at a time. Or you can dig around and underneath the plant and lift it out all at once, shake off the extra soil, and lay the plant on the ground or a tarp where you can work with it.

Some plants, such as boltonia, yarrow, and most ferns, are easy to divide. They almost fall apart when you dig them up. Others, such as astilbe, daylily, and most grasses, have very tough or tangled roots and you'll have to wrestle with them, chop them with a sharp butcher knife, pry them apart with a strong screwdriver or garden fork, or even cut through the roots with a hatchet or pruning saw. However you approach the job, before you insert any tool, take a close look at the plant right at ground level, and be careful to divide *between*, not *through*, the biggest and healthiest

buds or shoots. Using a hose to wash loose mulch and soil away makes it easier to see what you're doing.

Don't make the divisions too small; they should be the size of a plant that you'd want to buy, not just little scraps. If you have more divisions than you need or want, choose just the best-looking ones to replant and discard or give away the others. Replant new divisions as soon as possible in freshly prepared soil. Water them right away, and water again

whenever the soil dries out over the next few weeks or months, until the plants are growing again.

Divide hardy bulbs such as daffodils and crocuses every few years by digging up the clumps after they have finished blooming but before the foliage turns yellow. Shake the soil off the roots, pull the bulbs apart, and replant them promptly, setting them as deep as they were buried before.

DIVIDING PERENNIALS

You can divide a clump or patch of perennials by cutting down into the patch with a sharp spade, like slicing a pie or a pan of brownies, then lifting out the separate chunks.

Or you can dig up the whole clump, shake the extra soil off the roots, then pull or pry it apart into separate plantlets.

Problem Solving

Some plants are much more susceptible than others to damage by severe weather, pests, or diseases. In this book, we've recommended plants that are generally trouble-free, especially after they have had a few years to get established in your garden. But even these plants are subject to various mishaps and problems. The challenge is learning how to distinguish which problems are really serious and which are just cosmetic, and deciding how to solve—or, better yet, prevent—those problems that are serious.

Pests, large and small

Deer, rabbits, and woodchucks are liable to be a problem if your property is surrounded by or adjacent to fields or woods. You may not see them, but you can't miss the damage they do—they bite the tops off or eat whole plants of hostas, daylilies, and many other perennials. Deer also eat the leaves and stems of maples, azaleas, arborvitae, and many other trees and shrubs. Commercial or homemade repellents that you spray on the foliage may be helpful if the animals aren't too hungry. (See the box bottom right for deer-resistant plants.) But in the long run, the only solution is to fence out deer and to trap and remove smaller animals.

Chipmunks and squirrels are cute but naughty. They normally don't eat much foliage, but they do eat some kinds of flowers and several kinds of bulbs, they dig up new transplants, and they plant nuts in your flower beds and lawns. Voles and field mice can kill trees and shrubs by stripping the bark off the trunk, usually in the winter when the ground is covered with snow, and they eat away at many perennials, too. Moles don't eat plants, but their digging makes a mess of a lawn or flower bed. Persistent trapping is the most effective way to control all of these little critters.

Insects and related pests can cause minor or devastating damage. Most plants can afford to lose part of their foliage or sap without suffering much of a setback, so don't panic if you see a few holes chewed in a leaf. However, whenever you suspect that insects are attacking one of your plants, try to catch

Indentify, then treat

Don't jump to conclusions and start spraying chemicals on a supposedly sick plant before you know what (if anything) is actually wrong with it. That's wasteful and irresponsible, and you're likely to do the plant as much harm as good. Pinpointing the exact cause of a problem is difficult for even experienced gardeners, so save yourself frustration and seek out expert help from the beginning.

If it seems that there's something wrong with one of your plants—for example, if the leaves are discolored, have holes in them, or have spots or marks on them—cut off a sample branch, wrap it in damp paper towels, and put it in a plastic bag (so it won't wilt). Take the sample to the nursery or garden center where you bought the plant, and ask for help. If the nursery can't help, contact the nearest office of your state's Cooperative Extension Service or a public garden in your area and ask if they have a staff member who can diagnose plant problems.

Meanwhile, look around your property and around the neighborhood, too, to see if any other plants (of the same or different kinds) show similar symptoms. If a problem is widespread, you shouldn't have much trouble finding someone who can identify it and tell you what, if anything, to do. If only one plant is affected, it's often harder to diagnose the problem, and you may just have to wait and see what happens to it. Keep an eye on the plant, continue with watering and other regular maintenance, and see whether the problem gets worse or goes away. If nothing more has happened after a few weeks, stop worrying. If the problem continues, intensify your search for expert advice.

Plant problems stem from a number of causes: insect and animal pests, diseases, and poor care, particularly in winter. Remember that plant problems are often caused by a combination of these; all the more reason to consult with experts about their diagnosis and treatment.

Deer-resistant plants

Deer may nibble these plants, but they're unlikely to strip them bare. If you live in an area where deer populations are high, consider substituting some of these plants for others that are specified in a design.

Trees and Shrubs

Andromeda	Dogwood	Magnolia
Barberry	Forsythia	Pine
Boxwood	Holly	Spirea
Daphne	Lilac	Spruce

Perennials

Astilbe	Grasses	Russian sage
Bee balm	Heuchera	Sage
Blazing star	Iris	Veronica
Bluebeard	Lamb's ears	Yarrow
Daffodil	Lavender	
Ferns	Lenten rose	
Geranium	Peony	

one of them in a glass jar and get it identified, so you can decide what to do.

There are several new kinds of insecticides that are quite effective but much safer to use than the older products. You must read the fine print on the label to determine whether an insecticide will control your particular pest. Carefully follow the directions for how to apply the product, or it may not work.

Diseases

Several types of fungal, bacterial, and viral diseases can attack garden plants, causing a wide range of symptoms such as disfigured or discolored leaves or petals, powdery or moldy-looking films or spots, mushy or rotten stems or roots, and overall wilting. As with insect problems, if you suspect that a plant is infected with a disease, gather a sample of the plant and show it to someone who can identify the problem before you do any spraying.

In general, plant diseases are hard to treat, so it's important to take steps to prevent problems. These steps include choosing plants adapted to your area, choosing disease-resistant plants, spacing plants far enough apart so that air can circulate between them, and removing dead stems and litter from the garden.

Perennials that would otherwise be healthy are prone to fungal infections during spells of hot humid weather, especially if the plants are crowded together or if they have flopped over and are lying on top of each other or on the ground. Look closely for moldy foliage, and if you find any, prune it off and discard (don't compost) it. It's better to cut the plants back severely than to let the disease spread. Plan to avoid repeated problems by dividing the perennials, replanting them farther apart, and pruning them early in the season so they don't grow so tall and floppy again. Crowded shrubs are also subject to fungal problems in the summer and should be pruned so that air can flow around them.

Winter protection

More plants are damaged or killed in the winter than in any other season, but severe cold is usually not the problem. All of the plants in this book's designs can tolerate the coldest temperatures likely to occur in the Mid-Atlantic region. They probably won't freeze to death, but they may get broken by snow or ice, dried out, or drowned. There are a few steps you can take to prevent winter damage.

Plant shrubs far enough away from a street, driveway, or building that they won't get crushed by the extra snow that accumulates from shoveling or slides off a roof. (Where designs in this book call for plantings in these kinds of areas, we've selected plants that hold up well.) Use stakes to mark the edge or corners of any planting that's adjacent to a walk or driveway, so you can avoid hitting the plants with a snowblower or shovel.

Spray evergreen shrubs with an anti-transpirant in late fall to keep their leaves from dehydrating in the cold winter winds. Or you can erect burlap tents around young shrubs, to protect them from November until April. Drive four stakes in the ground and staple burlap to the sides. Leave the top open.

Any small or medium-size perennial or shrub that is planted in the fall is liable to be pushed up out of the ground, or frost-heaved, if the soil repeatedly freezes and thaws, and that means its roots get dried out. To prevent this, cover the ground around these plants with a loose mulch such as evergreen boughs (limbs from discarded Christmas trees are good) as soon as the soil has frozen hard, and don't remove the covering until midspring.

Many more plants die from being too wet in winter than from getting too cold. Any plants growing where water collects and the ground stays saturated in winter are liable to rot. If you're thinking about planting in a low spot, prevent this kind of loss by preparing the site before you plant. Dig deep to loosen compacted subsoil, and add more topsoil to raise the surface of the bed so that water will drain both down and away from the root zone.

Erect burlap tents around small to medium-size shrubs to protect them from cold, dry winds in winter.

WINTER PROTECTION

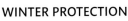

To avoid hitting plants with a snowblower or shovel, mark plantings near sidewalks and driveways before they are snow-covered.

Glossary

A

Amendments. Organic or mineral materials such as peat moss, perlite, or compost that are used to improve the soil.

Annual. A plant that germinates, grows, flowers, produces seeds, and dies in the course of a single growing season; a plant that is treated like an annual and grown for a single season's display.

Antitranspirant. A substance sprayed on the stems and leaves of evergreen plants to protect them from water loss caused by winter winds.

B

Balled-and-burlapped. Describes a tree or shrub dug out of the ground with a ball of soil intact around the roots; the ball is then wrapped in burlap and tied for transport.

Bare-root. Describes a plant dug out of the ground and then shaken or washed to remove the soil from the roots.

C

Compound leaf. A leaf with two or more leaflets branching off a single stalk.

Container-grown. Describes a plant raised in a pot that is removed before planting.

Crown. That part of a plant where the roots and stem meet, usually at soil level.

Cultivar. A cultivated variety of a plant, often bred or selected for some special trait such as double flowers, compact growth, cold hardiness, or disease and pest resistance.

D

Deadheading. Removing old flowers during the growing season to prevent seed formation and to encourage the development of new flowers.

Deciduous. Describes a tree, shrub, or vine that drops all its leaves in winter.

Division. Propagation of a plant by separating it into two or more pieces, each of which has at least one bud and some roots. Used mostly for perennials, grasses, ferns, and bulbs.

Drainage. The movement of water down through the soil. With good drainage, water disappears from a planting hole in just a few hours. If water remains standing overnight, the drainage is poor.

Drip line. An imaginary line on the soil around a tree that mirrors the circumference of the canopy above. Many of the tree's roots are found in this area.

Dry-laid. Describes a masonry path or wall that is installed without mortar.

Espalier

E

Edging. A shallow trench or physical barrier of steel, plastic, brick, or boards used to define the border between a flower bed and adjacent turf.

Espalier. The training of a plant to grow flat along wires, often against a wall or framework. A plant so trained may be called an espalier.

Exposure. The intensity, duration, and variation in sun, wind, and temperature that characterize any particular site.

F

Feeder roots. Slender branching roots that spread close to the soil surface and absorb most of the nutrients for a tree or shrub.

Formal. Describes a style of landscaping that features symmetrical layouts, with beds and walks related to adjacent buildings, and often with plants sheared to geometric or other shapes.

Foundation planting. Traditionally, a narrow border of evergreen shrubs planted around the foundation of a house. Contemporary foundation plantings often include deciduous shrubs, grasses, perennials, and other plants as well.

Frost heaving. A disturbance or uplifting of soil, pavement, or plants caused when moisture in the soil freezes and expands.

Full shade. Describes a site that receives no direct sun during the growing season.

Full sun. Describes a site that receives at least eight hours of direct sun each day during the growing season.

G

Garden soil. Soil specially prepared for planting to make it loose enough for roots and water to penetrate easily. Usually requires digging or tilling and the addition of some organic matter.

Grade. The degree and direction of slope on a piece of ground.

Ground cover. A plant such as ivy, liriope, or juniper used to cover the soil and form a continuous low mass of foliage. Often used as a durable substitute for turfgrass.

H

Habit. The characteristic shape or form of a plant, such as upright, spreading, or rounded.

Hardiness. A plant's ability to survive the winter without protection from the cold.

Hardiness zone. A geographic region where the coldest temperature in an average winter falls within a certain range, such as between 0° and –10°F.

Hardscape. Parts of a landscape constructed from materials other than plants, such as walks, walls, and trellises made of wood, stone, or other materials.

Building a "hardscape."

Herbicide. A chemical used to kill plants. Preemergent herbicides are used to kill weed seeds as they sprout, and thus to prevent weed growth. Postemergent herbicides kill plants that are already established and growing.

Hybrid. A plant resulting from a cross between two parents that belong to different varieties, species, or genera.

I

Interplant. To combine plants with different bloom times or growth habits, making it possible to fit more plants in a bed, thus prolonging the bed's appeal.

Invasive. Describes a plant that spreads quickly, usually by runners, and mixes with or dominates adjacent plantings.

L

Landscape fabric. A synthetic fabric, sometimes water-permeable, spread under paths or mulch to serve as a weed barrier.

Lime, limestone. White mineral compounds used to combat soil acidity and to supply calcium for plant growth.

Loam. An ideal soil for gardening, containing plenty of organic matter and a balanced range of small to large mineral particles.

M

Mass planting. Filling an area with one or a few kinds of plants spaced closely together. Often done to create a bold dramatic effect or to reduce maintenance.

Microclimate. Local conditions of shade, exposure, wind, drainage, and other factors that affect plant growth at any particular site.

Mowing strip. A row of bricks or paving stones set flush with the soil around the edge of a bed, and wide enough to support one wheel of the lawn mower.

Mulch. A layer of bark, peat moss, compost, shredded leaves, hay or straw, lawn clippings, gravel, paper, plastic, or other material, spread over the soil around the base of plants. During the growing season, a mulch can help retard evaporation, inhibit weeds, and moderate soil temperature. In the winter, a mulch of evergreen boughs, coarse hay, or leaves is used to protect plants from freezing.

N

Native. Describes a plant that occurs naturally in a particular region and was not introduced from some other area.

Nutrients. Nitrogen, phosphorus, potassium, calcium, magnesium, sulfur, iron, and other elements needed by growing plants. Nutrients are supplied by the minerals and organic matter in the soil and by fertilizers.

O

Organic matter. Plant and animal residues such as leaves, trimmings, and manure in various stages of decomposition.

P

Peat moss. Partially decomposed mosses and sedges, mined from boggy areas and used to improve garden soil or to prepare potting soil.

Perennial. A plant that lives for a number of years, generally flowering each year. By "perennial," gardeners usually mean "herbaceous perennial," although woody plants such as vines, shrubs, and trees are also perennial.

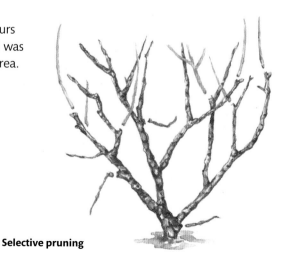

Selective pruning

Pressure-treated lumber. Softwood lumber treated with chemicals that protect it from decay.

Propagate. To produce new plants by sowing seeds, rooting cuttings, dividing plant parts, layering, grafting, or other means.

R

Retaining wall. A wall built to stabilize a slope and keep soil from sliding or eroding downhill.

Rhizome. A horizontal underground stem, often swollen into a storage organ. Both roots and shoots emerge from rhizomes. Rhizomes generally branch as they creep along and can be divided to make new plants.

Root ball. The mass of soil and roots dug with a plant when it is removed from the ground; the soil and roots of a plant grown in a container.

Rosette. A low, flat cluster of leaves arranged like the petals of a rose.

S

Selective pruning. Using pruning shears to remove or cut back individual shoots, in order to refine the shape of a shrub, maintain its vigor, or limit its size.

Severe pruning. Using pruning shears or loppers to cut away most of a shrub's top growth, leaving just short stubs or a gnarly trunk.

Severe pruning

Shearing. Using hedge shears or an electric hedge trimmer to shape the surface of a shrub, hedge, or tree and produce a smooth, solid mass of greenery.

Specimen plant. A plant placed alone in a prominent position, to show it off.

Spike. An elongated flower cluster, with individual flowers borne on very short stalks or attached directly to the main stem.

Standard. A plant trained to grow a round bushy head of branches atop a single upright stem.

T

Tender. Describes a plant that is damaged by cold weather.

V

Variegated. Describes foliage that is marked, striped, or blotched with color other than green.

Index

NOTE: Page numbers in
bold italic *refer to illustrations.*

Photo Credits

Front Cover: *(main image)* Karen Bussolini; *top left* Jerry Pavia; *top right* Saxon Holt

Back Cover: *both* Jerry Pavia

page 1: Jerry Pavia

page 7: Charles Mann

page 12: Shutterstock.com: Al Teich

page 13: *left* Shutterstock.com: imamchits; *right* Shutterstock.com: Giovanni Bertagna

pages 20-21: Karen Bussolini, design: Sydney Eddison

page 25: *all* Jerry Pavia

page 29: *top left* Karen Bussolini; *right & bottom* Jerry Pavia

page 33: *top left* Jerry Pavia; *top right & bottom* Karen Bussolini, *(bottom)* design: Tramontano & Rowe

page 37: *top* Jerry Pavia; *bottom right* Saxon Holt; *bottom left* Charles Mann

page 40: *top & bottom left* Jerry Pavia; *bottom right* Saxon Holt

page 45: *all* Jerry Pavia

page 48: *all* Jerry Pavia

page 52: *top left* Karen Bussolini; *top right & bottom* Jerry Pavia

page 56: *all* Jerry Pavia

page 61: *all* Jerry Pavia

page 64: *top left* Jerry Pavia; *top right & bottom* Karen Bussolini, *(top)* design: Wesley Rouse, *(bottom)* design: Rita Buchanan

page 69: *all* Jerry Pavia

page 72: *top left* Jerry Pavia; *top right & bottom* Karen Bussolini, *(bottom)* design: Sydney Eddison

page 77: *top left & bottom right* Jerry Pavia; *top right & bottom left* Karen Bussolini, *(top)* design: Katie Brown

page 81: *top* Jerry Pavia; *bottom left & right* Karen Bussolini, *(left)* design: Dickson DeMarche

page 85: *top left & bottom* Karen Bussolini; *top right* Jerry Pavia

page 88: *top & center* Jerry Pavia; *bottom* Karen Bussolini, design: Juanita Flagg

page 92: *all* Jerry Pavia

page 97: *top left & top right* Jerry Pavia; *bottom* Karen Bussolini, design: Fred & Mary Ann McGourty

page 101: *all* Jerry Pavia

page 105: *top left* Karen Bussolini, design: Wayne Renaud; *top right & bottom both* Jerry Pavia

page 109: *all* Jerry Pavia

page 113: *all* Jerry Pavia

pages 114-115: Jerry Pavia

page 116: *top* Shutterstock.com: Media Marketing; *center* Shutterstock.com: Volodymyr Petryshyn; *bottom* Shutterstock.com: EQRoy

page 117: *bottom left & top right* Karen Bussolini; *center right* Galen Gates; *bottom right* Charles Mann

page 118: *top* Galen Gates; *center & bottom left* Jerry Pavia; *bottom right* Rita Buchanan

page 119: *top & bottom left* Galen Gates; *right center* Charles Mann; *left center* Rita Buchanan

page 120: *top & bottom right* Galen Gates; *center* Jerry Pavia; *bottom left* Rita Buchanan

page 121: *top left* Carole Ottesen; *top right* Jerry Pavia; *center* Galen Gates; *bottom* Lauren Springer

page 122: *top* Saxon Holt; *center & bottom* Galen Gates

page 123: *top left & bottom right* Charles Mann; *top middle* Rita Buchanan; *top right* Karen Bussolini; *bottom left* Jerry Pavia

page 124: *top left & bottom* Carole Ottesen; *top right & middle* Saxon Holt

page 125: *top left & top right* Galen Gates; *middle* Ruth Rogers Clausen; *bottom* Jerry Pavia

page 126: *top left & center both* Charles Mann; *top right & bottom* Saxon Holt

page 127: *top left* Rita Buchanan; *top right & bottom* Galen Gates; *center right* Karen Bussolini; *center left* Jerry Pavia

page 128: *top* Charles Mann; *center* Rita Buchanan; *bottom* Shutterstock.com: James W. Thompson

page 129: *top left* Galen Gates; *top center* Saxon Holt; *top right & bottom right* Charles Mann; *bottom center* Jerry Pavia; *bottom left* Karen Bussolini

page 130: *top left* Jerry Pavia; *top right* Lauren Springer; *bottom* Galen Gates

page 131: *top left* Rick Mastelli; *top right* Charles Mann; *bottom right* Galen Gates; *bottom left* Jerry Pavia

page 132: *top & bottom left* Jerry Pavia; *bottom right* Rita Buchanan; *bottom center* Saxon Holt

page 133: *top* Lauren Springer; *center* Rita Buchanan; *bottom both* Charles Mann

page 134: *top & center* Charles Mann; *bottom* Rita Buchanan

page 135: *top left* Saxon Holt; *top center* Galen Gates; *top right* Jerry Pavia; *bottom all* Charles Mann

page 136: *top & left center* Karen Bussolini; *right center & bottom* Charles Mann

page 137: *top left* Rita Buchanan; *top right* Karen Bussolini; *right center & bottom right* Lauren Springer; *left center & bottom left* Galen Gates

page 138: *top & bottom right* Galen Gates; *right center* Saxon Holt; *bottom left* Jerry Pavia

page 139: *top* Charles Mann; *middle right* Michael Dirr; *middle center & bottom* Jerry Pavia; *middle left* Lauren Springer

page 140: *top left* Galen Gates; *top right* Charles Mann; *bottom right* Rick Mastelli; *bottom left* Lauren Springer

page 141: *top left & bottom right* Charles Mann; *top center* Galen Gates; *top right & bottom left* Jerry Pavia

page 142: *top left & center* Jerry Pavia; *top right* Galen Gates; *bottom* Saxon Holt

page 143: *top left* Rita Buchanan; *top right* Charles Mann; *center* Jerry Pavia; *bottom* Ruth Rogers Clausen

page 144: *top left* Jerry Pavia; *top center* Rita Buchanan; *top right* Saxon Holt; *bottom* Galen Gates

page 145: *top left & center* Jerry Pavia; *top right* Karen Bussolini; *bottom both* Galen Gates

page 146: *top left* Shutterstock.com: Nahhana; *top right & bottom both* Galen Gates

page 147: *top left & bottom* Jerry Pavia; *top right* Galen Gates; *center* Charles Mann

page 148: *top left, center & bottom* Galen Gates; *top right* Charles Mann

page 149: *top left* Carole Ottesen; *top right* Saxon Holt; *center* Galen Gates; *bottom* David McDonald

page 150: *left both* Charles Mann; *right* Jerry Pavia

page 151: *top & bottom* Karen Bussolini; *center both* Galen Gates

page 152: *left all* Jerry Pavia; *top right* Dency Kane; *bottom right* Saxon Holt

page 153: Charles Mann

page 154: *top & center* Saxon Holt; *bottom left* Lauren Springer; *bottom right* Galen Gates

page 155: *top left* Charles Mann; *top right* Karen Bussolini; *left center* Shutterstock.com: Razumhelen; *right center & bottom* Shutterstock.com: photowind

page 156: *top left* Jerry Pavia; *top center & bottom* Rita Buchanan; *top right* Galen Gates

page 157: *top left* Saxon Holt; *bottom left* Jerry Pavia; *top right & both middle right* Rita Buchanan; *bottom right* Galen Gates

page 158: *top left & middle* Galen Gates; *bottom* Saxon Holt

page 159: *top left* Shutterstock.com: Olga_Ionina; *top right & bottom* Rick Mastelli

pages 160–161: Jerry Pavia

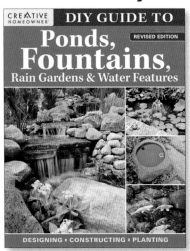

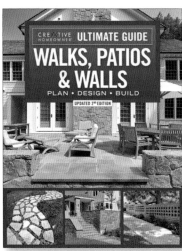